AMERICAN COUNTRY FURNITURE

PROJECTS FROM THE WORKSHOPS OF
DAVID T. SMITH

by Nick Engler and Mary Jane Favorite

FOX CHAPEL
PUBLISHING

Original edition © 1986 AW Media LLC
Revised edition © 2009 by Fox Chapel Publishing Company, Inc.

An American Woodworker book
www.americanwoodworker.com

American Country Furniture is an original work, first published in 1997 by Rodale Press, Inc., and revised in 2009 by Fox Chapel Publishing Company, Inc. This revision includes new color photographs. The furniture designs contained herein are copyrighted by The Workshops of David T. Smith. Readers may make copies of these patterns for personal use. The patterns themselves, however, are not to be duplicated for resale or distribution under any circumstances. Any such copying is a violation of copyright law. Reproduction of furniture from the designs contained herein for sale or profit is forbidden by law without written permission of The Workshops. This includes (but is not limited to) sales by religious and nonprofit organizations.

Photography by Karen Callahan and Mitch Mandel
Color photographs used with permission from David T. Smith

ISBN 978-1-56523-432-1

Library of Congress Cataloging-in-Publication Data

Engler, Nick.

   American country furniture / by Nick Engler and Mary Jane Favorite.

      p. cm.

   Reprint. Originally published: Emmaus, PA : Rodale Press, 1997.

   ISBN: 978-1-56523-432-1

   1. Furniture making. 2. Country furniture--United States. I. Favorite, Mary Jane, 1942- II. Workshops of David T. Smith (Firm) III. Title.

   TT194.E54 2009

   684'.08--dc22

                        2008054421

To learn more about the other great books from Fox Chapel Publishing, or to find a retailer near you, call toll-free 800-457-9112 or visit us at *www.FoxChapelPublishing.com*.

Note to Authors: We are always looking for talented authors to write new books in our area of woodworking, design, and related crafts. Please send a brief letter describing your idea to Acquisition Editor, 1970 Broad Street, East Petersburg, PA 17520.

Printed in China
First printing: May 2009

THE WORKSHOPS OF DAVID T. SMITH

The Workshops of David T. Smith are a unique business, perhaps the only one like it in America. The craftsmen and craftswomen at the Workshops make reproductions of historical furniture, pottery, ironware, and other household items that were used by our pioneer ancestors during the eighteenth and nineteenth centuries — what we now call *American country* artifacts.

The Workshops are just that — a collection of crafts shops on a farm in Warren County, Ohio, near the village of Morrow. The area has been an important crossroads in the country furniture trade for years. Nearby are the historic towns of Lebanon and Waynesville. Waynesville supported four country cabinetmakers in the early nineteenth century; Lebanon supported over a dozen. Today, each town does a booming business in the antique trade. Just a few miles farther down the

road is Cincinnati, the center of commerce (and furnituremaking) for the Midwest before the Civil War. Also nearby are the sites of three Shaker communities that flourished in the nineteenth century — Union Village and Watervaliet, Ohio, and White Water, Indiana. These communities also produced furniture. The Workshops have built their business on this rich country heritage.

David T. Smith is the founder, chief designer, and driving force behind the Workshops. He began building furniture in the 1960s when he married. At first, he built out of necessity — he had no money to buy furniture. His father lent him a table saw, some hand tools, and a few hundred board feet of cherry lumber. With these, he began to furnish his house.

THE WORKSHOPS OF DAVID T. SMITH

Around this same time, David attended a local auction and, at the advice of his father, picked up a table for $11. He repaired it, cleaned up the finish — and shortly thereafter a local antique dealer offered him $350 for it! He didn't sell the table (he still has it), but he did start a part-time business repairing and restoring antiques. Dealers, museums, and individuals brought him worn or broken furniture to make whole again. At first, David simply bought old wood and old furniture parts to use for restoration. Then, as he gained more experience, he purchased antiques that were

only partially complete — the base of a two-piece cupboard, for example — and rebuilt them. He experimented with finishing techniques until he could match the old finishes perfectly. He also devised methods of treating new hardware to make it look old and worn. He became so adept that his customers couldn't tell what part of an antique was original and what was replaced.

As time went on, prices for antiques escalated. So did the prices for parts of antiques — or antiques with parts missing. Prices rose so high that it began to cost David more for an antique in need of restoration than he could make by restoring it. This forced him to make a decision: "I thought to myself," says David, "if I can build half of a piece of furniture, I can build all of it. So I did just that."

At first, he built furniture pieces from old wood. When old wood became scarce, he switched to new wood and perfected his finishing techniques to make the new stock look old. The new pieces were almost indistinguishable from the antiques he had restored.

In early 1980, the demand for David's furniture had grown so large, he became a full-time cabinetmaker. Almost immediately he got his first big order: 200 tables and 400 benches for a nearby recreational park. He expanded to fill this order, hiring additional craftsmen. David T. Smith became "David T. Smith and Company, Furniture Makers and Grainers." David was also interested in antique redware pottery, ironware, and other household artifacts. So he built a pottery shop, then a blacksmith shop among his cabinetmaking and finishing shops. David T. Smith and Company became "The Workshops of David T. Smith." For other items, he sought craftsmen and craftswomen who worked in the old, country manner or who made accurate reproductions of rugs, brooms, toys, woodcarvings, pewterware, decoys, and so on. Some of these people work on the premises; others work in their own shops and sell their wares through the Workshops.

Although they use modern power tools, the crafts-people at the Workshops build accurate reproductions of American country furniture from the eighteenth and nineteenth centuries.

THE WORKSHOPS OF DAVID T. SMITH

Today, the Workshops employs almost three dozen people, over half of whom make furniture, pottery, brooms, and ironware. This doesn't include the many associated craftspeople and cabinetmaking shops elsewhere who create everything from Windsor chairs to pewter spoons. Together, these folks have gained a countrywide reputation for highly accurate reproductions of early American artifacts. The editors of magazines and journals have praised them not only for design and workmanship, but for their "museum-quality" finishes. A curator from the Winterthur Museum in Winterthur, Delaware, after inspecting furniture and pottery from the Workshops, commented that the reproductions were "done so well [that] in some cases, we couldn't say for sure whether or not these are reproductions unless we could break them open or take them apart."

All of this has been accomplished by careful attention to details and faithfulness to history and tradition. At the Workshops, the craftspeople not only build furniture that's similar to what their great-great-grandfathers might have built, they build it in the same manner. The Workshops operate very much like the old-time cabinetmaking shops that they emulate. The craftspeople don't *manufacture* furniture; there is no assembly line. A single craftsman builds each piece, from start to finish. On large pieces, such as a corner cabinet, two craftsmen might team up.

Sometimes people with exceptional skills are called on to make certain parts of a piece — turned legs or spindles, carved moldings and ornaments, inlay and other decoration. At the Workshops, finishing has also developed into a fine skill. Some craftspeople specialize in applying museum-quality finishes. This, too, is similar to the old-time way of working. Country cabinetmakers often employed turners, carvers, inlay artists, and other specialists for specific jobs.

The unique organization of the Workshops allows them to take on both large and small jobs.

The Workshops have a large enough base of craftspeople and associated shops to make 200 tables for a customer. However, they can also make one-of-a-kind pieces at a profit. This is similar to the way an eighteenth- or nineteenth-century country cabinetmaker conducted his business. He had to take his work where he could find it; no job was too small or too large. He handled small jobs himself. For large jobs, he called on his friends.

The projects in this book were developed by David T. Smith and other craftspeople at the Workshops. Some of them are one-of-a-kind pieces, made for this book or special clients. Others are "stock" pieces — popular designs that are reproduced again and again. Some are precise copies of historical pieces that can be found in museums or collections of fine furniture. Others are inspired by traditional forms. Whatever the piece, each is built as American country furniture was built centuries ago.

The Workshops are best known for their museum-quality finishes, which duplicate the worn finishes on real country antiques.

CONTENTS

CONSTRUCTION

FOR EATING AND DRINKING

FOR READING AND WRITING

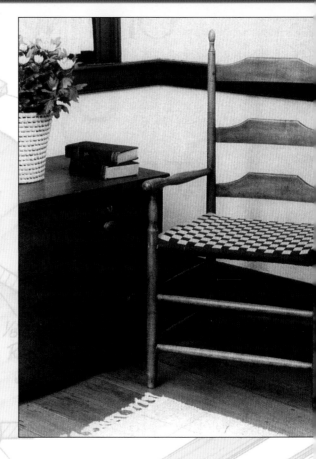

FOR DRESSING AND SLEEPING

FOR SITTING AND REFLECTING

FOR COOKING AND BAKING

FOR STORING AND KEEPING

FINISH

CONSTRUCTION

Tools, Materials, and Techniques

The construction of American Country furniture, while not particularly difficult, is exacting, detailed work. This comes as no great surprise to most woodworkers; all fine furnituremaking is exacting. However, there are several special details to keep in mind when making country furniture. You must use the same wood and hardware that a country cabinetmaker might have used, assemble the piece with the same joinery, and make it look as if you had used the same tools.

SELECTING LUMBER AND HARDWARE

There were more species of wood in Colonial eastern American forests suitable for furnituremaking than any other place in the world. Country cabinetmakers found that certain woods worked better for specific kinds of projects. They also found that different woods — or combinations of woods — produced different aesthetic effects.

Some were considered attractive, *formal* woods to be used for special projects. Because their wood grain was especially beautiful, these were usually finished with clear oil, beeswax, varnish, shellac, or lacquer. Others were common, *utilitarian* woods for projects that saw everyday use. These were often painted, since the wood grains weren't considered appealing. Utilitarian woods were also used as *secondary* woods (for inside, unseen parts) on large, formal case pieces. Here's a brief profile of a dozen common country furniture woods:

White Pine — Initial color is white, becoming light brown as it ages. The settlers found American white pine was soft, lightweight, easy to work, and surprisingly strong. Once it had been properly dried, it was fairly stable and durable. It has a subtle to moderate grain pattern. They used pine mostly for scooped chair seats, carved boxes or panels, and utilitarian furniture, especially painted benches, chests, and cupboards. It was also used as a secondary wood.

The pine lumber from 150 years ago and what you buy today are almost two different species. Old pine was cut from virgin timber and had small, tightly spaced growth rings. Because of this, it was very stable. Today's pine is harvested from fast-growing, hybrid trees. The growth rings are extremely wide, sometimes ¼" or more. This makes the wood very unstable — not well suited for furniture. If you must use pine for a project, look for old lumber or lumber with small growth rings. If not, use poplar instead.

Yellow Poplar — Initial color is a light yellow, becoming streaked with various shades of brown as it ages. Poplar has an extremely subtle grain pattern. It's slightly harder, more durable, and more stable than pine, but much more difficult to carve. Because of the tulip-shaped flowers on the trees, poplar was called *tulipwood* by the settlers, and was used as a utilitarian or secondary wood, like pine. If you need wide planks for a project, poplar is often your best choice. You can still find boards up to 18" wide.

Walnut — Initial color is deep purple-brown, lightening somewhat as it ages. Walnut is handsome, soft, durable, and easily worked wood. It has a moderate grain pattern, but lumber cut from a crotch or the tap root of the tree is often highly figured. Country cabinetmakers used it for formal pieces. They often made panels of figured walnut. Because they could easily carve it, they sometimes substituted walnut for imported mahogany on classic furniture with shell carving, ball-and-claw feet, and so on.

If you can, purchase *air-dried* walnut. Most kiln-dried walnut is steamed to disperse the brown color throughout the light-colored sapwood. This makes more of the lumber usable, but the color isn't as rich.

Cherry — Initial color is light pink, becoming a dark red-brown as it ages. Cherry has a subtle to moderate grain pattern and develops a rich patina in just a few years. It's not as hard as walnut, not as easily worked, but many woodworkers consider it easier to finish. However, it was used much like walnut, as a formal wood. You can sometimes find curly or figured cherry. The figuring isn't as pronounced as walnut or maple figuring, but it was highly regarded by country cabinetmakers.

Elm — Initial color is light red-brown, becoming darker with age. The wood is hard, not particularly strong, but it bends well. The grain pattern is subtle to moderate. The wood is considered a formal wood, but it was used little by cabinetmakers. It's not very stable — it expands and contracts more than other species. It was, however, popular with chairmakers, who used it both for seats and bent parts.

Hard Maple — Initial color is white, becoming light brown as it ages. The grain is sometimes figured, showing jewel-like curls, burls, or bird's-eyes. These become more prominent as the wood ages. It's extremely hard but moderately easy to work. Settlers used it for both utilitarian and formal furniture and sometimes as a secondary wood. It was a favorite of chairmakers, who used it to make long, slender spindles, legs, and rungs. It was commonly used to make objects that were expected to see a lot of wear, such as tabletops, bowls, pivots, and bentwood boxes. Tool handles and plane stocks in a country cabinetmaker's shop were often made of hard maple.

Soft Maple — Initial color is white, becoming light brown as it ages. Like hard maple, the grain is sometimes figured. The lumber is moderately soft and only moderately stable. Maple with ordinary grain was used as both a utilitarian and secondary wood; maple with figured grain was used as a formal wood.

Note: Highly figured woods often have to be worked down slowly with hand planes and sanders.

Power planers and jointers sometimes tear the grain.

Birch — Initial color is white, becoming light brown as it ages. This wood has many of the same characteristics and grain pattern as hard maple, but it's not as easy to work with hand tools. Consequently, cabinetmakers used it little, and only as a utilitarian or secondary wood. Chairmakers sometimes used it for turning. After birch has been aged a few years, it's indistinguishable from maple without microscopic analysis.

Oak — Initial color is white or light pink, becoming a deep brown as it ages. There are several species of oak, but they all have similar properties and uses. Oak is very hard, flexible, and has a very prominent grain pattern. Because of its large, open pores, it's not very stable. Up until the eighteenth century, oak (especially white oak) was considered a formal wood, but it fell out of favor with fine cabinetmakers. The grain pattern was too strong to be used with the intricate, flowing designs of the Queen Anne and Chippendale periods. During the country-furniture era, oak was used mostly as a utilitarian wood, although it was sometimes used in formal Pennsylvania German pieces. Chairmakers used oak for both turned and bent parts.

Ash — Initially a light tan color, becoming only slightly darker as it ages. Ash is lightweight, strong, flexible, and fairly easy to work. Depending on the species, it's hard to moderately hard, and has a moderate grain pattern. It was considered a utilitarian wood by cabinetmakers, who also used it for tool handles. It was more often used by chairmakers, who found it could be easily bent.

Chestnut — Initially a light brown color, becoming a rich nut-brown with age. It's a very soft wood, but flexible and highly resistant to rot. It has a prominent grain pattern. Chestnut was used as a formal wood up until the early eighteenth century, then fell out of favor for the same reason as oak. However, it continued to be a popular utilitarian wood throughout the country-furniture era, because it was so easy to work. It was used by chairmakers for both turning and bending.

Although there are no lumber-size living chestnut trees today, you can still purchase chestnut lumber. A blight killed the trees in the early part of this century, but because the wood is so rot resistant, many of the standing dead trees are still sound.

Hickory — Initially light reddish brown, becomes darker with age. Hickory has a moderate grain pattern. It's not particularly stable, but it is extremely hard — much harder than any other wood on this list. For this reason, it was often used for pegs and "tree nails," pinning wooden parts together. As such, it was primarily a utilitarian wood. Despite its hardness, it also bends easily.

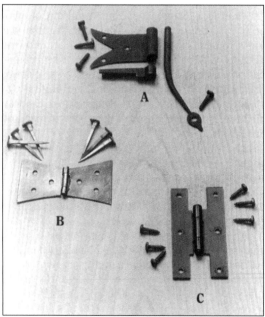

During the early country-furniture era, the most common types of hinges were all surface-mounted. Shown here are three popular styles: rat-tail hinge (*a*), butterfly hinge (*b*), and H-hinge (*c*).

Chairmakers used hickory for both turning and bending.

For an authentic reproduction, do not use plywood or particleboard, even for the backs of cupboards and cabinets. Plywood was not commercially available until the late nineteenth century, and particleboard not until the twentieth century.

In addition to wood, country cabinetmakers also used metal hardware. The type (and the amount) of hardware depended on when the furniture was made.

In rural eighteenth-century America, hardware was used sparingly, because it was expensive and added needlessly to the cost of the project. Pulls and latches were almost always fashioned from wood; the only metal parts in a typical country furniture piece were locks, hinges, nails, and perhaps a few blunt-end screws. These were usually made of iron by a local blacksmith. Brass hardware, while it was readily available in the larger American cities, had to be imported into rural areas. This extra transportation cost made *brasses*, as they were called, much more expensive than iron hardware.

The most visible pieces of hardware on an eighteenth-century piece were the hinges. The most common were surface mounted — butterfly, rat-tail, and various other shapes. These had been used since medieval times not just as hinges, but as metal gussets to strengthen a project. A cabinetmaker often mounted them to straddle the joints of a door frame and help hold it together. He usually attached these surface hinges with nails, driving them through the wood and clinching them over on the back side.

Mortised or *butt* hinges — the type that we take for granted nowadays — were less common. They were harder to make and install. However, like brasses, they were considered the mark of a fine piece of furniture. For a special project in which appearance was paramount, the cabinetmaker spent the extra money and effort for butt hinges, brasses, and screws to mount them.

The late eighteenth century saw rapid advances in metallurgy, including new technologies for working both iron and brass. As America was industrialized, hardware became less expensive, and country furniture used more of it. By the early nineteenth century, country cabinetmakers used manufactured brasses regularly — pulls, latches, and escutcheons as well as locks and latches. At the same time, screws began to replace nails as common fasteners.

Hardware designs — particularly brasses — evolved over time, like furniture. Hardware styles went in and out of vogue with furniture styles. For example, ornate "cloud-form" drawer pulls were popular only during the Queen Anne and Chippendale periods. By the Federal period, brass pulls had become simple ovals and shields. Consult the chart to see what hardware styles were popular during what periods.

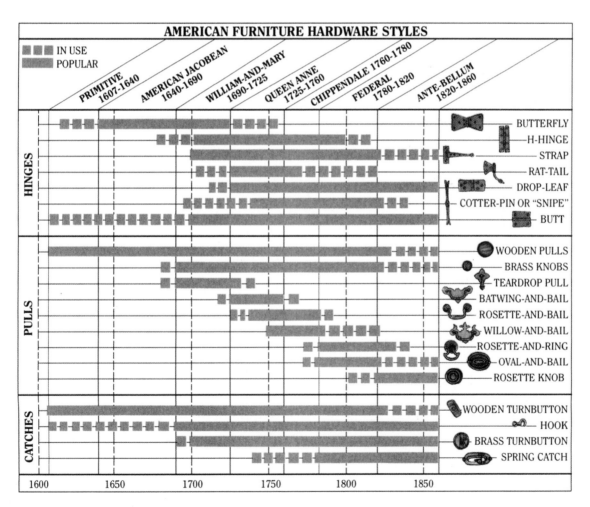

AMERICAN FURNITURE HARDWARE STYLES

To help select the proper materials for a country piece, give some thought to its history. How, where, and when was the furniture used? What period was it built? Did the cabinetmaker intend it as a formal or utilitarian piece? Would he have painted it or finished it naturally? Would he have used ordinary iron hardware or spent the money for fancy brasses? The answers to these questions will help you select the appropriate wood and hardware.

COUNTRY CONSTRUCTION TECHNIQUES

If you study a well-constructed piece of country furniture, you'll see that it's built like a three-dimensional puzzle. All the wood and hardware fit together in such a way that, even if the glue fails, the piece will remain whole. A Shaker chair is a prime example: All the wooden parts — legs, rungs, posts, stretchers, and slats — were assembled with round mortises and tenons, glued together. The top slat was mortised *and* pegged in the back posts, and the seating material — rush, reed, or cloth tape — was woven around the stretchers. Even if the glue failed in all the joints, the pegs and woven seat held the chair together.

Good construction also lets the wood "breathe." Wood breathes in moisture during hot, humid weather, expanding slightly. During cold, dry weather, it exhales this moisture and contracts. Furthermore, because of the way in which wood cells are shaped, wood swells and shrinks approximately ten times more *across* the grain than *with* it. For instance, if you cut a board 12" wide and 12" long in the winter, it may swell to 12¼" wide and $12\,^1\!/_{64}$" long in the summer. This movement isn't noticeable when the wood is under 3" wide, but it becomes an important consideration on large panels.

Good country joinery allowed for the movement of wide boards. Where possible, the wood grain was oriented so all the parts would swell and shrink in the same direction. When this couldn't be arranged, cabinetmakers "floated" the wide parts in the assembly or cut them up into smaller parts. In a frame-and-panel door, for instance, the wide panel floats in the grooved edges of the frame members. On a table, the top floats on the aprons. The wide backs of cabinets and cupboards were cut into narrow, overlapping boards, so each could expand and contract separately.

In some cases, hardware helped compensate for the movement of the wood. Small nails and screws are flexible — they will bend slightly with the movement of the wood. When the grain directions of two parts opposed each other, cabinetmakers sometimes nailed (but did *not* glue) the parts together. For example, moldings were sometimes nailed to the sides of cupboards and cabinets. The grain of the molding was horizontal, while that of the sides was vertical. But as the broad sides expanded and contracted, the nails holding the moldings flexed slightly. The moldings remained in place without restricting the wood movement.

All of the joinery was simple, no different than many of the joints we use today — rabbets, dadoes, grooves, mortises, tenons, and dovetails. Country cabinetmakers kept their construction simple because they used simple tools. You can duplicate most of these joints with contemporary power tools. Modern tools can also make some joints that weren't possible in an old-time cabinetry shop. A country cabinetmaker couldn't make dowel joints or "biscuit" joints. He didn't have a doweling jig, power drill, or plate joiner. If you do use modern tools, be careful not to add modern touches.

There are a few operations that can *only* be done with hand tools. For instance, you must use hand methods to make dovetail joints with narrow pins and wide tails — the style that was popular during the last half of the country-furniture era. There are commercial router jigs that will cut many different types of dovetail, but none that will cut pins narrow enough to duplicate those in many fine country antiques.

This isn't to say that you shouldn't use power tools when making country furniture. Most professional craftsmen couldn't survive in today's economy without using power tools to speed up woodworking operations. And most amateurs can't invest the time necessary to become proficient with hand tools. Use whatever tools do the best job for you. However, to preserve the accuracy of a reproduction, use the same joinery and construction techniques that a country cabinetmaker might have used.

A COUNTRY CABINETMAKER'S TOOLS

A fine reproduction should also look as if it were built with hand tools, even if you don't use them. Hand tools and power tools work very differently. Power tools arrive at the desired shape in a different manner from hand tools, and leave a different set of marks upon the surface. As you build, consider how an old-time cabinetmaker's tools cut or shaped the wood.

What sorts of tools did this cabinetmaker use? You would be surprised at how short the list is. Even the best cabinetmakers of Philadelphia, New York, or Newport had fewer tools than a well-equipped amateur, by today's standards. Consider the shop of John Hedges, a successful cabinetmaker in Circleville, Ohio, during the first part of the nineteenth century. Hedges ran a busy shop, employing four apprentices. When he died at age 49, at the peak of his career, the inventory of his estate listed these tools:

- 5 workbenches (one for himself, and one for each apprentice)
- 10 handscrew clamps and other miscellaneous clamps
- 1 grindstone
- 1 lathe

- 1 set of lathe chisels
- 1 hand saw
- 1 saw buck and ax
- 1 lot miscellaneous cabinetmaker's tools (valued at $5.00)
- 1 lot miscellaneous carpenter's tools (also valued at $5.00)
- 5 gallons of varnish

The lots of miscellaneous tools probably included a dozen or more planes, several chisels and gouges, some scrapers, two or three different gauges, one or two rules, a try square, a mallet, a drawknife or spokeshave, a rasp or a file, perhaps a hammer and a frame saw, and some nails and hardware. In addition, some of the apprentices probably had their own tools, and these weren't listed in the inventory. Even so, there weren't a great many tools for a busy shop.

This is a re-creation of a typical early nineteenth-century country cabinetmaker's shop at Ohio Historical Village in Columbus, Ohio. Craftsmen from the country era worked almost exclusively with hand tools. *Courtesy Ohio Historical Society.*

The most abundant tool in a country cabinetmaker's shop were his planes. There were usually at least a dozen, and often more than thirty, all handmade by the cabinetmaker himself. He used these to plane, joint, trim, smooth, and shape stock — operations we now perform mostly with power tools. *Courtesy Ohio Historical Society and Thomas Clark.*

The only tools in a country cabinetmaking shop that worked with a rotary motion were the gimlets, augers, brace and bits, and lathe *(not shown)*. All other tools worked with a linear motion. Each type of motion leaves distinctive marks on the wood.

However, the most important difference between nineteenth- and twentieth-century woodworking shops is not the relative number of tools, but *how these tools worked*. Almost all the tools in the Hedges inventory operated with a *linear* motion. For example, the most abundant tool in an old-time cabinetmaker's shop were his planes. He often had thirty or more, and used them during all phases of construction to plane, smooth, joint, trim, or shape the wood. All of these cut in a *straight line*. Only the lathe and the drilling tools (augers, gimlets, braces and bits) shaped the wood with a *rotary* motion. Today, all our power tools, (except the band saw, jigsaw, and saber saw) *rotate*.

These two cutting motions — linear and rotary — each produce a distinct surface on the stock. Hand saws leave uneven, straight lines; circular saws leave consistent, arched lines. When properly sharpened and adjusted, a hand plane leaves a glass-smooth surface. Most rotary power tools, including the jointer, planer, shaper, and router, leave wavelike *mill marks*.

For a truly accurate country-furniture reproduction, you must reproduce the effects of hand tools — or, at least, disguise the effects of power tools. If the cut surface is to be left rough, use a band saw or reciprocating saw instead of a circular saw. After planing, jointing, shaping, or routing surfaces that will be seen on the finished piece, carefully sand and scrape away the mill marks. If you wish, make a few passes with a hand plane to thoroughly disguise the machined surface. This doesn't take a lot of extra time — just some extra thought.

FOR EATING & DRINKING

TRESTLE TABLE

For hundreds of years before the discovery of America, European country folk made tables by placing a long, thick board across two or more trestle supports. (A medieval trestle was a horizontal beam supported by legs, much like a modern sawhorse.) In the sixteenth century, joiners (medieval woodworkers) began to fasten the boards permanently to the trestles. By using the trestle to hold the board flat, they could make the tabletops much thinner. They also simplified the trestles, building flat assemblies joined by long stretchers. Today, we remember this design as the trestle table.

Trestle tables continued to be used by country folk on both sides of the Atlantic. Because space was so precious in a pioneer home, most seventeenth-and eighteenth-century trestles and boards were disassembled and stored away when not in use. But as America became more settled and homes grew larger, trestle tables followed the European lead — they were built to stay assembled.

In the nineteenth century, the United Society of Believers in Christ's Second Appearing — the Shakers — used trestle tables for communal dining.

They often built tables 20 feet long or more! The table shown is a shortened version of a table built by Shaker cabinetmakers in Union Village, Ohio.

It's interesting that these trestle dining tables were one of the few pieces of Shaker furniture (other than chairs) that had stretchers. Shakers discouraged stretchers because folks were tempted to put their feet on them. This, in turn, caused the furniture to wear prematurely. Note that the stretcher on this table is placed too high to comfortably rest your feet on.

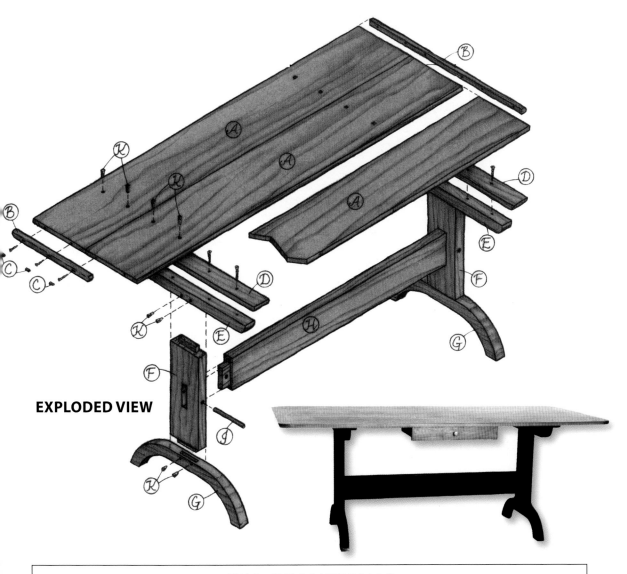

EXPLODED VIEW

BILL OF MATERIALS

WOODEN PARTS/*FINISHED DIMENSIONS*

A.	Top boards (3)	$7/8" \times 12" \times 75\frac{1}{2}"$
B.	Breadboards (2)	$7/8" \times 1\frac{1}{4}" \times 36"$
C.	Breadboard caps (12)	$3/8" \times 1\frac{1}{2}" \times 1\frac{1}{4}"$
D.	Trestle tops (2)	$7/8" \times 3\frac{1}{2}" \times 33\frac{1}{2}"$
E.	Braces (2)	$2" \times 2" \times 28\frac{3}{4}"$
F.	Posts (2)	$2" \times 6" \times 20\frac{1}{4}"$
G.	Feet (2)	$2" \times 7" \times 25\frac{1}{2}"$

H.	Stretcher	$2" \times 6" \times 49\frac{1}{2}"$
J.	Pins (2)	$5/8"$ dia. $\times 6"$
K.	Pegs (20)	$3/8" \times 3/8" \times 1\frac{1}{4}"$

HARDWARE

#8 × 1¾" Flathead wood screws (8)

#12 × 3½" Roundhead wood screws and washers (12)

PLAN OF PROCEDURE

1

Plane, rip, and cut the parts to the sizes shown in the Bill of Materials.

2

Cut the joinery needed to assemble the table:

- 1"-wide, 4"-long mortises through the posts, as shown in the *Post Layout/End View*

- 1"-wide, 1"-deep, 4"-long mortises in the braces and feet, as shown in the *Brace Layout* and *Foot Layout*

- 1"-thick, 2"-long, 4"-wide tenons on the ends of the stretcher, as shown in the *Stretcher Layout*

- 1"-thick, 1"-long, 4"-wide tenons on the ends of the posts, as shown in the *Post Layout*

- ⅜"-wide, ¾"-deep, 1¼"-long mortises in the outside edges of the breadboards, as shown in the *Breadboard Joinery Detail* and *Breadboard Layout/ End View*

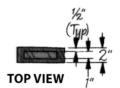

TOP VIEW

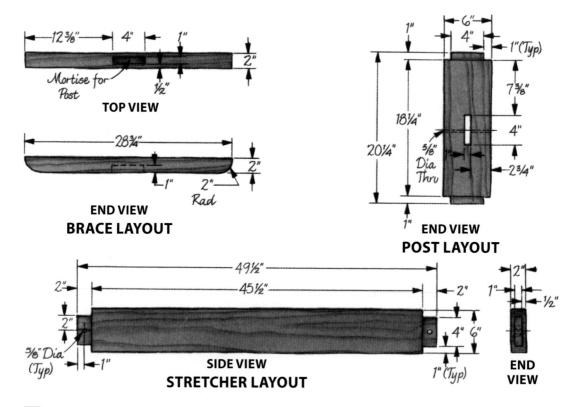

TOP VIEW
BRACE LAYOUT

END VIEW
BRACE LAYOUT

END VIEW
POST LAYOUT

SIDE VIEW
STRETCHER LAYOUT

END VIEW

3

Notch the edges of the post and stretcher tenons, creating "shoulders." Fit the tenons to their respective mortises.

4

Lay out the shape of the feet on the stock and cut the shapes. Sand the sawed edges.

5

Round over the ends of the braces and trestle tops, as shown in the *End View* and *Brace Layout/End View*.

6

Finish sand the feet, posts, braces, trestle tops, and stretcher. Join the feet, posts, braces, and trestle tops with glue to make two trestle assemblies. Reinforce the glue

joints between the braces and trestle tops with #8 × 1¾" flathead wood screws. Countersink the heads of the screws.

7

Joint both edges of the top boards. Lightly chamfer or "break" the hard corners along the edges, as shown in the *Tabletop Joinery Detail*. Glue the boards together, edge to edge, so the end grains cup up.

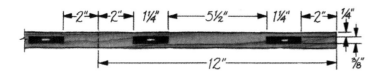

END VIEW
BREADBOARD LAYOUT

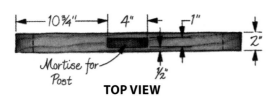

Mortise for Post

TOP VIEW

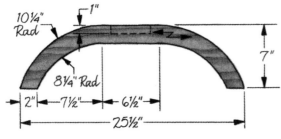

10¼" Rad
8¼" Rad

END VIEW
FOOT LAYOUT

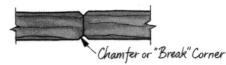

Chamfer or "Break" Corner

TABLETOP JOINERY DETAIL

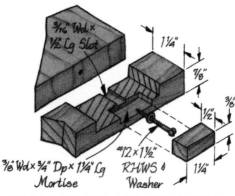

³⁄₁₆" Wd × ½" Lg Slot
³⁄₈" Wd × ¾" Dp × 1¼" Lg Mortise
#12 × 1½" RHWS & Washer

BREADBOARD JOINERY DETAIL

PLAN OF PROCEDURE

8

While the glue is drying on the tabletop assembly, position the trestles on each end of the stretcher. Glue the stretcher to the posts, then drill a ⅝"-diameter hole through the mortise-and-tenon joint in each post, as shown in the *Side View*. Glue a ⅝"-diameter dowel in each hole to peg each tenon in its mortise. Sand the dowel ends flush with the edges of the posts, and the tenon ends flush with the faces.

9

Finish sand the tabletop assembly, then lay it across the trestles. Center it and make sure the end grain cups up.

10

Round the bottom portion of the pegs, as shown in the *Peg Detail*. Drill ⅜"-diameter, 1¼"-deep holes through the top boards where shown in the *Top View*. Drive a peg into each hole. Do *not* glue the tabletop to the trestles.

11

Attach the breadboards to the ends of the tabletop with #12 × 1½" roundhead wood screws and flat washers, as shown in the *Breadboard Joinery Detail*. Glue breadboard caps in the breadboard mortises to hide the screw heads. Sand the caps flush with the edges of the breadboards.

12

Do any necessary touch-up sanding, then apply a finish to *all* sides — top and bottom — of the entire table.

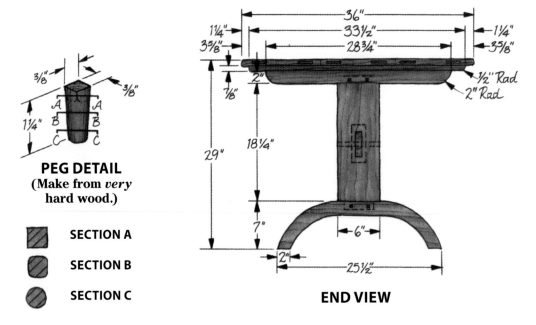

PEG DETAIL
(Make from *very* hard wood.)

▨ **SECTION A**

◍ **SECTION B**

◉ **SECTION C**

END VIEW

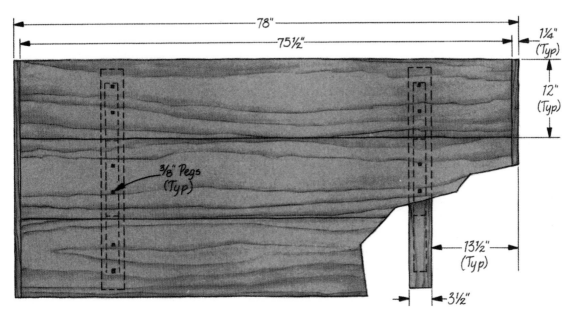

TOP VIEW

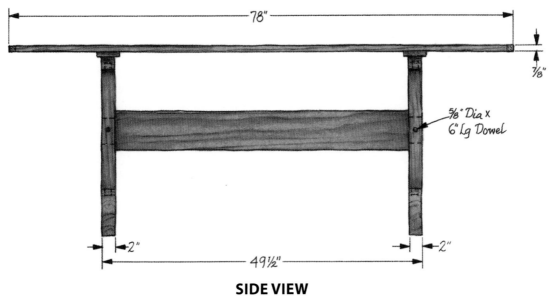

SIDE VIEW

COUNTRY CRAFTSMAN'S KNOW-HOW:
JOINING BREADBOARD ENDS

To prevent wide boards from cupping, cabinetmakers often attached "breadboards" to the ends. While these controlled cupping, they sometimes created other problems. Because the boards were fastened so the wood grains were perpendicular, the breadboards restricted the normal movement of the wider board. As it expanded and contracted with changes in humidity, it often split or popped the joints.

To correct this, use the following *nontraditional* method for joining breadboards to tabletops and other wide parts. It controls cupping *and* allows the wide boards to shrink and swell. You can disguise the hardware used in this joinery to look like traditional mortises and tenons.

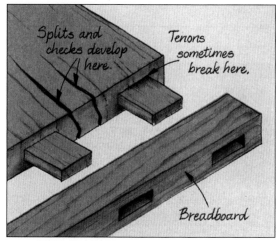

1 There were several traditional methods for joining breadboards, but one of the most common was mortise-and-tenon joints. The cabinetmaker cut tenons in the wide board and fit them to mortises in the breadboards. In some cases, the joints were pegged. This restricted the movement of the wide board, eventually causing the board to split or the tenons to break.

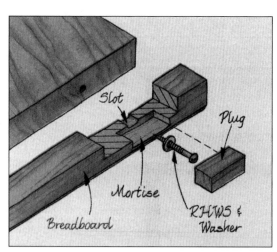

2 To prevent this from happening, attach the breadboards with roundhead screws. Drive these screws through slots in the breadboards. As the wide board shrinks and swells, the screws move slightly in the slots. The breadboards, however, remain securely fastened.

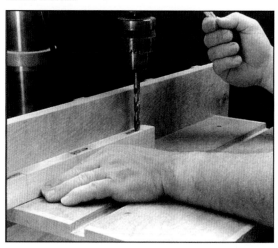

3 Mortise the edge of the breadboard for screws by drilling a line of overlapping holes. These holes should be about twice the diameter of the head of the screw. Clean up the edges of the mortise with a chisel.

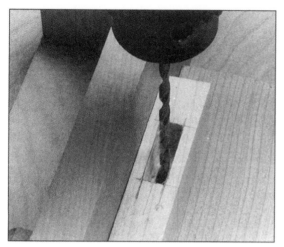

4 Cut the screw slots in the same manner — drill a line of holes in the bottom of each mortise. The diameter of the holes should be the same size as or slightly larger than the screw shaft.

5 When you have made the mortises and slots, clamp the breadboard to the end of the wider board. Drill pilot holes, then put flat washers over the screw shanks and drive the screws through the slots and into the board. Tighten each screw so it's snug, but not so tight that it presses the washer into the wood.

6 Make wooden plugs for the mortises to hide the screws and washers. Glue each plug in place so the end grain faces *out*.

7 After the glue dries, sand the plug flush with the edge of the breadboard. The breadboard will appear as if it's held to the wider board with mortises and tenons.

SHAKER DINING BENCH

There were more than 100 religious experiments in communism — communal ownership and living — in eighteenth- and nineteenth-century America. One of the most successful was the United Society of Believers in Christ's Second Appearing, better known as the *Shakers*. From just eleven followers, newly arrived from England in 1774, the sect had over 1,000 members in eleven separate communities by 1800 and 6,000 in eighteen communities by 1850.

Because Shaker life was communal, they designed and built many pieces of furniture for group activities. Among them was this *dining bench,* used by several communities in their dining halls and schoolrooms. It was an original invention, a variation on a traditional five-board bench. The Shaker craftsmen extended the legs to support a slender backrest. The result was a piece that was more comfortable — and more elegant — than an ordinary bench.

The design for this dining bench was inspired by a similar bench built at the Shaker community in Hancock, Connecticut, and used in their dining room. It's now on display at the Metropolitan Museum of Art in New York City.

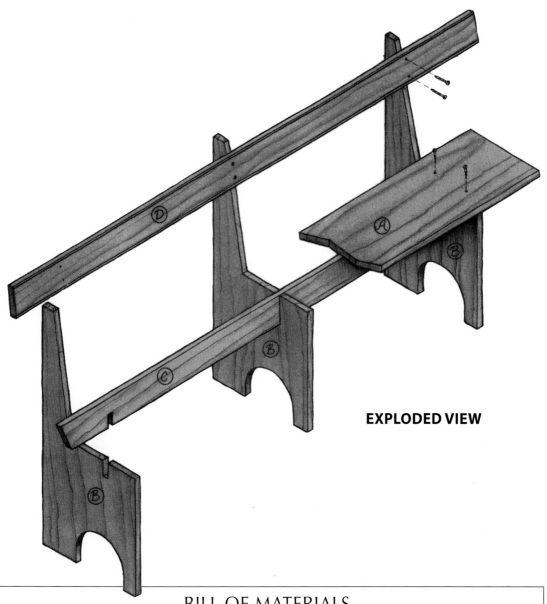

EXPLODED VIEW

BILL OF MATERIALS

WOODEN PARTS/_FINISHED DIMENSIONS_

A.	Seat	⅞" × 11¾" × 78"
B.	Legs (3)	⅞" × 15¼" × 34¼"
C.	Rail	⅞" × 4" × 74"
D.	Backrest	⅞" × 4" × 78"

HARDWARE

#12 × 1¾" Flathead wood screws (12)

PLAN OF PROCEDURE

1

If necessary, glue up wide stock for the legs and seat. Plane, rip, and cut the parts to the sizes shown in the Bill of Materials.

2

Lay out and cut the shape of the legs, as shown in the *End View*. Sand the sawed edges.

3

Miter the ends of the rails at 60°, as shown in the *Front View*.

4

Cut three ⅞"-wide, 2"-long notches in the bottom edge of the rail and cut matching notches in the top ends of the legs, where the seat attaches, as shown in the *Rail-to-Leg Joinery Detail*.

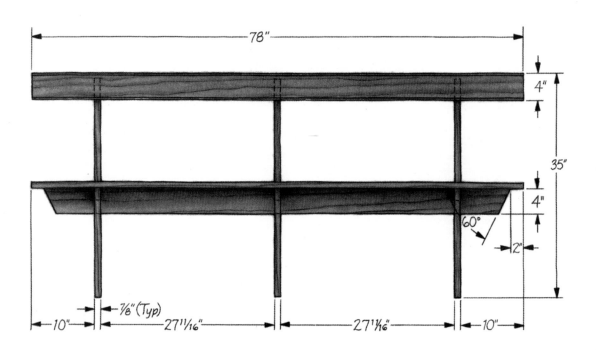

FRONT VIEW

5

Rout or cut beads in the front face of the backrest, near the edges, as shown in the *Backrest Profile.*

6

Finish sand the parts of the bench and dry assemble them to check the fit of the joints. Reassemble the parts with glue and flathead wood screws. Counterbore and countersink the screws, then cover their heads with putty.

7

Do any necessary touch-up sanding and apply a finish to the completed project.

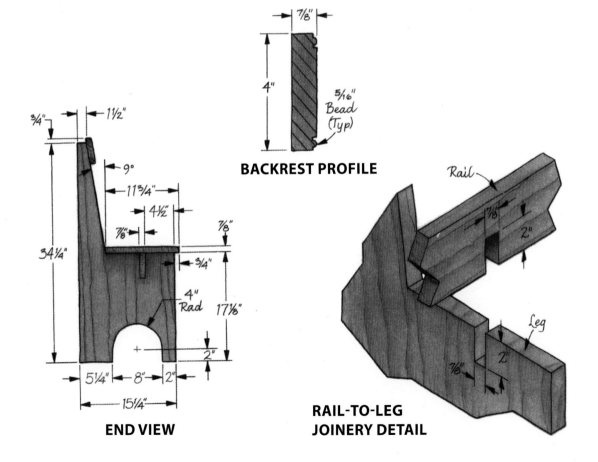

BACKREST PROFILE

END VIEW

RAIL-TO-LEG JOINERY DETAIL

SHOE-FOOT SETTLE TABLE

During the Middle Ages, a unique piece of furniture began to appear in English taverns. It combined several medieval furniture forms — settle, chest, and trestle table — to provide extra seating, storage, or table space, depending on the needs of the innkeeper. Two trestles supported a chest and a pivoting top piece. When the top was vertical, folks could sit on the chest or put things in it. When it was horizontal, it became a large table. These settle tables, or "monk's chairs," were among the earliest examples of convertible furniture.

The popularity of the piece gradually declined in England, but in the seventeenth and eighteenth centuries, American colonists revived and refined it. They found it was a useful design not just for taverns and inns but for many country homes where space was at a premium. Between meals, when a table was not needed, the top tilted up and the settle table was stored against a wall. This freed the room to be used for other purposes.

The settle table shown is similar to one now on display at Old Sturbridge Village in Massachusetts. The chest and seat are supported by distinctive shoe-shaped feet. As on many tables that survive from this period, the base is painted, while the top is natural wood. Originally, the entire piece may have been painted. However, years of scrubbing and scouring removed the paint from the top.

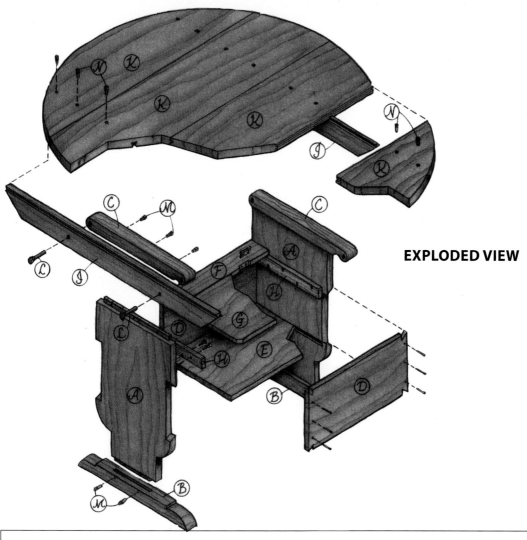

EXPLODED VIEW

BILL OF MATERIALS

WOODEN PARTS/*FINISHED DIMENSIONS*

A.	Trestles (2)	$\frac{7}{8}" \times 15" \times 26\frac{1}{8}"$
B.	Shoe feet (2)	$2" \times 2" \times 22"$
C.	Armrests (2)	$2" \times 2" \times 20"$
D.	Chest front/back	$\frac{7}{8}" \times 9\frac{1}{8}" \times 21\frac{3}{4}"$
E.	Chest bottom (2)	$\frac{7}{8}" \times 13\frac{1}{4}" \times 20\frac{3}{4}"$
F.	Seat	$\frac{7}{8}" \times 3\frac{1}{2}" \times 20"$
G.	Seat lid	$\frac{7}{8}" \times 12\frac{1}{2}" \times 19\frac{7}{8}"$
H.	Lid supports (2)	$\frac{7}{8}" \times 1\frac{1}{2}" \times 13\frac{1}{4}"$
J.	Braces (2)	$\frac{7}{8}" \times 3\frac{7}{16}" \times 41\frac{5}{8}"$

K.	Top boards (4)	$\frac{7}{8}" \times 12\frac{3}{8}" \times 48"$
L.	Pivots (4)	$1\frac{3}{8}"$ dia. $\times 4"$
M.	Long pegs (10)	$\frac{3}{8}" \times \frac{3}{8}" \times 1\frac{3}{4}"$
N.	Short pegs (16)	$\frac{3}{8}" \times \frac{3}{8}" \times 1\frac{1}{4}"$

HARDWARE

#10 × 1½" Flathead wood screws (8)
1¾" × 3" Butt hinges and mounting screws (1 pair)
6d Square-cut nails (16–20)

Plan of Procedure

1

If necessary, glue up wide stock to make the trestles and other parts. Plane, rip, and cut the parts to the sizes shown in the Bill of Materials, except the pivots. Cut these 1"–2" longer than specified.

2

Lay out the shape of the trestle, feet, and armrest, as shown in the *Trestle Layout, Shoe Foot Layout,* and *Armrest Layout.* However, don't cut the shapes yet.

3

Cut or rout the joinery necessary to build the base:

- ⅞"-wide, ⅜"-deep, 13¼"-long double-blind dadoes in the inside faces of the trestles, as shown in the *Trestle Layout/ Side View*

- ⅜"-wide, 1"-deep, 7"-long mortises in the top surfaces of the feet, as shown in the *Shoe Foot Layout/Top View.*

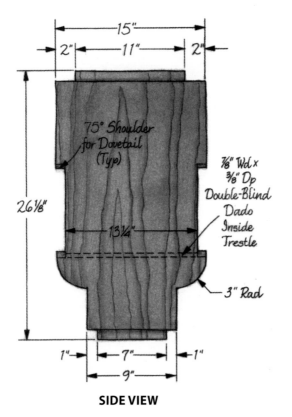

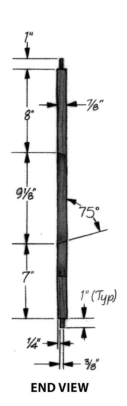

SIDE VIEW   **END VIEW**

TRESTLE LAYOUT

- ⅜"-wide, 1"-deep, 11"-long mortises in the bottom surfaces of the armrests, as shown in the *Armrest Layout/Bottom View*

- ⅜"-thick, 1"-long tenons along the entire width of the top and bottom ends of the trestles

4

Using a band saw or saber saw, cut the shapes of the trestles. Notch the tenons so they fit their respective mortises.

5

Using a band saw, remove as much waste as possible from the dovetail notches. Cut the angled shoulders of the notches with a chisel, as shown in the *Trestle Layout/End View*. Sand the sawed edges.

6

Lay out and cut the chest front and back, as shown in the *Chest Front/Back Layout*, to fit in the dovetail notches.

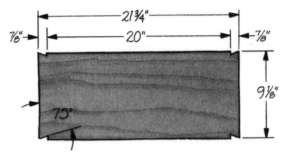

CHEST FRONT/BACK LAYOUT

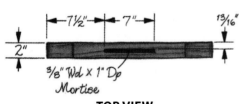

TOP VIEW

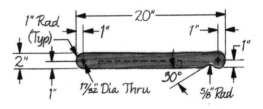

SIDE VIEW

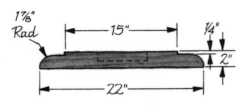

SIDE VIEW
SHOE FOOT LAYOUT

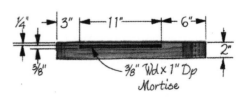

BOTTOM VIEW
ARMREST LAYOUT

PLAN OF PROCEDURE

7

Drill $^{17}/_{32}$"-diameter holes through the armrest, as shown in the *Armrest Layout/Side View*.

8

Cut the shapes of the feet and armrests. Sand the sawed edges.

9

Finish sand the trestles, feet, armrests, chest bottom, front, and back. Dry assemble the parts to check the fit of the joints, then reassemble the trestles, feet, and armrest with glue.

10

Round the bottom portion of the long pegs, as shown in the *Peg Detail*.

11

Drill ⅜"-diameter, 1¾"-deep holes through the mortise-and-tenon joints that hold the feet and armrests to the trestles, as shown in the *Side View*. Drive the long pegs into the holes from the outside. Leave about ¹⁄₁₆" of each peg protruding.

12

Glue the chest bottom in the dadoes in the trestle assemblies and glue the front and back to the bottom. Do *not* glue the front and back to the trestles. (The trestles' grain direction opposes that of the front and back. Glue joints would keep the front and back from expanding and contracting properly.) Instead, attach the front and back to the trestles with square-cut nails.

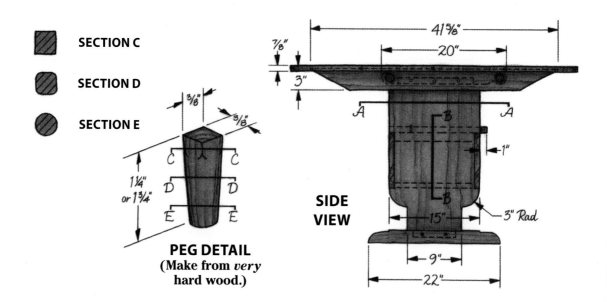

SECTION C

SECTION D

SECTION E

PEG DETAIL
(Make from *very* hard wood.)

SIDE VIEW

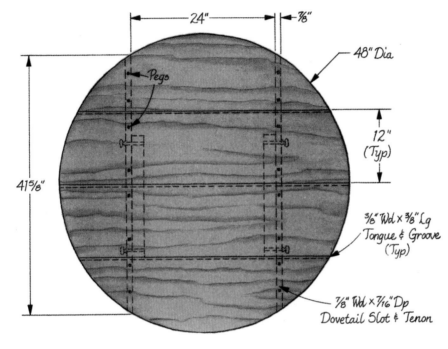

TOP VIEW

24"

⅞"

Pegs

48" Dia

41⅝"

12" (Typ)

⅜" Wd × ⅜" Lg
Tongue & Groove
(Typ)

⅞" Wd × ⁷⁄₁₆" Dp
Dovetail Slot & Tenon

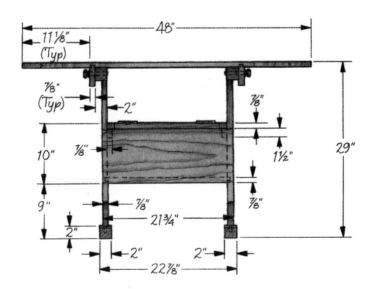

FRONT VIEW

48"

11⅛" (Typ)

⅞" (Typ)

2"

⅞"

10"

⅞"

1½"

9"

⅞"

⅞"

29"

2"

21¾"

2"

2"

22⅞"

PLAN OF PROCEDURE

13

Finish sand the lid supports and fasten them to the inside surfaces of the trestles with flathead wood screws. Countersink the screws, so the heads are flush with the surface of the supports. Do *not* glue the supports to the trestles — the grain directions oppose each other.

14

Cut off the front corners of the lid, as shown in the *Lid Layout*. Sand the sawed edges.

15

Mortise the adjoining edges of the lid and seat for hinges.

16

Finish sand the lid and seat, then fasten the seat to the back and lid supports with glue and nails. Mount the lid to the seat.

17

Set all the nails, then cover the heads with putty.

18

Cut a ⅜"-wide, ⅜"-deep groove in one edge of each top board and a matching ⅜"-thick, ⅜"-long tongue in the other edge. Clamp the boards together, edge to edge, with the tongues fitted in the grooves. However, do *not* glue them up.

19

With a string or a beam compass, lay out the circular shape of the top and the positions of the braces, as shown in the *Top View*.

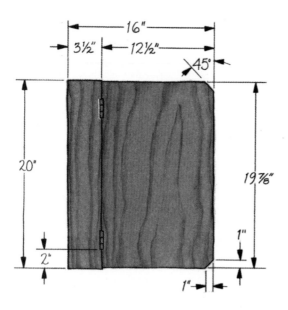

LID LAYOUT

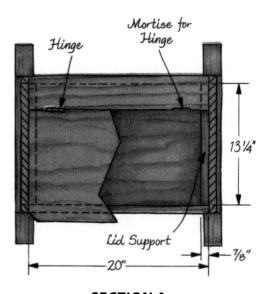

SECTION A

20

Rout two ⅞"-wide, ⁷⁄₁₆"-deep dovetail grooves across all four boards (perpendicular to the tongue-and-groove joints), where you wish to mount the braces. Using a table-mounted router, rout matching dovetails in each brace.

21

Miter the ends of the braces at 60°, as shown in the *Top Brace Layout/Side View.*

22

Disassemble the top boards. Finish sand the boards and the braces. Clamp the boards back together, edge to edge, lining up the dovetail slots. Slide the braces into the slots. *Do not* apply glue.

23

Turn the top assembly over, so the top side faces up. Saw the circular shape and sand the sawed edges.

24

Place the top assembly on the settle, so the braces straddle the armrests. Center the top on the settle, then reach through the holes in the armrests with a pencil or an awl to mark the inside surface of the braces.

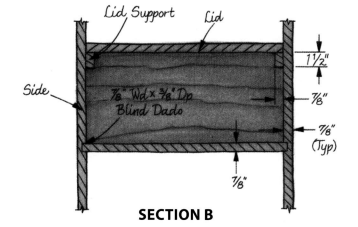

SECTION B

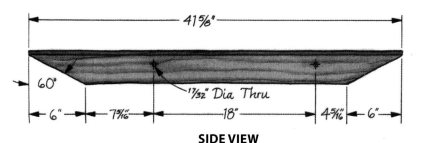

SIDE VIEW

TOP BRACE LAYOUT

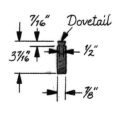

END VIEW

PLAN OF PROCEDURE

25

Remove the top and disassemble it. Drill $^{17}/_{32}$"-diameter holes through the braces at each of the marks, then reassemble the top.

Note: There should be two holes in each brace, front and back. The back hole should be 13½" from the back end, and the front hole should be 10½" from the front end.

26

Turn the shapes of the pivots, as shown in the *Pivot Layout*.

27

Reposition the top assembly on the settle, lining up the front and back holes in the braces with those in the armrests. Slide the pivots through the braces and into the armrests.

28

Round the bottom portion of the short pegs, as shown in the *Peg Detail*.

29

Drill ⅜"-diameter, 1¼"-deep holes through the top boards into the braces. Drive the short pegs into the holes, leaving about ¹⁄₁₆" of each peg protruding.

30

Check the tilting action of the top. Remove the front pivots and tilt the top up until it's vertical. It should move easily and remain vertical with no need to brace it. Make any necessary adjustments.

31

Remove all the pivots and take the top off the base. Also remove the lid and the hinges. Do any necessary touch-up sanding, then apply a finish to the completed settle table. After the finish dries, replace the lid and the top.

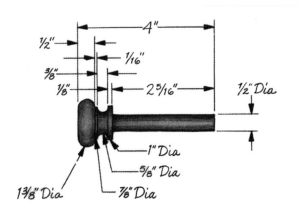

PIVOT LAYOUT

SPOON RACK

At the country table, spoons were the most important utensils. The early settlers rarely used forks and employed knives just for cutting and spearing. Most of the actual eating was accomplished with spoons.

Consequently, the cook kept the spoons ready. Many plate racks, pewter benches, and cupboards had notches in the front edges of the shelves to hold the spoons where they could be easily reached. It was also common to find the spoons arranged on their own special rack, hung on the kitchen or eating room wall.

The spoon rack shown is a copy of an old country design. Three notched bars hold a dozen spoons — a king's ransom in spoons for many pioneer families.

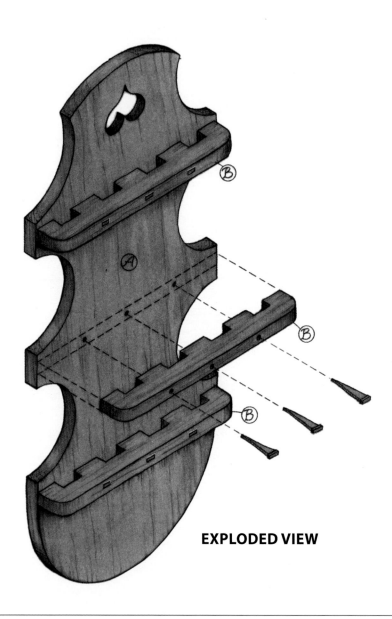

EXPLODED VIEW

BILL OF MATERIALS

WOODEN PARTS/*FINISHED DIMENSIONS*
A. Backboard   ½" × 9¼" × 21½"
B. Holders (3)   ½" × 1¼" × 9¼"

HARDWARE
6d Square-cut nails (9)

PLAN OF PROCEDURE

1

Plane, rip, and cut the parts to the sizes shown in the Bill of Materials.

2

Cut 1"-wide, ½"-deep notches in the holders, as shown in the *Holder Detail*.

3

Lay out and cut the *Backboard Pattern*. Sand the sawed edges.

4

Finish sand the parts of the spoon rack, then glue the holders to the backboard.

5

Let the glue dry, then drill pilot holes for square-cut nails. Drive the nails through the holders and into the backboards, but don't set or cover the heads — let them show.

6

Do any necessary touch-up sanding and apply a finish to the completed project.

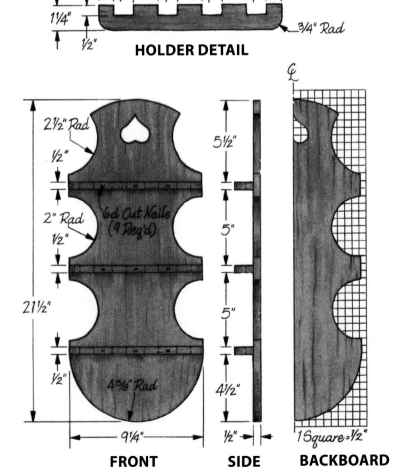

HOLDER DETAIL

FRONT VIEW

SIDE VIEW

BACKBOARD PATTERN

KNIFE CADDY

Country folks made all sorts of carryalls and containers to help them organize their lives. This "knife caddy" was one of the most common. It was not unusual for a family to have a dozen or more of these carriers, which they used to hold everything from dinner-ware to sewing notions to gardening tools.

The knife caddy looks like a small, contemporary toolbox or "tote." It's made in much the same way — just a shallow box with a handle that also serves as a divider. Like most utilitarian pieces, it's fairly plain. The only decorative feature is the heart-shaped handle cutout. Hearts have been a common folk ornament since medieval times.

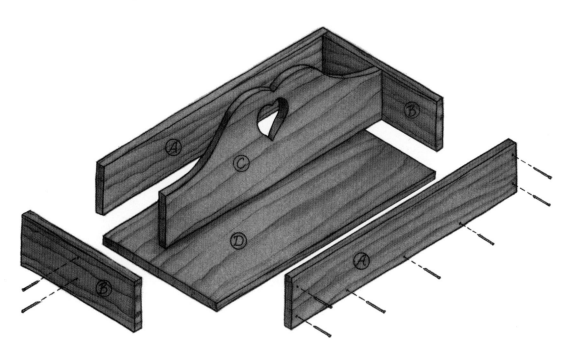

EXPLODED VIEW

BILL OF MATERIALS

WOODEN PARTS/*FINISHED DIMENSIONS*

A.	Sides (2)	⅜" × 2¼" × 14"
B.	Ends (2)	⅜" × 2¼" × 7"
C.	Divider	⅜" × 4⅞" × 13¼"
D.	Bottom	¼" × 7" × 13¼"

HARDWARE
1¼" Headless brads (24–30)

Plan of Procedure

1

Plane, rip, and cut the parts to the sizes shown in the Bill of Materials.

2

Lay out and cut the shape of the divider, as shown in the *Divider Pattern*. Sand the sawed edges.

3

Finish sand the parts of the knife caddy and dry assemble them to check the fit. Reassemble the parts with glue and headless brads. Set the heads of the brads and cover them with putty.

4

Do any necessary touch-up sanding and apply a finish to the completed project.

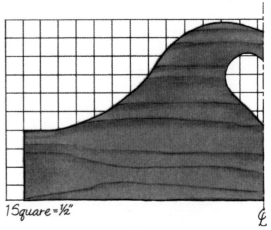

1 Square = ½"

DIVIDER PATTERN

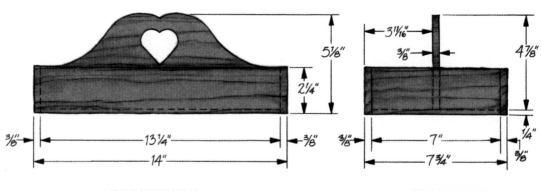

FRONT VIEW

SIDE VIEW

FOR READING
& WRITING

LAP DESK

During the Middle Ages, the few literate folks in western Europe who could read and write often used a *writing box* — a small chest with a flat, slanted lid. The writing box was a storage chest, a tabletop desk, and a book stand all in one. The box had compartments for paper, pens, and ink. The lid provided a writing surface or supported books at a comfortable angle for reading.

This basic design continued to be used through the eighteenth century in England and longer in her colonies. In America, folks called it a *lap desk*, although they rarely used it on their laps. They rested the box on a table when it was needed and set it aside on a shelf or in a cabinet when it wasn't. As the American public became more and more schooled and reading and writing became a part of everyday life, the lap desk gave way to larger desks with legs attached to them.

The lap desk shown is patterned after one made in the Shaker community in New Lebanon, New York, during the first part of the nineteenth century. It has several clever features: A small drawer on the right side serves as an inkwell and a larger drawer on the left holds extra paper. Under the lid, there is space for books or additional writing materials and a ledge or *till* for pens, pencils, and nibs.

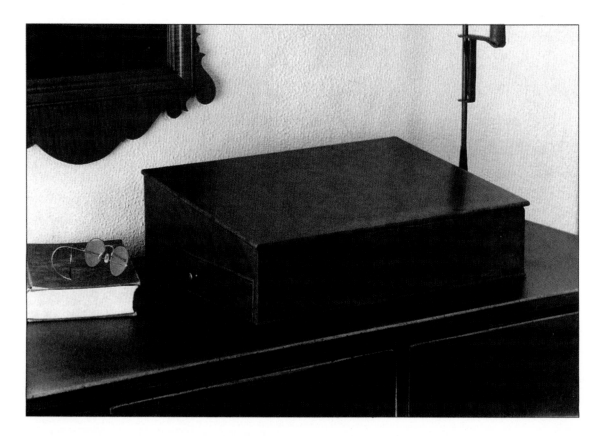

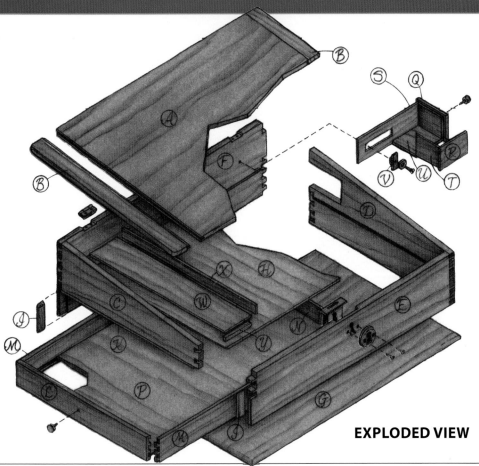

EXPLODED VIEW

BILL OF MATERIALS

WOODEN PARTS/*FINISHED DIMENSIONS*

A.	Lid	$5/_{16}$" × 13⅛" × 17⅜"
B.	Breadbords (2)	$5/_{16}$" × 1$3/_{16}$" × 13⅛"
C.	Left side	⅜" × 3⅝" × 12¾"
D.	Right side	⅜" × 3⅝" × 12¾"
E.	Front	⅜" × 3$15/_{16}$" × 18¾"
F.	Back	⅜" × 5⅝" × 18¾"
G.	Bottom	$3/_{16}$" × 13" × 19"
H	Shelf	¼" × 12⅜" × 18$3/_{16}$"
J.	Side bead molding (2)	⅛" × $9/_{16}$" × 2"
K.	Top bead molding	⅛" × $9/_{16}$" × 12¼"
L.	Paper drawer front	⅜" × 11$3/_{16}$" × 11$15/_{16}$"
M.	Paper drawer sides (2)	¼" × 1$13/_{16}$" × 18$3/_{16}$"
N.	Paper drawer back	¼" × 1$7/_{16}$" × 11$15/_{16}$"
P.	Paper drawer bottom	¼" × 11⅝" × 18⅛"
Q.	Ink drawer front	⅜" × 2⅛" × 2⅝"
R.	Front ink drawer side	⅛" × 1$13/_{16}$" × 2⅝"
S.	Back ink drawer side	⅛" × 1$13/_{16}$" × 5⅝"

T.	Ink drawer back	⅛" × 1$11/_{16}$" × 2$1/_{16}$"
U.	Ink drawer bottom	⅛" × 2$1/_{16}$" × 2⅝"
V.	Ink drawer keeper	$5/_{16}$" × $5/_{16}$" × 1½"
W.	Pencil till bottom	⅛" × 2$5/_{16}$" × 12"
X.	Pencil till lip	⅛" × ¾" × 12"
Y.	Pencil till glue blocks (2)	$5/_{16}$" × $5/_{16}$" × 2$7/_{16}$"

HARDWARE

½" -dia. Brass drawer pulls (2)
Small lock and latch
Escutcheon
⅞" Wire or headless brads (24–36)
#6 × ⅝" Roundhead wood screw
#6 Flat waser

PLAN OF PROCEDURE

1

Plane, rip, and cut the front, back, sides, bottom, lid, breadboards, and shelf to the sizes shown in the Bill of Materials. Bevel the top edges of the front and back at 8°, as shown in *Section A*. Plane and rip the bead molding stock to the specified thickness and width, but don't cut it to length yet. You can plane the stock needed for the other parts, but don't cut them to length or width.

Note: The smaller assemblies in this project — the paper drawer, ink drawer, and pencil till — should be fitted to the desk *after* it's built. If the dimensions of the desk change slightly from what's shown as you assemble it, the size of these smaller pieces must change also.

2

Cut the opening for the ink drawer in the right side, as shown in the *Right Side Layout*.

3

Lay out and cut the dovetails that join the front, back, and sides. For instructions on how to cut these dovetails, refer to Making Hand-Cut Dovetails, page 48.

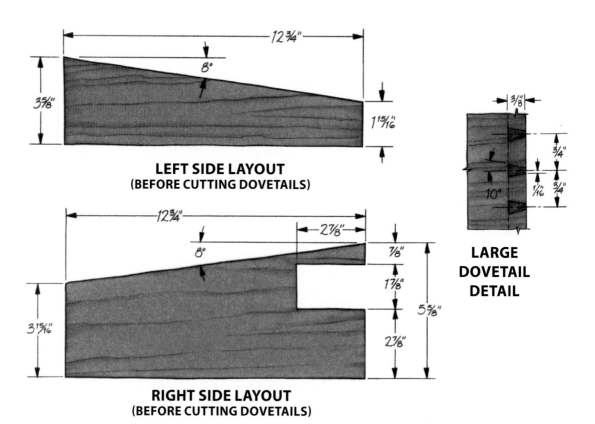

LEFT SIDE LAYOUT
(BEFORE CUTTING DOVETAILS)

RIGHT SIDE LAYOUT
(BEFORE CUTTING DOVETAILS)

LARGE DOVETAIL DETAIL

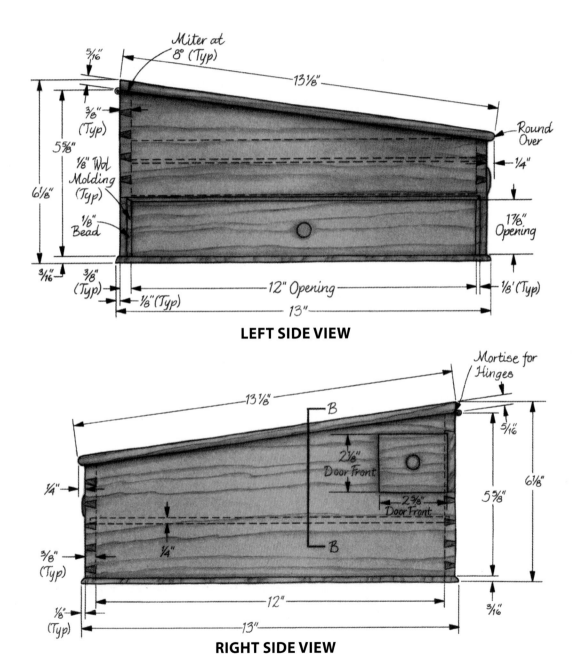

Miter at 8° (Typ)

5/16"

13 1/8"

3/8" (Typ)

Round Over

5 5/8"

1/4"

1/8" Wd Molding (Typ)

6 1/8"

1 7/8" Opening

1/8" Bead

3/16"

3/8" (Typ)

12" Opening

1/8" (Typ)

1/8" (Typ)

13"

LEFT SIDE VIEW

Mortise for Hinges

13 1/8"

B

5/16"

2 1/8" Door Front

1/4"

6 1/8"

2 5/8" Door Front

5 5/8"

1/4"

3/8" (Typ)

B

12"

1/8" (Typ)

3/16"

13"

RIGHT SIDE VIEW

PLAN OF PROCEDURE

4

Cut or rout the remaining joinery necessary to assemble the desk:

- ¼"-wide, ³⁄₁₆"-deep double-blind grooves in the front, back, and right side to hold the shelf, as shown in *Section A* and *Section B* (stop these grooves ³⁄₁₆" from the ends of the parts; do *not* cut through to the ends)

- ½"-wide, ⅛"-deep, 2"-long blind rabbets in the left ends of the front and back to hold the bead molding, as shown in the *Left Side/Molding Detail*

- ⅛"-wide, ⅛"-deep rabbet in the left edge of the shelf, to house the bead molding

- ⅛"-wide, ³⁄₁₆"-deep grooves in the ends of the lid, to hold the breadboards, as shown in the *Breadboard Joinery Detail*

- ⅛"-wide, ³⁄₁₆"-long tenons in the inside edges of the breadboards, to fit the grooves in the lid

- Mortises in the front, back, and lid for the hinges and lock (the dimensions of these mortises will depend on the hardware)

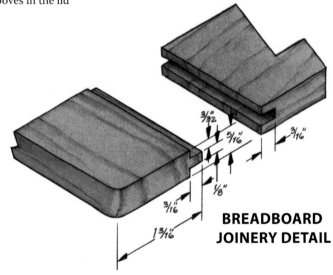

BREADBOARD JOINERY DETAIL

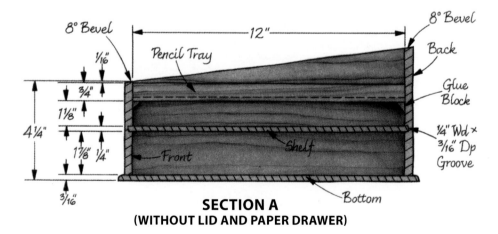

SECTION A
(WITHOUT LID AND PAPER DRAWER)

5

Drill a hole in the front so you can insert the key in the lock.

6

Assemble the lid and breadboards with glue. Let the glue dry, then sand the surfaces clean and flush.

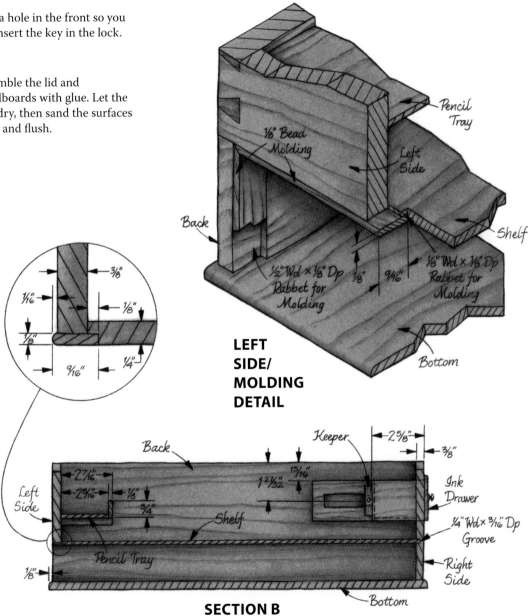

LEFT SIDE/ MOLDING DETAIL

Pencil Tray

Left Side

Shelf

Back

Bottom

⅛" Bead Molding

½" Wd × ⅛" Dp Rabbet for Molding

⅛"

9⁄16"

⅛" Wd × ⅛" Dp Rabbet for Molding

³⁄₈"

1⁄16"

⅛"

⅛"

9⁄16"

¼"

SECTION B (WITHOUT LID AND PAPER DRAWER)

Back

Keeper

2⅝"

³⁄₈"

15⁄16"

1²⁷⁄₃₂"

Ink Drawer

Left Side

2⁷⁄16"

2⅝⁄16"

⅛"

¾"

Shelf

¼" Wd × ³⁄16" Dp Groove

Pencil Tray

Right Side

⅛"

Bottom

PLAN OF PROCEDURE

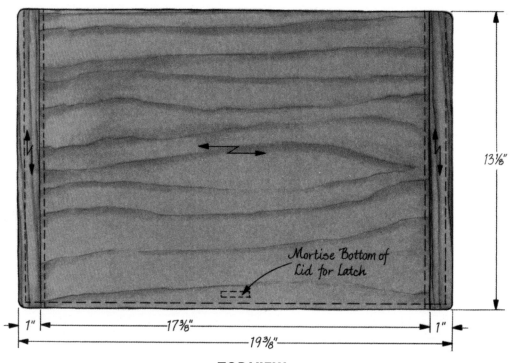

Mortise Bottom of
Lid for Latch

13⅛"

1"   17⅜"   1"

19⅜"

TOP VIEW

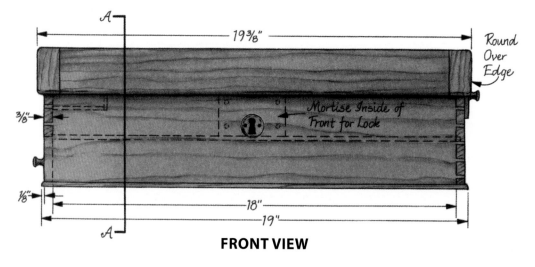

A

19⅜"

Round
Over
Edge

3/8"

Mortise Inside of
Front for Lock

⅛"

18"

19"

A

FRONT VIEW

7

Round over the outside edge of the bead molding stock, the side and front edges of the lid assembly, and all four edges of the bottom.

8

Dry assemble the front, back, sides, and shelf to test the fit of the joints. Adjust the fit as necessary, then cut the moldings to length. Miter the adjoining edges.

9

Finish sand all the parts you've made so far. Assemble the front, back, sides, shelf, and moldings. Glue all parts except the shelf. Let it float in its grooves.

10

Attach the bottom to the front, back, and right side with brads. You may glue the bottom to the front and back, but do *not* glue it to the right side. Set the heads of the brads.

11

Attach the lid to the desk assembly.

12

Install the lock and escutcheon. When the lock is installed, measure the location of the latch on the lid.

13

Cut a mortise for the latch, and install it in the lid.

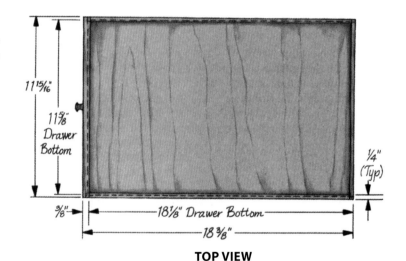

TOP VIEW

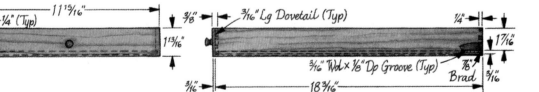

FRONT VIEW **PAPER DRAWER** **SIDE VIEW**

PLAN OF PROCEDURE

14

Measure the opening for the paper drawer and determine the proper dimensions for the drawer. (It should be approximately ¹⁄₁₆" smaller than the width and height of the opening when finished. You may wish to build it slightly large, then plane or sand it to fit.) Cut the paper drawer parts to size.

15

Lay out and cut the dovetails that join the drawer front, back, and sides. Note that the dovetails that join the front to the sides are *half-blind,* so they can't be seen when the drawer is closed.

16

Rout or cut ³⁄₁₆"-wide, ⅛"-deep grooves in the inside surfaces of the drawer front and sides to hold the drawer bottom, as shown in the *Paper Drawer/ Side View.*

17

Dry assemble the drawer to test the fit of the joints, and adjust them as necessary.

18

Finish sand the parts of the paper drawer, then assemble the front, back, and sides with glue. Using a handplane, "relieve" the edges and front ends of the drawer bottom so the bottom tapers to ³⁄₁₆" thick, as shown on the *Paper Drawer Joinery Detail.* Slide the bottom into its grooves and tack it to the back with brads. Do *not* glue the bottom in place; let it float in the grooves. Sand the drawer joinery clean and flush.

19

Install one of the drawer pulls on the front and test its fit in the desk. If it binds, sand or plane stock from the drawer parts to adjust the fit.

20

Measure the ink drawer opening and determine the proper dimensions for the drawer, as you did with the paper drawer. Cut the ink drawer parts to size.

21

Rout or cut ⁹⁄₃₂"-wide, ³⁄₁₆"-deep rabbets in the ends and bottom edge of the drawer front. Cut a ⁵⁄₃₂"-wide, ³⁄₁₆"-deep rabbet in the top edge, as shown in the *Ink Drawer/Side View* and *Ink Drawer/Top View.*

22

Rout or cut a ⁹⁄₁₆"-wide, 2½"-long groove in the back side, as shown in the *Ink Drawer/ Side View.*

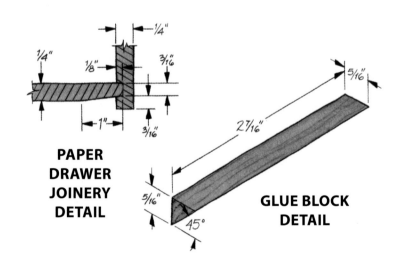

PAPER DRAWER JOINERY DETAIL

GLUE BLOCK DETAIL

23

Cut the keeper to fit the groove in the ink drawer side, as shown in the *Ink Drawer Keeper Detail*. Drill a ⅛"-diameter hole through the keeper.

24

Finish sand the ink drawer parts, then assemble them with glue and brads. Sand the joints clean and flush and install the remaining drawer pull on the front.

25

Slide the drawer into the opening to check the fit. If necessary, sand or plane the drawer until it slides smoothly in and out of the desk. Then install the keeper on the inside face of the back, holding it in place with a roundhead wood screw and flat washer. Do *not* glue the keeper in place, in case you want to remove it to repair the drawer.

26

Measure the space for the pencil till and cut the parts accordingly. Bevel the edges of the glue blocks, as shown in the *Glue Block Detail*.

27

Finish sand the parts of the pencil till. Glue the blocks inside the desk and glue the till lid to the till bottom. When the glue dries, attach the till inside the desk, gluing it to the blocks and the left side.

28

Remove the drawers from the desk and detach all hardware — hinges, pulls, lock, latch, and escutcheon. Apply a finish to the desk, then replace the drawers and hardware.

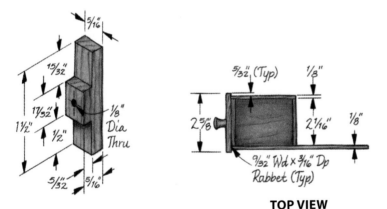

INK DRAWER KEEPER DETAIL

TOP VIEW

INK DRAWER

FRONT VIEW

SIDE VIEW

COUNTRY CRAFTSMAN'S KNOW-HOW:
MAKING HAND-CUT DOVETAILS

When assembling boxes — plank chests, cases, and drawers — cabinetmakers often used dovetails to join the front, back, and sides. These are extremely durable joints — the *pins* lock between the *tails*, so the joint holds tight even without glue or metal fasteners.

Old-time craftsmen cut these joints by hand, employing a chisel and a saw. Today, there are several commercial router jigs that will cut the dovetails with a machine, but so far, no one has produced a jig that can reproduce the slender pins and wide tails favored by eighteenth- and nineteenth-century cabinetmakers. The best way

to make these dovetails is still by hand. With a little practice, you can cut them manually as easily as with a router.

In addition to a chisel and a saw, you'll also need a small mallet (to strike the chisel), a marking gauge, a marking knife or scratch awl, and a template (to lay out the dovetails). You can purchase commercially made dovetail templates, make your own, or substitute a sliding T-bevel. The homemade template shown offers an advantage over commercial templates and T-bevels: You can also use it to guide the saw.

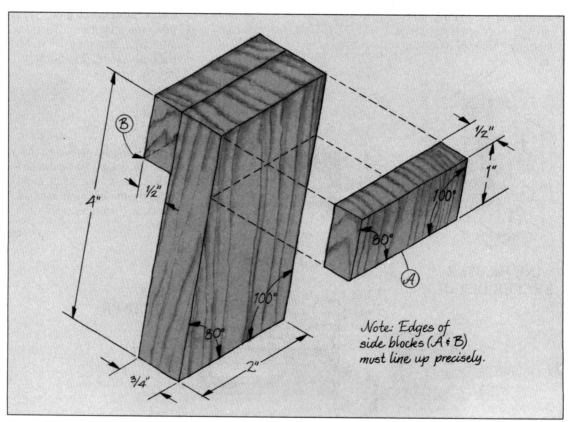

Dovetail Template and Guide (make from a very hard wood, such as maple or hickory)

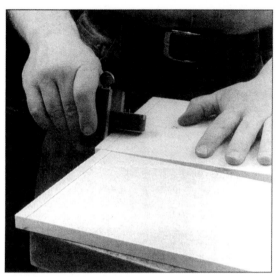

1 You can start with either the pins or the tails — most craftsmen prefer the tails. Using the marking gauge, scribe two lines — one on each face — near the end of the board. These lines indicate the length of the tails and are called "baselines." Through tails are as long as the adjoining board is thick; half-lap tails are half to two-thirds as long.

2 Using the template and a marking knife, draw the angled lines that mark the sides or "cheeks" of the tails. Once again, mark *both* sides of the board. Shade the area between the tails — the waste to be removed — with a pencil. Note that the tails are noticeably wider than the waste. This is not necessary, but, as mentioned previously, it's traditional.

3 Saw the cheeks of the tails down to the baselines, cutting on the waste side of the marks. If you wish, guide the saw with the template. Use a small, fine-toothed saw, such as a dovetail saw or a Dozuki saw, to do the cutting.

COUNTRY CRAFTSMAN'S KNOW-HOW:
MAKING HAND-CUT DOVETAILS—*CONTINUED*

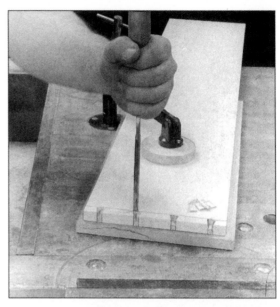

4 Once you have cut the cheeks, remove the waste between the tails with a *very* sharp chisel. Remove each bit of waste in two steps: First, use the chisel as a cutting tool. Hold it vertically and place the edge on the baseline. Strike it with a mallet, cutting $1/16$"– $1/8$" deep all along the line.

5 Next, use the chisel as a wedge. Hold it horizontally and put the edge against the waste at the end of the board, $1/16$"– $1/8$" below the face. Strike it with a mallet, lifting a small amount of waste.

6 Repeat this procedure until you've cut halfway through the board. Then turn the board over and remove waste from the other side. Continue until you have removed all the waste between the tails.

7 Scribe baselines on both sides of the adjoining board, then mark the pins. Use the completed tails as a template. (If you chose to make the pins first, you can use the completed pins to mark the tails.) Once again, shade the waste area.

8 Saw the cheeks of the pins down to the baselines, cutting on the waste side of the marks. (This prevents you from removing too much stock.) If you wish, guide the saw with the template.

9 Remove the waste with a chisel, using the same cutting and wedging technique as before. Cut halfway through the board, turn it over, and remove the remaining waste.

10 Test the fit of the joint. Because you cut on the waste side of the marks when making both the tails and the pins, the fit is likely to be tight. If it's too tight, shave a little bit of stock from the pins with the chisel.

BOOKSHELF

Until the mid-nineteenth century, the "library" of a typical country home would fit in a small box. Most families had but a single book — a Bible. Books, after all, were a luxury, and most country folks didn't know how to read.

In the early nineteenth century, two events changed that forever. The newly developed American system of public education, in little more than a generation, taught most of the nation's children to read, write, and cipher. For the first time in history, literacy became the rule rather than the exception. At the same time, the riot of innovation and invention that we remember

as the Industrial Revolution spawned a parade of fast, efficient printing presses. A tidal wave of inexpensive books washed over a literate public hungry for things to read. Almost overnight, home libraries expanded from one book to dozens.

This, in turn, created an inevitable problem — where to store the books? Country folks, with typical inventiveness, began to modify existing cupboards and racks — most of which had been used to keep cooking and eating utensils — to hold books. The bookshelf shown is an example. It's built in the same manner as a plate rack, but with wider shelves.

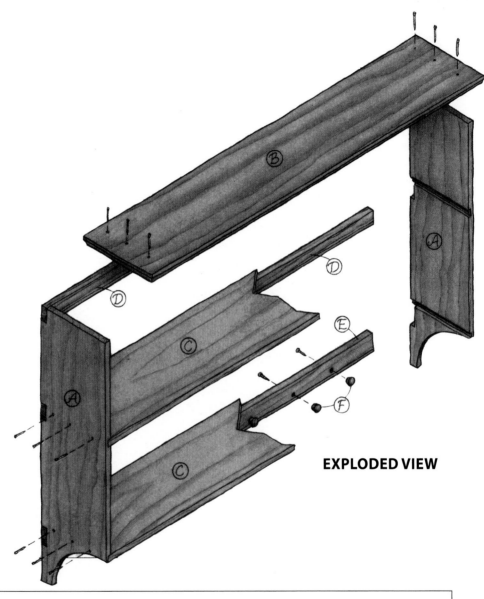

EXPLODED VIEW

BILL OF MATERIALS

WOODEN PARTS/*FINISHED DIMENSIONS*

A.	Sides (2)	¾" × 10¾" × 39¼"
B.	Top	¾" × 11¾" × 58"
C.	Shelves (2)	¾" × 10¾" × 55¼"
D.	Top/middle rails (2)	¾" × 2" × 56"
E.	Bottom rail	¾" × 3" × 56"
F.	Pegs (7)	1³/₈" dia. × 1⅛"

HARDWARE

#8 × 1½" Flathead wood screws (7)
6d Square-cut nails (24 – 30)

PLAN OF PROCEDURE

1

Plane, rip, and cut the parts to the sizes shown in the Bill of Materials. You can purchase pegs similar to those shown from some woodworking suppliers, or substitute Shaker pegs, which are handled by most suppliers. If you plan to turn these pegs, cut turning stock for each peg about 1" longer than specified.

2

Cut the joinery necessary to assemble the project:

- ¾"-wide, ⅜"-deep dadoes in the sides, as shown in the *Front View*, to hold the shelves
- ¾"-wide, 2"-long notches in the back edges of the sides, to hold the top and middle rails, as shown in the *Side View*
- ¾"-wide, 3"-long notch in the back edges of the sides to hold the bottom rail

3

Lay out and cut the shape of the sides, as shown in the *Side View*.

4

Rout or cut the molded shapes:

- $5/_{16}$"-diameter beads in the front face of the rails, near the bottom edge, as shown in the *Rail Profile*. This bead runs the full length of the rails.
- ½"-radius cove in the front edge and ends of the top, as shown in the *Top Profile*

5

If you're turning your own pegs, turn them to the profile shown in the *Peg Detail*.

6

Drill ⅛"-diameter, 1"-deep pilot holes, centered in the back ends of the pegs. Also drill ⅛"-diameter pilot holes through the bottom rail where you wish to mount these pegs. Countersink the pilot holes on the back surface of the rail.

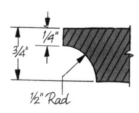

TOP PROFILE

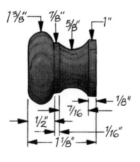

PEG DETAIL

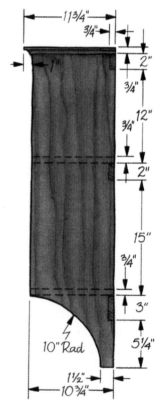

SIDE VIEW

7

Finish sand the parts of the bookshelf and dry assemble them to check the fit of the joints. Reassemble the sides, shelves, top, and rails with glue and square-cut nails.

8

Set the nails and cover the heads with putty.

9

Attach the pegs to the bottom rail with flathead wood screws. Drive the screws from the back of the rail into the pegs.

10

Do any necessary touch-up sanding and apply a finish to the completed project.

11

Hang the finished bookshelves on a wall by driving screws or Molly anchors through the top rail.

   Note: To support the weight of the books safely, fasten the shelves to *two* or more studs in the wall.

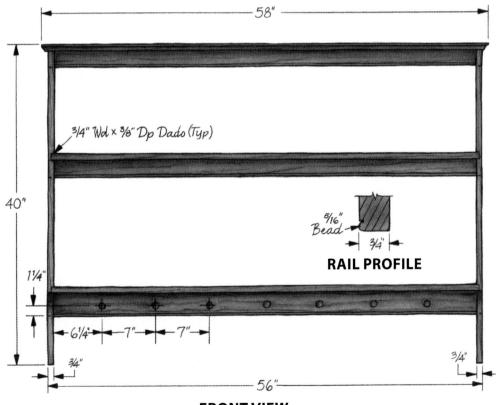

3/4" Wd x 3/8" Dp Dado (Typ)

58"

40"

1¼"

6¼" 7" 7"

3/4"

3/4"

56"

5/16" Bead

3/4"

RAIL PROFILE

FRONT VIEW

SHAKER CANDLE LEDGE

The United Society of Believers in Christ's Second Appearing — better known as the Shakers — developed an entire storage *system* around the simple peg. They lined the rooms in their community buildings with peg rails, then made clothes hangers, shelves, cupboards, and other small furniture pieces that could be hung on them.

This candle ledge is an example. It's patterned after a ledge made by the Shakers of Pleasant Hill, Kentucky. It's designed to be easily moved. If necessary, the Shakers could carry the candle ledge from room to room, hanging it on the wall wherever they wished.

They could also move the candle ledge around within a single room. Because they could place it anywhere there was a peg, and hang it at several different heights, a Shaker brother or sister could set the candle where its light was most needed. They might also use the ledge to hold other small items — kitchen utensils, sewing notions, tools, a water glass, or the personal effects that folks collect in their pockets.

The ledge is made in the same manner as Shaker bentwood boxes. The outside lip is a single piece of thin hardwood, bent into a hoop and pegged to a round bottom.

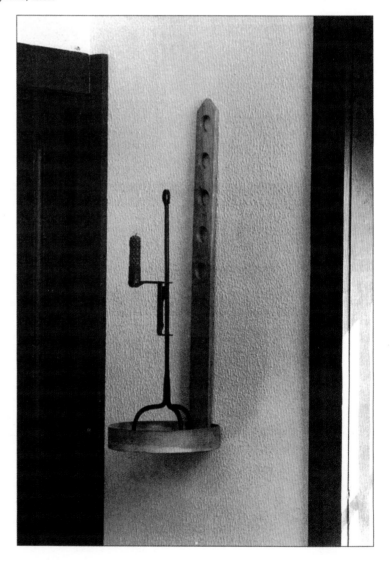

EXPLODED VIEW

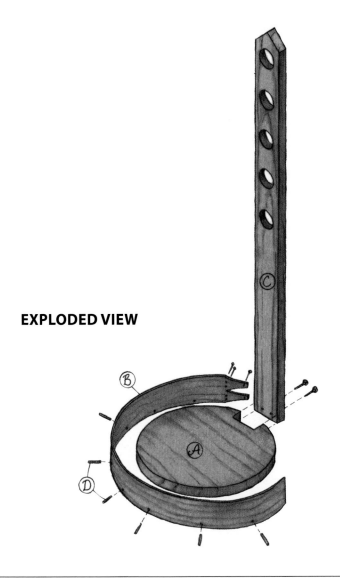

BILL OF MATERIALS

WOODEN PARTS/*FINISHED DIMENSIONS*

A.	Bottom	9" dia. × ⅝"
B.	Lip	³/₃₂" × 1¾" × 30¼"
C.	Post	½" × 2" × 28¾"
D.	Pegs (16–18)	¹/₁₆" dia. × ½"

HARDWARE
#6 × 1" Flathead wood screws (2)
#2 Copper tacks* (6)

You can purchase these tacks from:
   W. W. Cross Nail Company
   P.O. Box 365
   Jeffery, NH 03452

PLAN OF PROCEDURE

1

Plane, rip, and cut the parts to the sizes shown in the Bill of Materials.

Note: Most planers will only plane wood to ⅛" thick. To make the ³/₃₂"-thick stock for the lip, rip a thin slice from a wider board.

2

Mark the locations of the 1¼"-diameter holes on the post, as shown in the *Front View*, and drill them through the stock.

3

Miter the top of the post at 45°, so it comes to a point.

4

Bend the lip to form a 9"-diameter hoop, following the technique in Making Bentwood Boxes on page 60.

5

Cut the round bottom, beveling the edge at 5°, as shown in *Section A*. Fit the bottom to the lip, as described in Making Bentwood Boxes.

6

Remove the bottom from the lip and cut a 2"-wide, ½"-deep notch in the bottom, as shown in the *Top View*.

7

Finish sand the post and bottom. Fasten the post in the notch with flathead wood screws and glue. The end of the post should be flush with the bottom surface of the bottom.

8

Fit the lip to the bottom again, so it laps behind the post. Peg the bottom to the lip, as described in Making Bentwood Boxes. Sand the pegs flush with the surface of the lip.

9

Finish sand the lip and do any necessary touch up sanding to the other parts of the candle ledge. Apply a finish to the completed project.

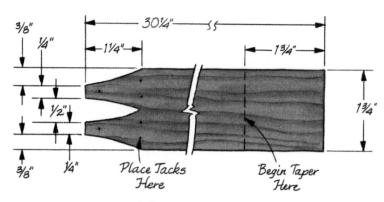

EDGING DETAIL

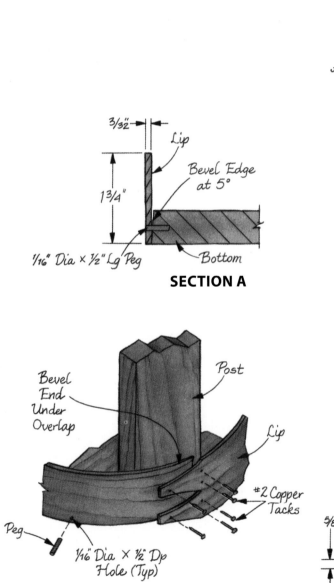

TOP VIEW

½"

³⁄₃₂"

9" Dia

A · A

SECTION A

³⁄₃₂"

Lip

Bevel Edge at 5°

1³⁄₄"

¹⁄₁₆" Dia × ½" Lg Peg

Bottom

LIP DETAIL

Bevel End Under Overlap

Post

Lip

#2 Copper Tacks

Peg

¹⁄₁₆" Dia × ½" Dp Hole (Typ)

FRONT VIEW

2"

2"

45°

1¼" Dia (Typ)

3" (Typ)

28¾"

⅝"

1³⁄₄"

COUNTRY CRAFTSMAN'S KNOW-HOW:
MAKING BENTWOOD BOXES

Sometime in the seventeenth century — perhaps earlier — craftsmen began to make round and oval bentwood boxes. These curved boxes, made from thin stock, were much lighter than rectangular boxes made from thicker boards. Yet, because the sides were curved, they were just as strong and durable. Country folks found many uses for these boxes — they made them into storage containers, shipping crates, trays, carryalls, and hanging shelves, such as the Shaker Candle Ledge. There are even records of these boxes being used as spitoons!

The box maker was a specialist, like the turner or chair bodger. As such, he had special tools. The most important were a steamer, or *poacher*, to make the wood pliable and bending forms (called *box molds*) to bend the wood to the proper shape. He also used a special *clinch anvil* to bend the points of the tiny tacks that held the wood together. Finally, he needed *dryers* to hold the shape of the wood until it cooled and dried. You can make all of these tools from scraps of hardwood, metal pipe, and metal guttering, as shown in the drawings.

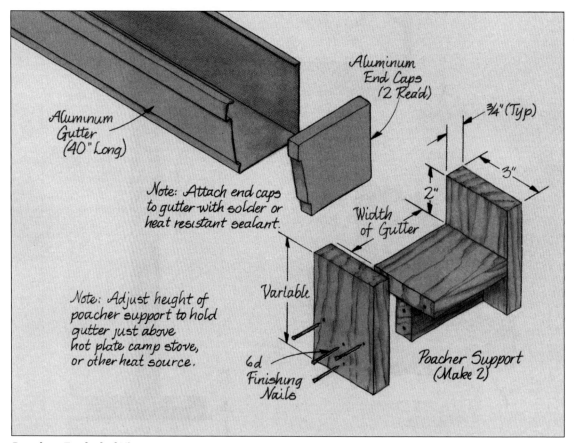

Aluminum End Caps (2 Req'd)

¾" (Typ)

3"

2"

Aluminum Gutter (40" Long)

Note: Attach end caps to gutter with solder or heat resistant sealant.

Width of Gutter

Note: Adjust height of poacher support to hold gutter just above hot plate camp stove, or other heat source.

Variable

6d Finishing Nails

Poacher Support (Make 2)

Poacher, Exploded View

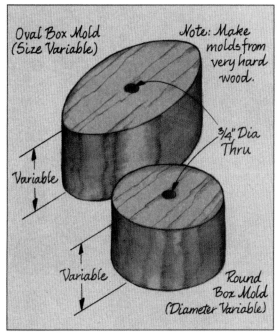

Oval Box Mold
(Size Variable)

Note: Make molds from very hard wood.

¾" Dia Thru

Variable

Variable

Round Box Mold (Diameter Variable)

Sample Box Molds

¾" Dia × 1½" Lg Dowel

12"

Note: Assemble frame with glue and nails Epoxy pipe in frame.

¾" Dia × ½" Dp Hole

12"

9"

1½" Dia Thru

4¼" ¾"

1½"

1½" OD × 18 Lg Steel Pipe

12"

Clinch Anvil, Exploded View

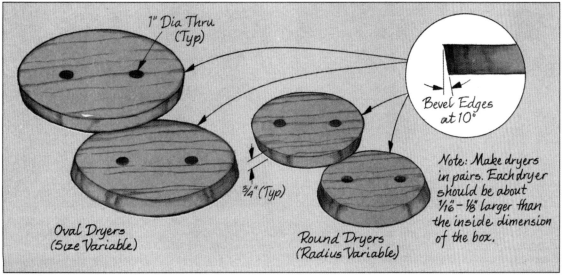

1" Dia Thru (Typ)

Bevel Edges at 10°

¾" (Typ)

Oval Dryers (Size Variable)

Round Dryers (Radius Variable)

Note: Make dryers in pairs. Each dryer should be about 1/16" – 1/8" larger than the inside dimension of the box.

Sample Dryers

COUNTRY CRAFTSMAN'S KNOW-HOW:
MAKING BENTWOOD BOXES—*CONTINUED*

1 First, cut the thin stock that forms the sides, or *bands,* of the boxes. You can use almost any stock, but box makers traditionally used maple. Depending on the size of the box, these bands should be $^3/_{64}$" – $^3/_{32}$" thick — the bigger the box, the thicker the band. Since most planers only plane to $^1/_8$" thick, cut the bands with a table saw and a hollow-ground planer blade.

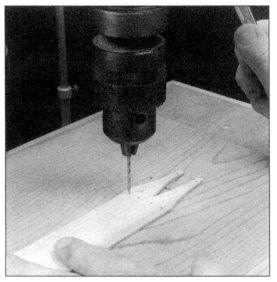

2 Where each band laps over itself, you must cut tapering fingers or *swallowtail joints* in the outside end. These swallowtails keep the band from splitting as the wood expands and contracts. Drill $^3/_{64}$"-diameter holes for the tacks in the swallowtails — this makes the tacks easier to drive.

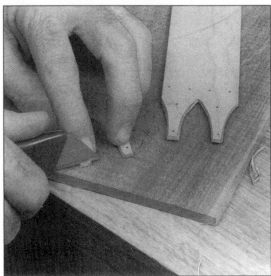

3 If you wish, chamfer the edges of the swallowtails with a bench knife. This is not necessary, but it does make a more attractive joint.

4 Taper the other end (opposite the swallowtails) with a belt sander. Use a thin scrap to press the inside surface of the wood against the abrasive belt, as shown. This protects your fingers from the heat generated by the friction of sanding. After making the taper, lightly sand the entire band to remove the saw marks.

5 Heat water in the poacher until it's as hot as you can get it without boiling. Let the band soak for 15–25 minutes, then take it out with a pair of tongs.

6 Before the wood cools, wrap it around the box mold as tightly as you can. If you're making an oval box, position the lapped portion of the band over the "side," where the elliptical curve is flattest. The swallowtails must end up on the outside, with the chamfers facing out.

COUNTRY CRAFTSMAN'S KNOW-HOW:
MAKING BENTWOOD BOXES—*CONTINUED*

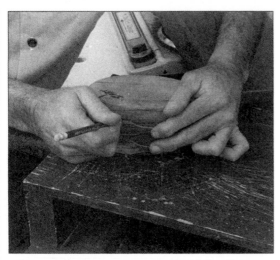

7 Mark the edges of the band across the lapped portion, near the base of the swallowtails. Loosen the band *slightly* and take it off the mold.

8 Put the band back together, so the marks on the edges line up. Place the band over the end of the anvil, then drive tacks through the swallowtails. The tacks will clinch over when the points hit the metal anvil. This, in turn, will hold the band together.

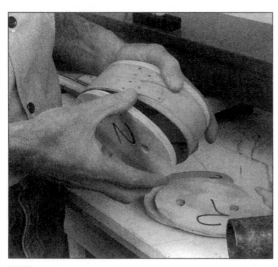

9 Press the dryers into the assembled band as you'd press a cork in a bottle. Use two dryers for each band, one in the top and one in the bottom. Leave the dryers in place while the band dries.

10 If you want to make a lid for the box, bend the lid band around the box band in the same manner that you bent the box band around the mold. Mark the lapped edges, tack the lid band together, and put it back over the box band to dry.

11 Cut the box bottom and lid from stock ¼" thick or thicker. You may want to use a softwood for these parts — box makers traditionally used white pine. Cut the part a little large, then sand it to size on a disk sander. As you sand, bevel the edge at 5° by tilting the sander's worktable.

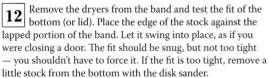

12 Remove the dryers from the band and test the fit of the bottom (or lid). Place the edge of the stock against the lapped portion of the band. Let it swing into place, as if you were closing a door. The fit should be snug, but not too tight — you shouldn't have to force it. If the fit is too tight, remove a little stock from the bottom with the disk sander.

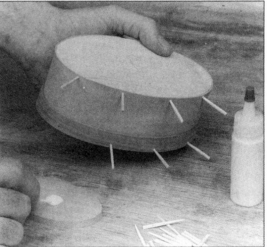

13 Adjust the bottom so it's flush with the edge of the band. Drill $1/_{16}$"-diameter, ½"-deep holes, spaced every 2"–3" around the circumference, through the band and into the bottom. (If you're making an oval box, do *not* drill holes at the points of the ellipse — this will weaken the box.) Dip round toothpicks in glue and insert the ends into the holes. Let the glue dry, then trim the toothpick pegs flush with the band.

RATCHET CANDLESTAND

One disadvantage of candlelight is that as a candle burns, it becomes shorter and the light gets lower. It strikes the page of the book — or whatever you're trying to see — at a more oblique angle, making the object harder to see. Because of this, the country folks who used candles invented several ingenious devices to raise the candle easily from time to time.

One of their favorite devices was a *ratchet candlestand*. This is a small table mounted on a telescoping pedestal. The sliding portion of the pedestal — the *ratchet* — has several teeth that point down. These engage a hinged *pawl* on the stationary part. This simple mechanism allows you to raise the stand a few inches at a time without having to loosen or tighten anything. Simply lift the top until the pawl drops under the next tooth on the ratchet — the pawl will prevent the top from sliding back down. To lower the top, lift the ratchet and let it slide back down.

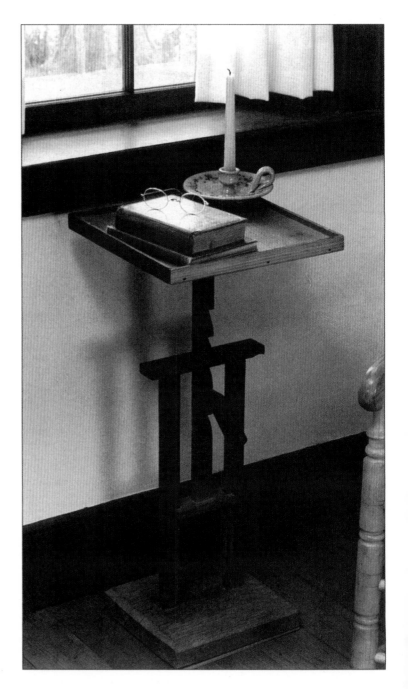

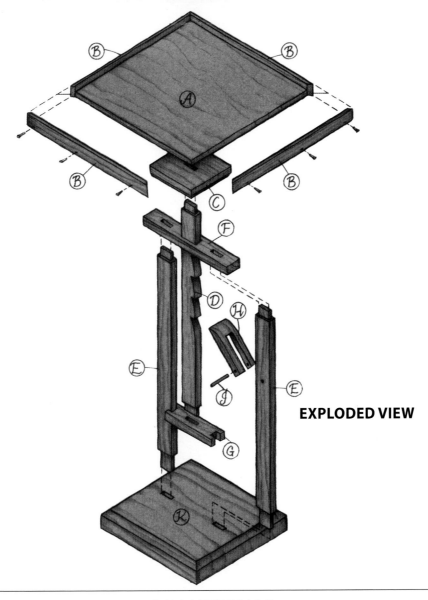

EXPLODED VIEW

BILL OF MATERIALS

WOODEN PARTS/*FINISHED DIMENSIONS*

A.	Top	½" × 14" × 14"
B.	Top trim (4)	¼" × 1" × 14½"
C.	Top mounting block	1" × 5" × 5"
D.	Ratchet	¾" × 1½" × 20¾"
E.	Legs (2)	¾" × 1½" × 2½"
F.	Stretcher	¾" × 1¾" × 10"

G.	Guide	¾" × 1¾" × 5¼"
H.	Pawl	¾" × 1¾" × 5⅝"
J.	Dowel	¼" dia. × 1¾"
K.	Base	1¾" × 10¾" × 11½"

HARDWARE

⅞" Square-cut headless brads (12–16)

PLAN OF PROCEDURE

1

If necessary, glue up stock to make the top. Then plane, rip, and cut the parts to the sizes shown in the Bill of Materials, except the top trim. Cut the trim ½"–1" longer than specified.

2

With a dado cutter or a table-mounted router, cut tenons in the ends of the rachet and legs, as shown in the *Ratchet Layout* and *Leg Layout*. Note that although the tenons are all the same thickness and width, their lengths differ.

3

Cut the mortises in the top mounting block, stretcher, guide, and base, as shown in the *Top Mounting Block Layout, Stretcher Layout, Guide Layout,* and *Base Layout*. As you cut, carefully fit the tenons on the ratchet and legs to the appropriate mortises. Note that all of these mortises go completely through the parts.

4

Chamfer the bottom edges of the top mounting block and the top edges of the base, as shown in the *Top Mounting Block Layout* and *Base Layout*.

5

Lay out the teeth on the ratchet, as shown in the *Ratchet Layout,* and cut them with a band saw or scroll saw. Sand the sawed edges.

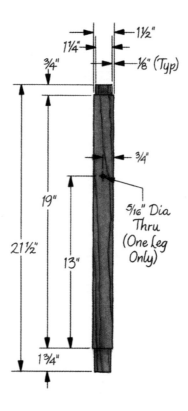

LEG LAYOUT

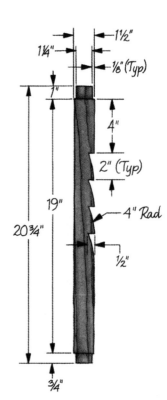

RATCHET LAYOUT

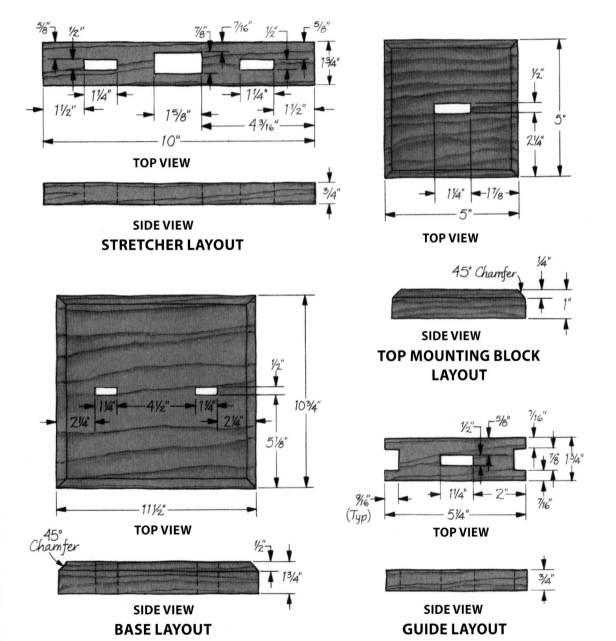

TOP VIEW

SIDE VIEW
STRETCHER LAYOUT

TOP VIEW

TOP VIEW

SIDE VIEW
TOP MOUNTING BLOCK
LAYOUT

TOP VIEW

SIDE VIEW
BASE LAYOUT

SIDE VIEW
GUIDE LAYOUT

PLAN OF PROCEDURE

6

Lay out the shape of the pawl, as shown in the *Pawl Layout,* and cut it on a band saw. First, cut the point with the pawl stock resting on its edge. Then cut the notch, with the stock resting on its face. Sand the sawed edges.

7

Lay out and cut the notches in the guide, and shown in the *Guide Layout.*

8

Finish sand all the parts of the stand. Position the top mounting block and the top so the grain of both parts are parallel, then glue them together.

9

When the glue dries, fit the trim around the circumference of the top. Miter the adjoining ends, as shown in the *Top View.* Attach the trim with brads or finishing nails and set the heads. Do *not* glue the trim to the top.

10

Drill a $5/16$"-diameter hole in one of the legs, as shown in the *Leg Layout.* Then attach the pawl to the leg with the dowel. Glue the dowel in the pawl, but *not* in the leg. The pawl must pivot freely in the leg.

11

Dry assemble the stand and check the ratchet action. The ratchet should slide up and down easily, and the weight of the pawl should keep it against the ratchet teeth. Make any necessary adjustments. When you're satisfied the parts fit and work properly, disassemble the stand.

12

Assemble the legs, stretcher, and base with glue. Let the glue dry, then sand the leg tenons flush with the surfaces of the base and stretcher.

13

Assemble the ratchet and the top assembly, gluing the 1"-long tenon in the top mounting block.

14

Place the guide so the notches straddle the legs. Pivot the pawl so it points up, and insert the ratchet through the stretcher. Glue the ratchet in the guide. When the glue dries, file the bottom ratchet tenon flush with the bottom surface of the guide.

15

Once again, check the ratchet action to be sure it operates properly. Do any necessary touch-up sanding on the stand, then apply a finish.

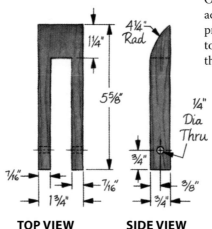

TOP VIEW   SIDE VIEW

PAWL LAYOUT

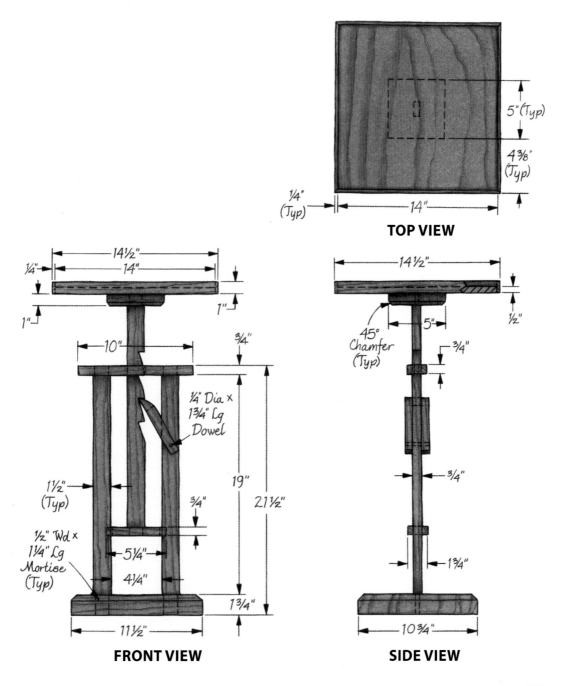

TOP VIEW

5" (Typ)

4⅜" (Typ)

¼" (Typ)

14"

14½"

14"

¼"

1"

1"

10"

¾"

¼" Dia × 1¾" Lg Dowel

19"

21½"

1½" (Typ)

¾"

½" Wd × 1¼" Lg Mortise (Typ)

5¼"

4¼"

1¾"

11½"

FRONT VIEW

14½"

5"

½"

45° Chamfer (Typ)

¾"

¾"

1¾"

10¾"

SIDE VIEW

MEAL BIN FILING CABINET

C ountry cooks often stored their flour in a meal bin. They mixed bread dough and let it rise in a similar bin called a "dough box." Both the meal bin and dough box were wooden chests with legs. When they weren't being used to make bread, these bins and boxes provided extra work surfaces. The lids were often split so the cook could move the items on them to one side, then open the other side of the lid.

As more and more Americans bought their bread from bakers and grocery stores, meal bins and dough boxes became less common. However, the general design remained useful. Bins and boxes were converted to store linens, records, wine, and many other small items.

Outwardly, this meal bin is a copy of an old country piece. However, the inside has been adapted to hold hanging letter-size files. These are suspended from pairs of metal rods that run side to side in the bin. Like all traditional meal bins, the lid is split. You can reach the files by raising one or the other half-lid. If you've placed something on top of the bin, simply move it aside to the portion of the lid you don't need to open.

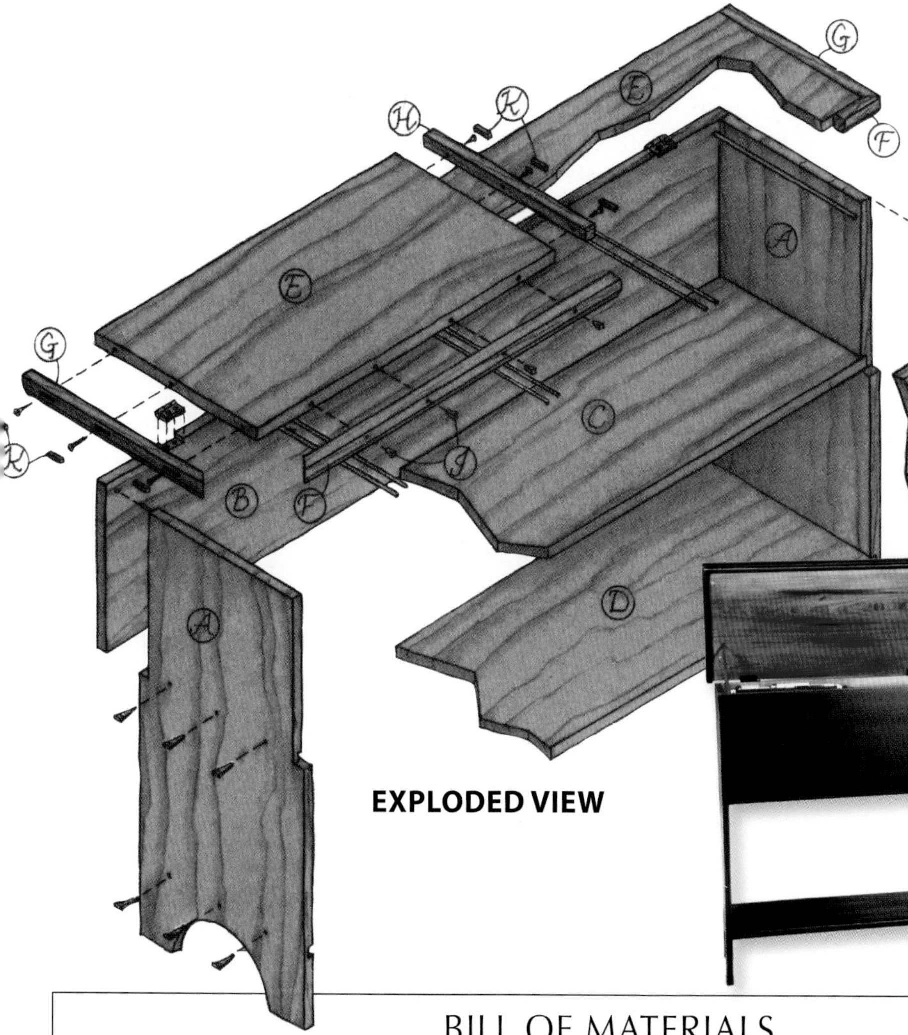

EXPLODED VIEW

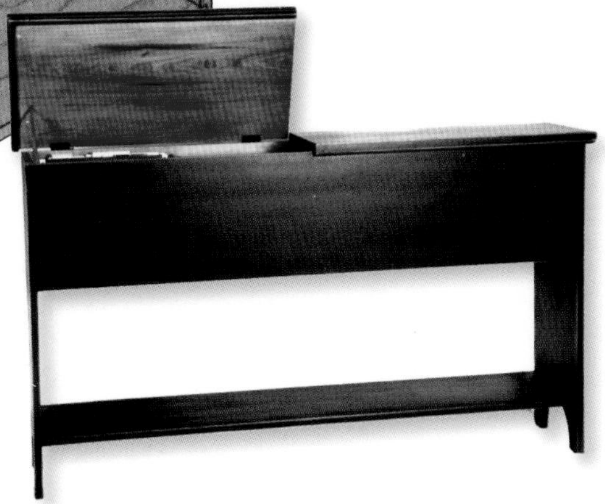

BILL OF MATERIALS

WOODEN PARTS/*FINISHED DIMENSIONS*

A.	Sides (2)	¾" × 14" × 31¾"
B.	Front/back (2)	¾" × 12" × 54"
C.	Bin bottom	¾" × 12½" × 53¼"
D.	Bottom shelf	¾" × 14" × 53¼"
E.	Lids (2)	¾" × 14 1/16" × 26⅛"
F.	Front outside moldings (2)	⅞" × 1" × 27⅞"
G.	Right/left outside moldings (2)	⅞" × 1" × 14 15/16"
H.	Right/left inside moldings (2)	¾" × ⅞" × 14 1/16"
J.	Pegs (8)	5/16" × 5/16" × 1¼"
K.	Caps (12)	⅜" × ½" × 1¼"

HARDWARE

#12 × 1¼" Roundhead wood screws and flat washers (12)
½" × 2" Butt hinges and mounting screws (2 pairs)
¼"-dia. × 13¼" Metal rods (8)
6d Square-cut nails (24 – 30)

PLAN OF PROCEDURE

1

Plane, rip, and cut the parts to the sizes shown in the Bill of Materials, except the moldings. Cut these to the proper thickness and width, but wait to cut them to length. They must be fitted to the lids.

2

Cut ¾"-wide, ⅜"-deep dadoes in the sides, as shown in the *Side Layout.*

3

Lay out and cut the shapes of the sides. Sand the sawed edges.

4

Drill ¼"-diameter, ⅜"-deep holes in the *inside* face of the front and back, as shown in the *Front/Back Layout/Inside View.* These holes will hold the file suspension rods.

5

Finish sand the sides, front, back, bin bottom, and bottom shelf. Glue the sides, bin bottom, and shelf together. Reinforce the joints with nails.

6

Check that the assembly is square. Glue the back to the bin bottom, then nail the back to the sides. Do *not* glue the back to the sides.

7

Insert the metal rods into the holes in the back. Glue the front to the bin bottom, inserting the rods into the holes in the front. Nail the front to the sides.

8

Sand the ends of the front and back flush with the sides. Set the heads of all the nails and cover them with putty.

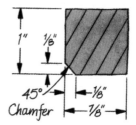

OUTSIDE MOLDING PROFILE

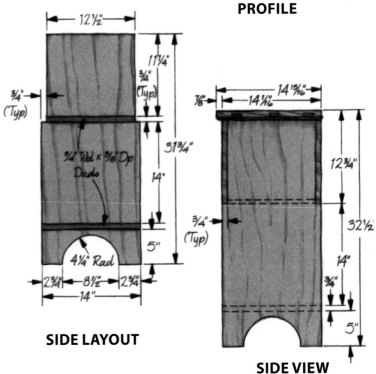

SIDE LAYOUT

SIDE VIEW

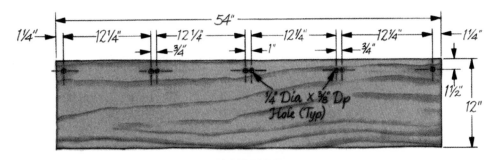

INSIDE VIEW
FRONT/BACK LAYOUT

¼" Dia X ⅜" Dp
Hole (Typ)

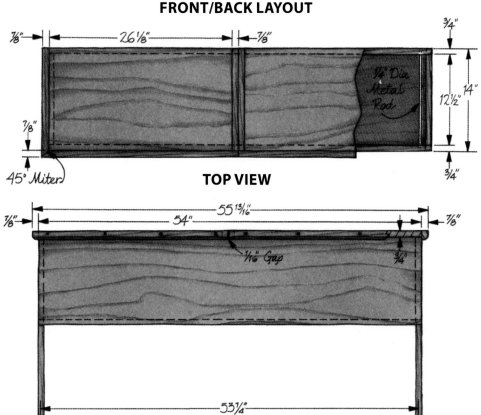

TOP VIEW

¼" Dia
Metal
Rod

45° Miter

FRONT VIEW

1/16" Gap

¾" Wd X ⅜" Dp
Dado

¾"(Typ)

PLAN OF PROCEDURE

9

Chamfer the lower corner of the outside molding stock, as shown in the *Outside Molding Profile.*

10

Miter the moldings to fit the lids and make ⅜"-wide, ¾"-deep, 1¼"-long mortises in the right and left moldings, as shown in the *Side View* and *Right/Left Molding Joinery Detail.* Cut a ³/₁₆"-wide, ½"-long slot at the base of each mortise.

11

Attach the right and left moldings to the ends of the lids with #12 × 1¼" roundhead wood screws and flat washers, as shown in the *Right/Left Molding Joinery Detail.* Do *not* glue the right or left moldings to the lids. Glue caps in the mortises to hide the screw heads. Sand the caps flush with the edges of the moldings.

12

Glue the front outside molding to the lids.

13

Round the bottom portion of the pegs, as shown in the *Peg Detail.* Drill four ⁵/₁₆"-diameter, 1¼"-deep holes through each of the front moldings, as shown in the *Front View.* Drive a peg into each hole.

14

Finish sand the lids. Cut mortises for the hinges and mount the lids to the bin.

15

Remove the lids from the bin and the hinges from the lids. Do any necessary touch-up sanding, then apply a finish to the completed meal bin. When the finish dries, reassemble the lids and bin.

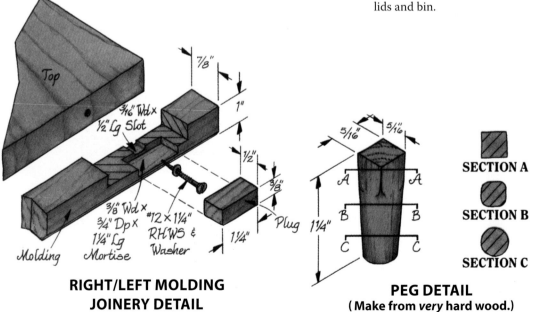

RIGHT/LEFT MOLDING JOINERY DETAIL

PEG DETAIL
(Make from *very* hard wood.)

SHAKER CANDLESTAND

Small, portable pieces of country furniture, particularly stools and tables, often had just three legs. The reason was threefold: First, a tripod always sets solidly, no matter how uneven the floor or ground might be. Second, the economy of legs makes the piece lighter and easier to move. Finally, when not in use, a three-legged piece can be conveniently stored in an out-of-the-way corner.

The tripod design is ancient — archaeologists have found three-legged furniture in Egyptian tombs dating back to the third millennium B.C. But it became particularly popular in the late eighteenth and early nineteenth centuries. Craftsmen on both sides of the Atlantic turned out thousands of *pedestal tables* — small tables with a turned central support and three spreading feet. These small stands were used for everything from serving wine to supports for lamps and candles. Perhaps the best remembered are the "candlestands" made by United Society of Believers in Christ's Second Appearing — also known as the Shakers.

Shaker candlestands were without decoration, since the beliefs of the religious order forbid unnecessary ornament. Nonetheless, the simple, Spartan lines were often strikingly elegant. Because of this, many historians and collectors consider these pedestal tables to be among the best examples of American country furniture. The crescent legs and urn-shaped pedestal of this small table is typical of many that were made in the Shaker furniture shops of New Lebanon, New York, during the first half of the nineteenth century.

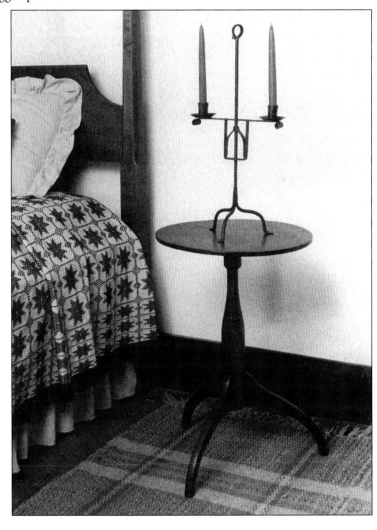

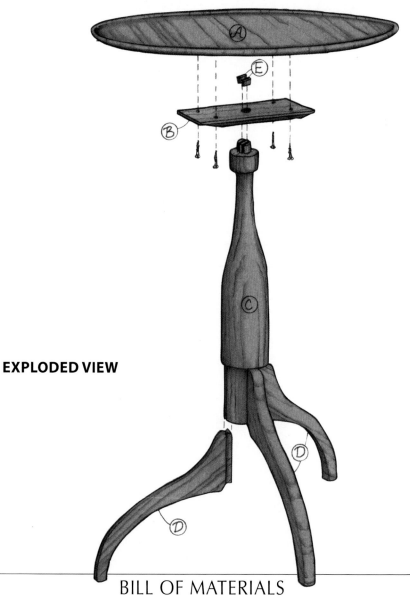

EXPLODED VIEW

BILL OF MATERIALS

WOODEN PARTS/*FINISHED DIMENSIONS*

A.	Tabletop	20" dia. × ¾"
B.	Brace	¾" × 5" × 13¾"
C.	Pedestal	2¾" dia. × 18¾"
D.	Feet (3)	¾" × 5" × 14¾"
E.	Wedges (2)	⁵/₃₂" × ¾" × 1"

HARDWARE

#8 × 1¼" Flathead wood screws (4)

PLAN OF PROCEDURE

1

If necessary, glue up wide stock for the top. Plane, rip, and cut the parts to the sizes shown in the Bill of Materials, except the pedestal. Make this about ¼" thicker and wider than shown. Cut the wedges from a piece of very hard wood, such as maple or hickory, tapering them from ⁵/₃₂" at the top to about ¹/₁₆" at the bottom.

2

Turn the pedestal stock to a simple cylinder, 2¾" in diameter. Then turn the bottom portion of the cylinder to 2½" in diameter, creating a ⅛" step, as shown in the *Pedestal* Layout. Finish sand the 2½"-diameter portion.

3

Rout three ¾"-wide, ⅝"-deep, 3½"-long dovetail grooves in the bottom end of the cylinder, as shown in *Section B*; see Routing Dovetail Mortises and Tenons on page 82.

4

Enlarge the foot pattern, as shown in the *Side View*, and trace it on the stock. Cut the tenon faces *only* — the flat ends that attach to the pedestal.

5

Rout dovetail tenons in the top ends of the legs, fitting them to the mortises.

6

Turn the upper half of the pedestal and finish sand the completed pedestal on the lathe. Do *not* sand the bottom 2½"-diameter portion of the pedestal, where the feet will be attached.

7

Mount the top on the lathe, making sure the end grain curves up, as shown in the *Top Section*. Turn the top, as shown in *Section C*. If your lathe doesn't have a 20" swing, rout the recess in the top with a core-box bit. Shape the bottom edge with a quarter-round bit. Finish sand the top.

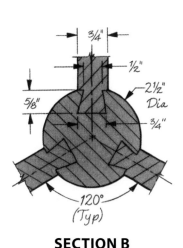

SECTION B

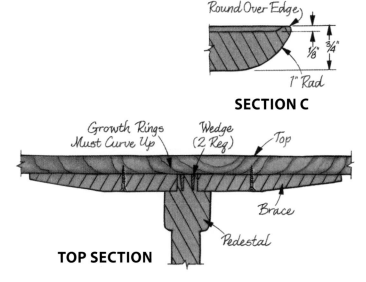

SECTION C

TOP SECTION

PLAN OF PROCEDURE

8

Chamfer the edges of the brace at 15°, as shown in the *Brace Detail.*

9

Drill a 1"-diameter round mortise in the brace to attach it to the pedestal.

10

Cut two ⅛"-wide, ¾"-deep slots in the tenon at the top of the pedestal.

11

Cut the shape of the feet and sand the sawed edges.

12

Finish sand the feet and brace. Glue the pedestal to the brace and drive the wedges into the slots at the top of the tenon.

Note: The wedges and slots must be *perpendicular* to the wood grain of the brace.

13

Glue the feet to the pedestal. Sand or file the bottom of the pedestal and the dovetail tenons clean and flush.

14

Turn the top upside down, and position the brace on it. Fasten the brace to the top with flat-head wood screws, countersinking the heads. Do *not* glue the brace to the top.

15

Using a file, round over the edges of the feet, as shown in *Section A.* Do any necessary touch up sanding to the table, and apply a finish.

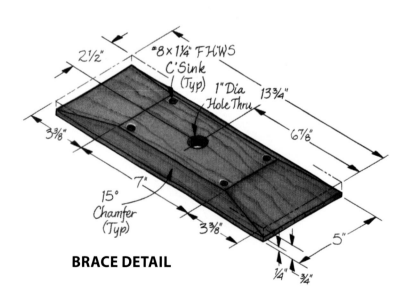

BRACE DETAIL

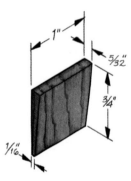

WEDGE DETAIL

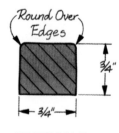

SECTION A

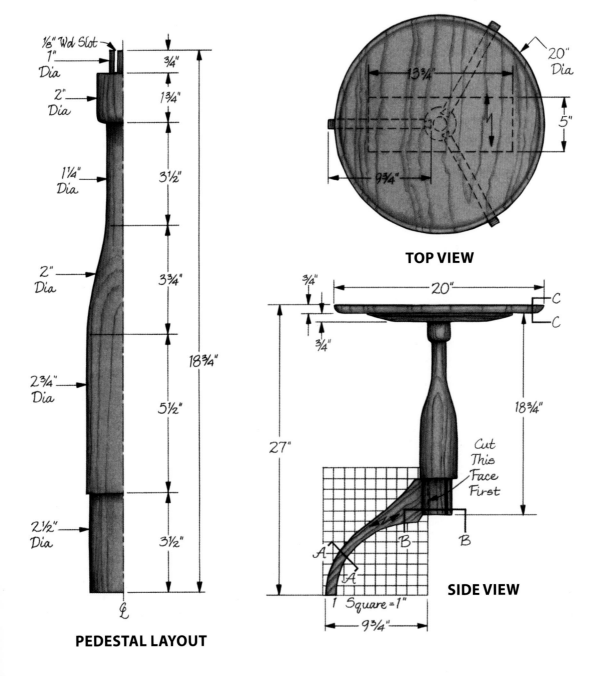

TOP VIEW

⅛" Wd Slot
1" Dia
¾"
2" Dia
1¾"
1¼" Dia
3½"
2" Dia
3¾"
2¾" Dia
5½"
18¾"
2½" Dia
3½"

PEDESTAL LAYOUT

20" Dia
13¾"
5"
9¾"

¾"
20"
C
C
¾"
27"
18¾"
Cut This Face First
B
B
A
A
1 Square = 1"
9¾"

SIDE VIEW

COUNTRY CRAFTSMAN'S KNOW-HOW:
ROUTING DOVETAIL MORTISES AND TENONS

Country craftsmen often used dovetail mortises and tenons. These were also called sliding dovetails (because the parts slid together) or, less commonly, French dovetails (for reasons that are lost to history). They cut these joints with a small saw and chisel — same tools they employed for making dovetails in drawers and boxes. You can duplicate these joints with a router and a dovetail bit.

The technique for routing a dovetail mortise and tenon in square stock is straightforward: Rout the mortise in the same manner you might rout a dado or groove, but use a dovetail bit instead of a straight bit. Then rout the tenon with the same dovetail bit.

The technique for routing these joints in round stock is more involved. You need a way to hold the round stock while you rout it and a way to guide the router. Some craftsmen use their lathe to hold the stock, then make a routing jig that mounts on the lathe. Others mount the stock in a V-block, then cut the mortises with an overhead routing jig, as shown in the drawings.

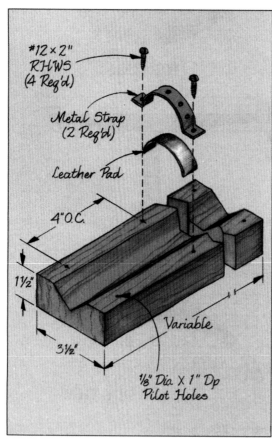

V-BLOCK

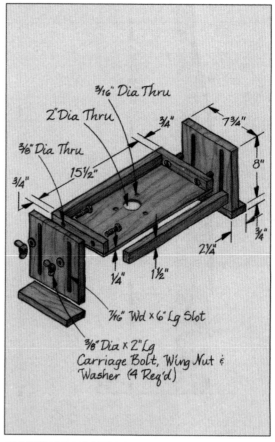

OVERHEAD ROUTING JIG

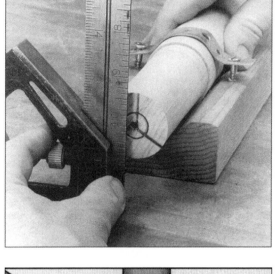

1 Before mounting the stock, carefully measure where you want to cut the mortises and mark them on the end of the stock — several straight lines through the diameter. Place the stock loosely in the V-block, and place the jig on your workbench. Rest a try square on the bench near the marked end, and turn the stock until the first mortise line is parallel to the edge of the square. Tighten the straps.

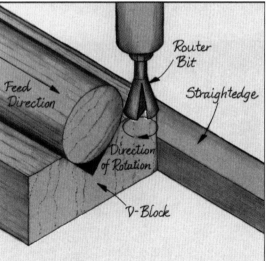

2 With a dovetail bit in the router, adjust the overhead routing jig to the proper height. Clamp a straightedge under the jig to guide the stock and clamp a block to the straightedge to stop the cut when the mortise is the proper length. Turn the router on and feed the stock slowly, keeping the V-block pressed against the straightedge. Repeat for each mortise.

3 When using an overhead routing jig, observe the same precautions that apply to a table-mounted router. Place the straightedge so the rotation of the bit helps to keep the V-block against the fence as you cut.

(Countinued) 83

COUNTRY CRAFTSMAN'S KNOW-HOW:
ROUTING DOVETAIL MORTISES AND TENONS—*CONTINUED*

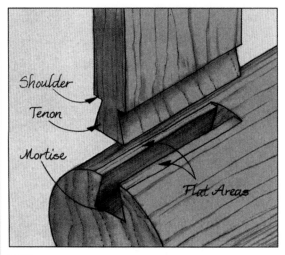

4 A dovetail tenon, like any other tenon, has flat shoulders. Because of this, you must cut flat areas on the cylinder, on either side of the dovetail mortises. Otherwise, the tenons won't mate properly with the mortises.

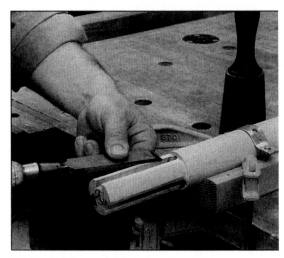

5 Cut these flats with the same setup used to make the mortise, but mount a straight bit in the router instead of a dovetail bit. After routing the flats, square them off with a chisel, if necessary.

6 Rout the dovetail tenons with a table-mounted router and the *same* dovetail bit used to make the mortises. Clamp a straightedge to the table to guide the stock. Cut each tenon in two passes — rout one face of the stock, then turn it over and rout the other.

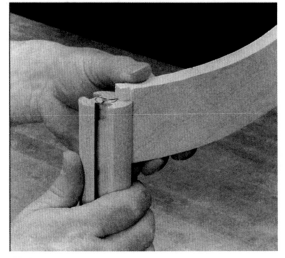

7 Slide the tenon into the mortise to test the fit. It should be snug, but not too tight. You may have to make several practice tenons until you cut one that fits just right.

PLANTATION DESK

Although well-to-do folks had desks as early as the sixteenth century, desks for country folks are a fairly recent development. Until the beginning of the nineteenth century, the typical country family could keep all of its important papers, letters, writing materials — its entire *library* — in a small box. The first country desks were, in fact, boxes like the Lap Desk and Keeping Box.

However, education was nurtured and encouraged in the years following the American Revolution. The public quickly became more literate, and families outgrew their desk boxes. At first, they simply made these boxes larger and put legs on them. Then they began to add shelves and dividers to help organize their paperwork.

A popular early desk was a simple cupboard placed on a table. Country folks favored this design because it was practical

and easy to build. Often, they simply joined two furniture pieces they already had on hand — a worktable and a wall cupboard. They sometimes added either a drawer or a compartment beneath the tabletop to provide extra storage space. Inside the cupboard, they added vertical dividers between the shelves, creating pigeonholes.

This marriage between a table and a cupboard was especially common in the rural South — Kentucky, Tennessee, and Georgia. For that reason, we remember it as a "plantation" desk.

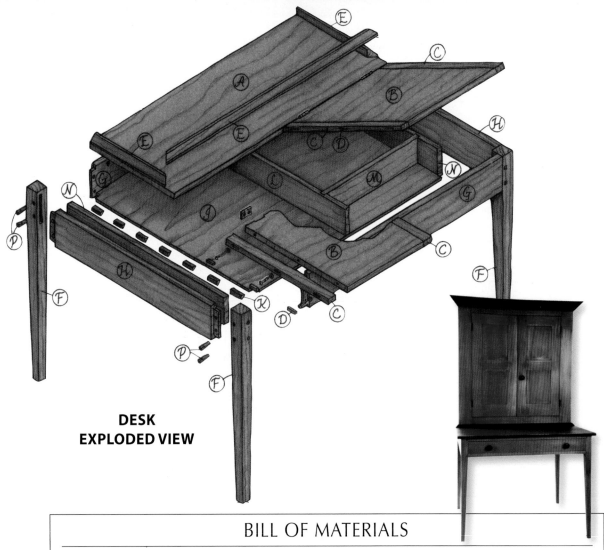

**DESK
EXPLODED VIEW**

BILL OF MATERIALS

WOODEN PARTS/_FINISHED DIMENSIONS_

Desk

A.	Desk top	¾" × 15¾" × 38"
B.	Lids (2)	¾" × 16¼" × 15⁷⁄₁₆"
C.	Breadboards (4)	¾" × 1¼" × 16¼"
D.	Breadboard caps (12)	⅜" × ½" × 1¼"
E.	Foot molding (total)	1" × 1" × 68"
F.	Legs (4)	1¾" × 1¾" × 28¼"
G.	Front/back aprons (2)	⅞" × 5" × 34"
H.	Side aprons (2)	⅞" × 5" × 29"
J.	Desk bottom	½" × 29¼" × 34¼"
K.	Small glue blocks (28)	¾" × ¾" × 2½"
L.	Front-to-back divider	¾" × 3¾" × 29¼"
M.	Side-to-side divider	¾" × 3¾" × 16⅝"
N.	Stiffeners (2)	⅞" × 3¾" × 27½"
P.	Small pegs (16)	⁵⁄₁₆" × ⁵⁄₁₆" × 1"*

Cabinet

P.	Small pegs (4)	¼" × ¼" × 1"*
Q.	Sides (2)	¾" × 12¼" × 39"
R.	Top/shelves (4)	¾" × 11¾" × 35¼"
S.	Narrow backboard	½" × 6¾" × 39"
T.	Wide backboards (4)	½" × 7½" × 39"
U.	Center shelf support	¾" × 11¾" × 23⅝"
V.	Pigeonhole dividers (8)	½" × 5¾" × 11¾"
W.	Adjustable shelves (2–4)	¾" × 11¾" × 16¾"
X.	Face frame stiles (2)	¾" × 4" × 39"

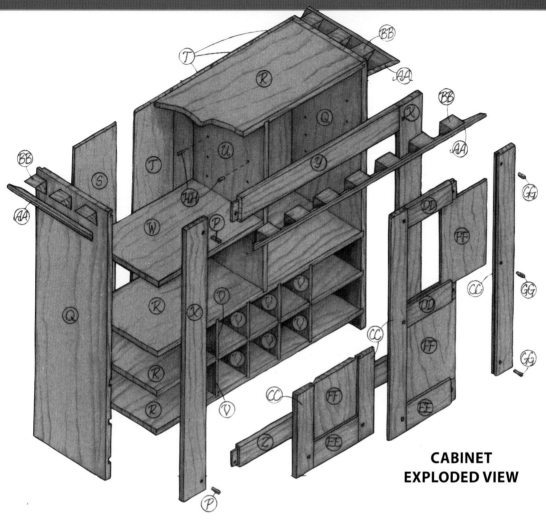

**CABINET
EXPLODED VIEW**

Y.	Face frame top rail	¾" × 4" × 30"
Z.	Face bottom rail	¾" × 3" × 30"
AA.	Crown molding (total)	¾" × 3⅝" × 74"
BB.	Large glue blocks (14)	1⁷⁄₁₆" × 1⁷⁄₁₆" × 2½"
CC.	Door stiles (4)	¾" × 3" × 31⅞"
DD.	Top/middle door rails (4)	¾" × 3" × 10¼"
EE.	Bottom door rails (2)	¾" × 4" × 10¼"
FF.	Door panels (4)	½" × 8⅞" × 11⅝"
GG.	Large pegs (12)	⅜" × ⅜" × 1¼"*
HH.	Shelving support pegs (8–16)	¼" dia. × ¾"

*Make the pegs at least this long, then trim them after
you install them.*

HARDWARE
6d Square-cut nails (¼ lb.)
4d Finishing nails (¼ lb.)
#12 × 1½" Roundhead wood screws and washers (12)
#10 × 1¼" Flathead wood screws (6)
1½" × 2" Butt hinges and mounting screws (4 pairs)
Door latch
Door catch
Door pull

Plan of Procedure

To help this project progress smoothly, build it in two parts — desk first, then the cabinet.

Making the Desk

1

Plane, rip, and cut the desk parts to the sizes shown in the Bill of Materials, except the foot molding and small glue blocks. Plane and rip the molding and glue block stock to the proper thickness and width, but don't cut them to length or shape them yet.

2

Cut the joinery needed to assemble the desk:

- ¾"-wide, ⅜"-deep dadoes in the front-to-back divider and right stiffener, as shown in *Section A*

- ⅜"-wide, ¾"-long tenons on the ends of the aprons, as shown in the *Leg-to-Apron Joinery Detail*

- ⅜"-wide, ¾"-deep, 4"-long mortises in the inside surfaces of the legs, as shown in *Section A*

- ⅜"-wide, ¾"-deep, 1¼"-long mortises in the outside edges of the breadboards, as shown in the *Breadboard Joinery Detail* and *Breadboard Layout/Side View*

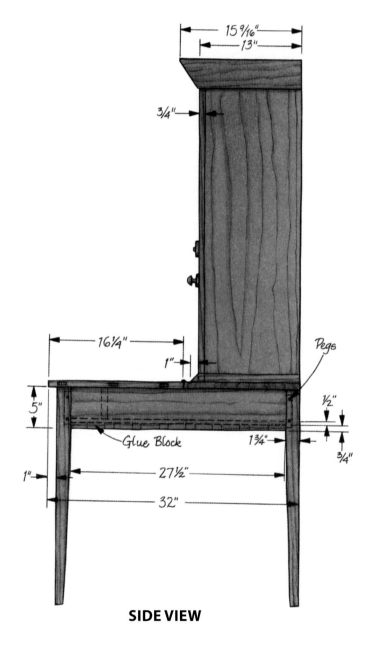

SIDE VIEW

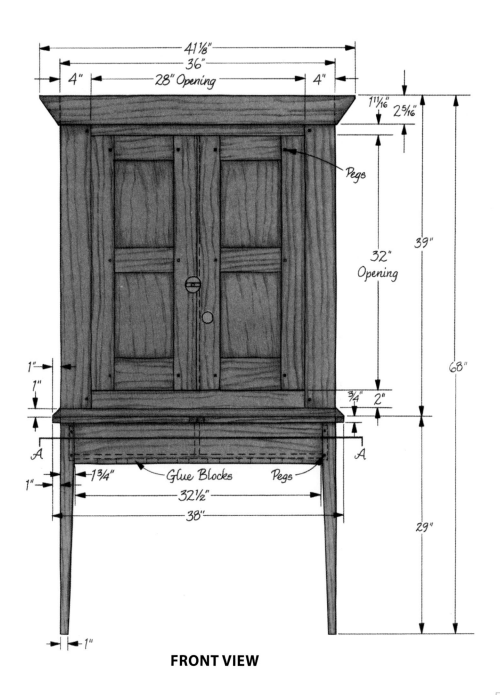

41⅛"
36"
4"
28" Opening
4"
1¹¹⁄₁₆"
2⁵⁄₁₆"
Pegs
39"
32"
Opening
68"
1"
1"
¾"
2"
A
A
1"
1¾"
Glue Blocks
Pegs
32½"
38"
29"
1"

FRONT VIEW

PLAN OF PROCEDURE

3

Notch the top and bottom edges of the apron tenons to fit in the leg mortises.

4

Drill screw pockets in the stiffeners and back aprons, as shown in *Section A*.

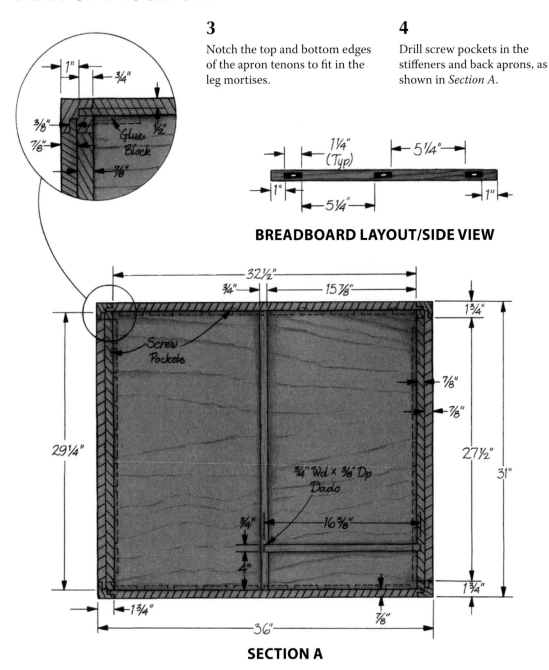

BREADBOARD LAYOUT/SIDE VIEW

SECTION A

5

Cut 2½° tapers in the *inside* surfaces of the legs, as shown in the *Leg Layout*.

6

Attach the breadboards to the lids with #12 × 1½" roundhead wood screws and flat washers, as shown in the *Breadboard Joinery Detail*. Glue breadboard caps in the breadboard mortises to hide the screw heads.

7

Finish sand the breadboard assemblies and the other parts of the desk. Assemble the legs and aprons with glue.

8

Round the bottom portion of the small pegs, as shown in the *Small Peg Detail*.

SECTION B

SECTION C

SECTION D

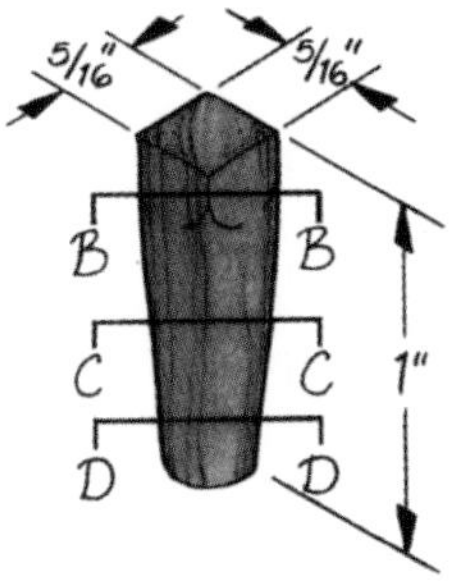

5/16"   5/16"

B   C   B

C   C   1"

D   D

SMALL PEG DETAIL
(Make from *very* hard wood.)

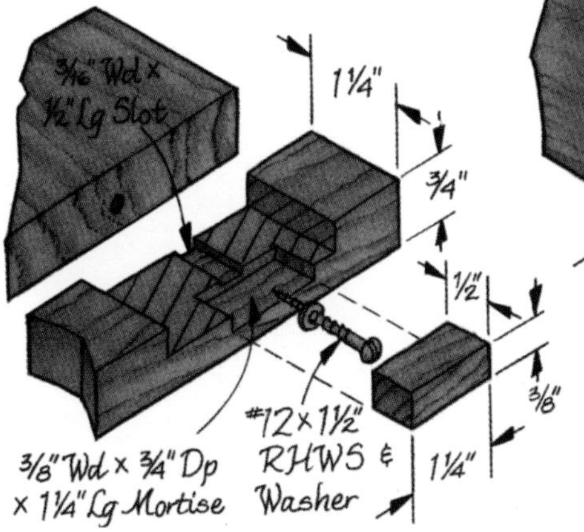

3⁄16" Wd × 1½" Lg Slot

1¼"

¾"

½"

3⁄8"

3⁄8" Wd × ¾" Dp × 1¼" Lg Mortise

#12 × 1½" RHWS & Washer

1¼"

BREADBOARD JOINERY DETAIL

½"   3⁄8"

½"

7⁄8"

1¾"

4"

5"

½"

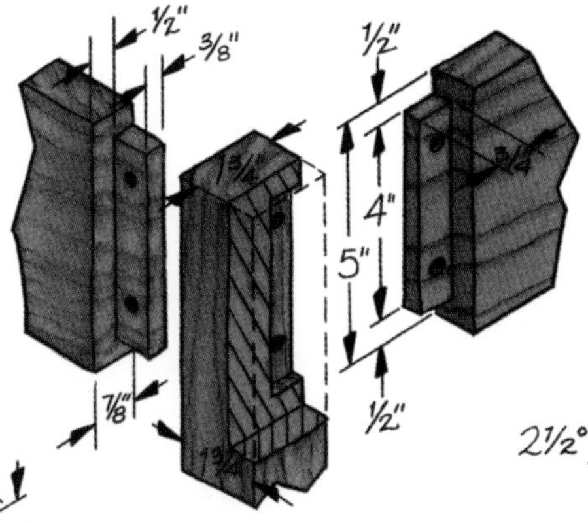

LEG-TO-APRON JOINERY DETAIL

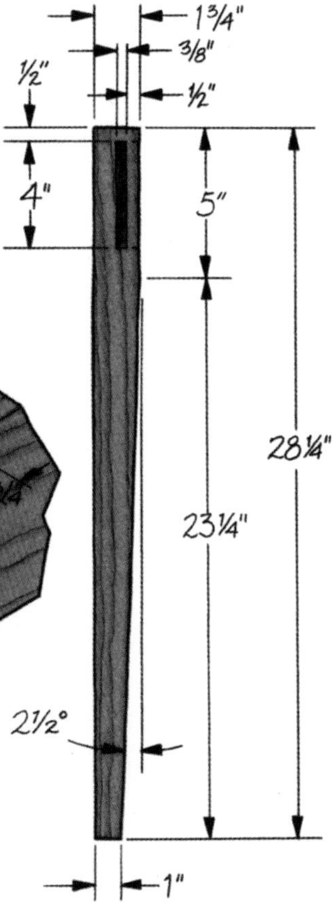

½"   1¾"
3⁄8"   ½"

½"

4"   5"

28¼"

23¼"

2½°

1"

LEG LAYOUT

PLAN OF PROCEDURE

9

Drill two ⁵/₁₆"-diameter, 1"-deep holes through each mortise-and-tenon joint that holds the legs to the aprons. Drive small pegs into each of the holes.

10

Attach the front-to-back divider to the front and back aprons with glue and square-cut nails. Make sure the dado is toward the front of the desk, and it faces right. Set the heads of the nails.

11

Glue the stiffeners to the side aprons. Make sure the screw pockets face up and toward the inside. Also make sure the stif-fener with the dado is on the right, and that the dado is directly opposite the dado in the front-to-back divider.

12

Rip a 45° bevel in the small glue block stock, as shown in the *Small Glue Block Detail,* then cut the blocks to length.

13

Turn the desk upside down and position it over the desk top. Attach the desk top to the desk with #10 × 1¼" flathead wood screws, driving the screws through the screw pockets and into the underside of the top.

14

Cut a notch in each corner of the bottom, as shown in the *Desk Bottom Notch Detail,* to fit around the legs.

15

While the desk is still upside down, put the bottom in place. Attach small glue blocks to the aprons to secure the bottom. Tack the bottom to the front-to-back divider with finishing nails. Set the nails.

16

Turn the desk right side up and install the side-to-side divider. Set it in the dadoes in the right stiffener and front-to-back divider, but do *not* glue it in place. Leave it loose, so that you can remove it if you need to.

17

Cut hinge mortises in the lids and desk top. Mount the lids on the desk.

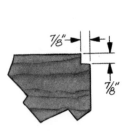

**DESK BOTTOM
NOTCH DETAIL**

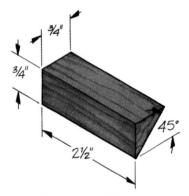

**SMALL GLUE BLOCK
DETAIL**

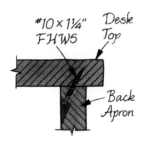

**SCREW POCKET
DETAIL**

18

Rip a bevel in one corner of the foot molding stock, as shown in the *Foot Molding Profile.* Then set the stock aside — *don't* attach it to the desk yet.

Making the Cabinet

Note: The pigeonholes and divider shown in the drawings are optional. If you wish, you can make a simpler cabinet with 2–3 adjustable shelves, as shown in the lead photograph.

19

Plane, rip, and cut the cabinet parts to the sizes shown in the Bill of Materials, except for the crown molding, large glue blocks, and pegs. Plane and rip the molding and glue block stock to the proper thickness and width, but don't cut them to length or shape them yet. Cut large and small pegs ¼"–½" longer than specified.

20

Cut the joinery needed to assemble the case:

- ¾"-wide, ⅜"-deep dadoes in the inside surfaces of the sides, as shown in the *Side Layout,* to hold the bottom, middle, and upper shelves

- ¾"-wide, ⅜"-deep dadoes in the inside surface of the top and the top surface of the upper shelf, to hold the center shelf divider, as shown in the *Cabinet/Front View*

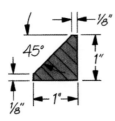

FOOT MOLDING PROFILE

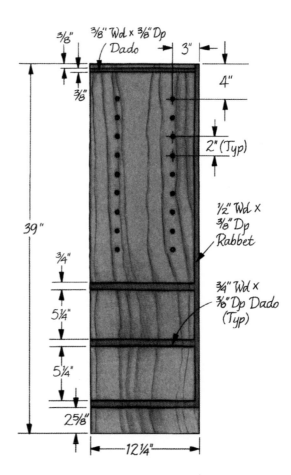

SIDE LAYOUT

PLAN OF PROCEDURE

- ½"-wide, ⅜"-deep rabbets in the back edges of the sides, to hold the backboards

- ½"-wide, ¼"-deep dadoes in the upper, middle, and bottom shelves to hold the pigeonhole dividers

- ⅜"-wide, ⅜"-deep dadoes in the inside surfaces of the sides to hold the top

- ⅜"-wide, ⅜"-deep rabbet in each end of the top

- ⅜"-wide, ¼"-deep rabbets in the edges of the backboards, as shown in the *Top View*

- ¼"-wide, 1"-long tenons in the ends of the face frame rails, as shown in the *Face Frame Joinery Detail*

- ¼"-wide, 1"-deep, 2"-long mortises in the inside edges of the face frame stiles, near the bottom end, as shown in the *Face Frame Joinery Detail*

- ¼"-wide, 1"-deep, 3"-long mortise in the inside edges of the face frame stiles near the top end

21

Notch the top and bottom edges of the face frame tenons to fit the mortises.

22

Drill ¼"-diameter, ½"-deep holes in the inside surfaces of the sides, as shown in the *Side Layout*. Drill ¼"-diameter holes following the same layout completely through the long divider. These holes will hold pegs to support the adjustable shelves.

23

Finish sand the parts of the cabinet you've made so far. Assemble the sides, shelves, top, center shelf support, and pigeonhole dividers with glue.

24

Attach the backboards to the case with finishing nails. Set the heads of the nails.

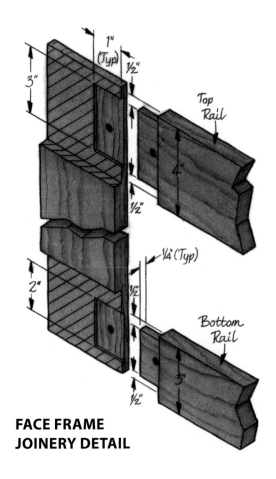

FACE FRAME JOINERY DETAIL

25

Assemble the face frame rails and stiles with glue.

26

Round the bottom portion of the small pegs, as shown in the *Small Peg Detail*.

27

Drill a ⁵⁄₆"-diameter hole through each mortise-and-tenon joint that holds the rails to the stiles. Drive small pegs into each of the holes. Cut the pegs off flush with the back surface of the face frame.

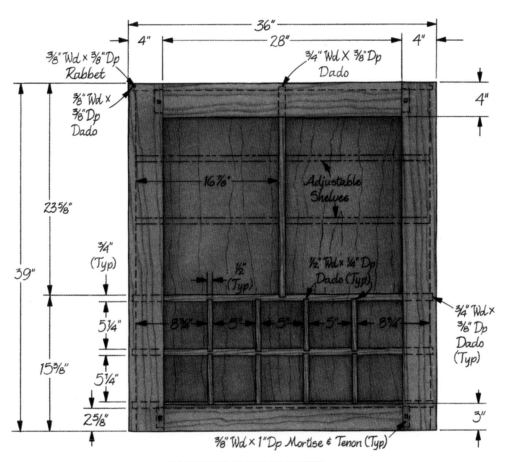

CABINET/FRONT VIEW
(WITHOUT DOORS AND MOLDING)

Plan of Procedure

28

Attach the face frame to the case with glue and square-cut nails. Set the nails.

29

Bevel the edges of the crown molding and large glue block stock, as shown in the *Crown Molding Detail* and *Large Glue Block Detail.*

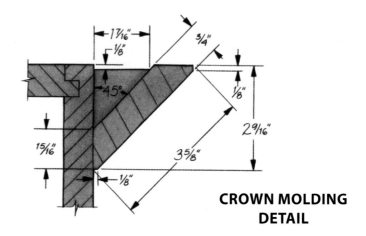

CROWN MOLDING DETAIL

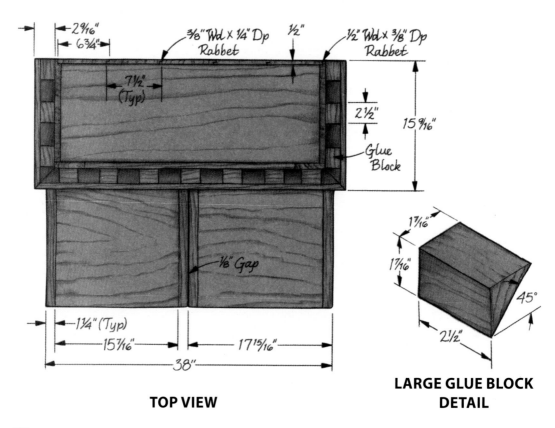

TOP VIEW

LARGE GLUE BLOCK DETAIL

30

Compound-miter the crown molding to fit the top of the case. Attach the molding with glue, large glue blocks, and finishing nails. Set the nails.

31

Cut the joinery needed to assemble the door, as shown in the *Door Assembly Detail:*

- ⅜"-wide, ⅜"-deep rabbets in the outside edges of the inside door stiles, so the doors will overlap

- ¼"-wide, ⅜"-deep grooves in the inside edges of the rails and stiles

- ¼"-wide, 1"-deep, 2¼"-long mortises in the upper ends and the middle of the stiles

- ¼"-wide, 1"-deep, 3¼"-long mortises in the lower ends of the stiles

- ¼"-wide, 1"-long tenons in the ends of the rails

32

Notch the tenons, as shown in the *Door Assembly Detail,* to fit the mortises.

33

Bevel the edges of the panels at 15°, as shown in the *Door/Panel Section.*

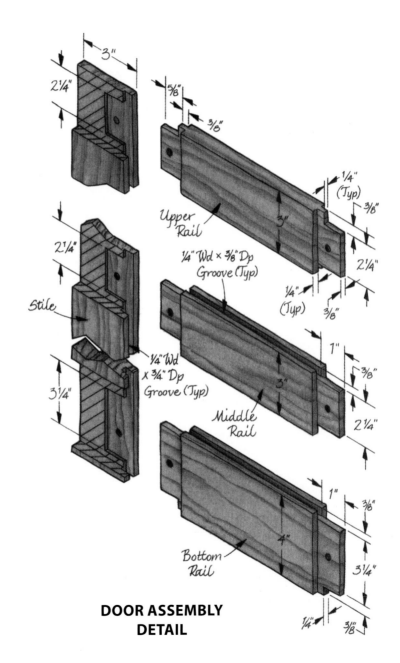

DOOR ASSEMBLY DETAIL

PLAN OF PROCEDURE

34

Finish sand the parts of the door. Assemble the rails and stiles with glue. Insert the panels in the grooves, beveled side facing in, but do *not* glue the panels in place. Let them float in the grooves.

35

Round the bottom portion of the large pegs, as shown in the *Large Peg Detail*.

36

Drill a ⅜"-diameter hole through each mortise-and-tenon joint in the doors, then drive the pegs through the holes from the outside. Cut the pegs off flush with the inside surface of the door frame.

37

Cut hinge mortises in the door frames and face frame, then mount the doors in the case.

38

Install the door catch on the inside of the cabinet, and the door latch and pull on the outside of the door frame.

Finishing Up

39

Place the completed cabinet on the desk. Miter the foot molding to fit around the base of the cabinet and attach it to the desk top with glue and finishing nails. Set the nails. Do *not* attach the molding to the cabinet itself.

40

Remove the cabinet from the desk. Disassemble the doors from the cabinet and the lids from the desk. Remove all hardware and set it aside.

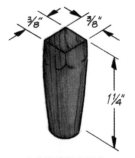

LARGE PEG DETAIL
(**Make from very hard wood.**)

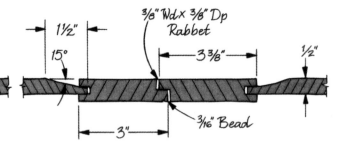

DOOR / PANEL SECTION

41

Do any necessary touch-up sanding, then apply a finish to *all* sides — inside and outside, top and bottom — of the desk, cabinet, lids, and doors.

42

Reassemble the completed project. Do *not* attach the cabinet to the desk, just let it sit inside the moldings. This will allow you to disassemble the components easily when you need to move or repair the project.

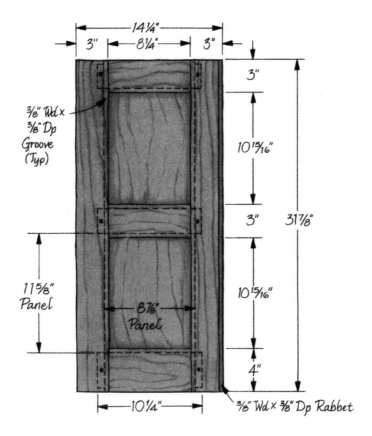

DOOR LAYOUT

COUNTRY CRAFTSMAN'S KNOW-HOW:
ATTACHING MOLDINGS

Country furniture is often decorated with *applied* moldings — narrow, molded strips of wood attached to the main assembly.

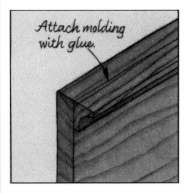

1 When the wood grain of the surface is parallel to the grain of the molding, you can simply glue the molding in place.

2 When the wood grain of the surface is perpendicular to that of the molding, attach the molding with wire brads or finishing nails. Brads and nails bend slightly as the wood expands and contracts beneath the molding. The molding remains in place, but it doesn't restrict the movement of the wood.

3 Set the heads of the finishing nails slightly below the surface of the molding, and cover the heads with wood putty, such as Durham's Water Putty. If you wish, mix the putty with stain or aniline dye to match the finish you will put on the project.

4 Never glue a molding to a surface so wood grains are perpendicular. The molding will buckle or the board to which it's applied will cup. Eventually, the glue bond will break and the molding will fall off.

5 Sometimes glue and finishing nails aren't enough. To help reinforce large moldings that angle out from the top of a piece, such as crown moldings and bed moldings, use glue blocks in addition to glue and nails.

FOR DRESSING & SLEEPING

KEEPING BOX

Early American households used dozens of chests and boxes of all sizes and shapes for storage. Sometimes a family member would make a small or medium-size box to keep his or her personal treasures — documents, jewelry, keepsakes, and so on. These were called, appropriately enough, keeping boxes.

While most storage boxes were constructed simply, craftsmen usually put forth extra effort when building keeping boxes. Most of these boxes were very sturdy — the keeping box shown is made from thick boards (for its size), which are dovetailed together. They were secure — this one has a metal latch and lock. Many were very stylish and ornately decorated. Craftsmen painted, carved, inlaid, or laced the surfaces with veneers and moldings. The extra pains that they took when making the boxes attested to the value of the things stored in them.

EXPLODED VIEW

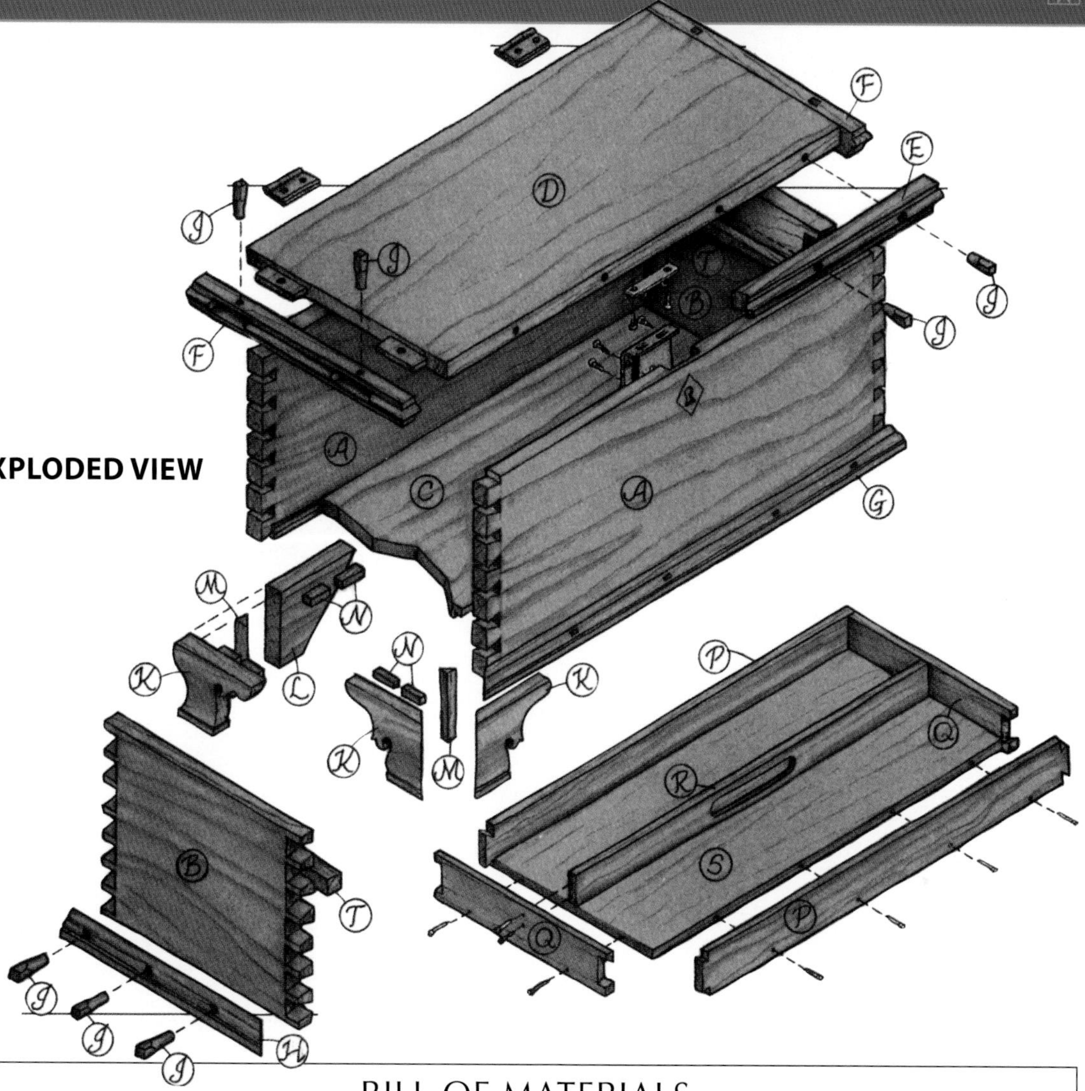

BILL OF MATERIALS

WOODEN PARTS/*FINISHED DIMENSIONS*

A.	Front/back (2)	⅝" × 8" × 20"
B.	Sides (2)	⅝" × 8" × 10"
C.	Bottom	⅝" × 9 3/16" × 19 ¼"
D.	Lid	⅝" × 10" × 21 ½"
E.	Front lid molding	¾" × 1" × 20"
F.	Breadboards (2)	¾" × 1" × 10 ¾"
G.	Front bottom molding	½" × ⅞" × 21"
H.	Side bottom moldings (2)	½" × ⅞" × 10 ½"
J.	Pegs (18)	¼" × ¼" × 1 ¼"
K.	Front/side feet (6)	¾" × 3" × 4 ¼"
L.	Back feet (2)	¾" × 3" × 3 ½"
M.	Long glue blocks (4)	¾" × ¾" × 3"
N.	Short glue blocks (16)	½" × ½" × 1"
P.	Tray front/back (2)	⅜" × 1 ¾" × 18 ⅝"
Q.	Tray sides (2)	⅜" × 1 ¾" × 8 ⅝"
R.	Tray divider	⅜" × 1 ⅜" × 17 ⅞"
S.	Tray bottom	⅜" × 7 ⅞" × 17 ⅞"
T.	Cleats (2)	⅝" × ⅝" × 8 ¾"

HARDWARE

⅞" Wire or headless brads (20–24)
1 ¼" × 2" Butt hinges and mounting screws (2)
Chest lock, latch, and mounting screws

PLAN OF PROCEDURE

1

Plane, rip, and cut the parts to the sizes shown in the Bill of Materials, except the moldings, breadboards, and feet. Plane and rip the top molding, breadboards, and feet to the proper thickness and width, but don't cut them to length yet. Plane stock to the proper thickness for the bottom moldings, but don't cut them to width or length.

2

Cut ¼"-wide, ¼"-deep double-blind grooves inside the front, back, and sides, near the bottom edge, as shown in the *Bottom Groove Layout*. Cut a ¼"-wide, ¼"-deep rabbet in the edges and ends of the bottom, as shown in the *Bottom-to-Box Joinery Detail*.

3

Lay out and cut the dovetails and pins in the front, back, and sides, as shown in the *Box Dovetail Detail*. Dry assemble the front, back, sides, and bottom.

4

Mark the lid and the back for the hinge mortises. Take the box apart and cut these mortises in both parts.

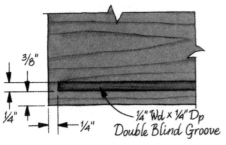

BOTTOM GROOVE LAYOUT

¾"

¼"

¼"

¼" Wd × ¼" Dp
Double Blind Groove

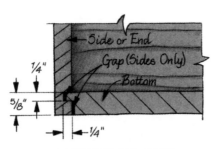

BOTTOM-TO-BOX JOINERY DETAIL

Side or End

Gap (Sides Only)

Bottom

¼"

⅝"

¼"

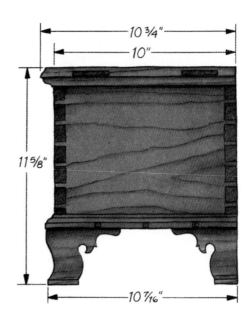

SIDE VIEW

10 ¾"

10"

11 ⅝"

10 ⁷⁄₁₆"

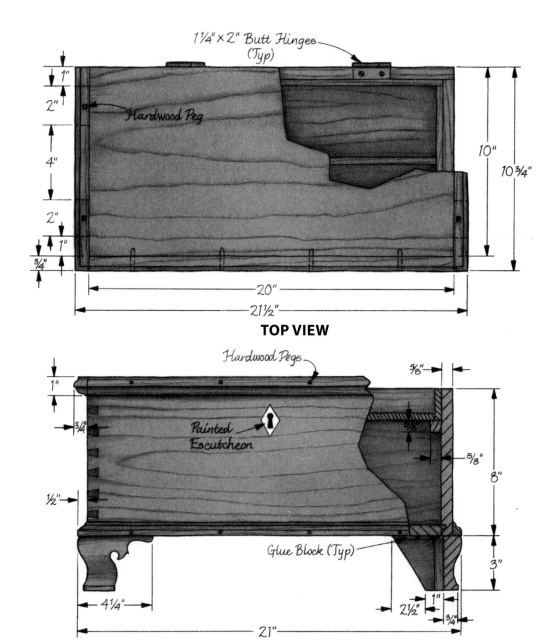

1¼" × 2" Butt Hinges (Typ)

Hardwood Peg

1"
2"
4"
2"
1"
¾"

10"
10¾"

20"
21½"

TOP VIEW

Hardwood Pegs

Painted Escutcheon

Glue Block (Typ)

1"
¾"
½"

5⁄8"
5⁄8"
5⁄8"
8"
3"

4¼"
21
2½"
1"
¾"

FRONT VIEW

PLAN OF PROCEDURE

5

Cut a mortise in the inside surface of the front for the chest lock, as shown in the *Lock Mortise Detail*. Also, drill a keyhole. The size of the lock mortise and the location of the keyhole will depend on the make of the lock.

6

Finish sand the front, back, sides, and bottom. Assemble the front, back, and sides with glue. Put the bottom in the box, but don't glue it — let it float in the grooves. After the glue dries, sand the joints clean and flush.

7

Temporarily hinge the lid to the box. Mark the location of the latch, then remove the lid from the box. Cut the mortise for the latch.

8

Cut ¼"-wide, ¾"-long tenons in the ends of the lid. Cut the tenon so it runs the entire width of each end, then notch these tenons, as shown in the *Lid Tenon Detail*, to make two split tenons in each end of thelid. Each tenon should be 2" long.

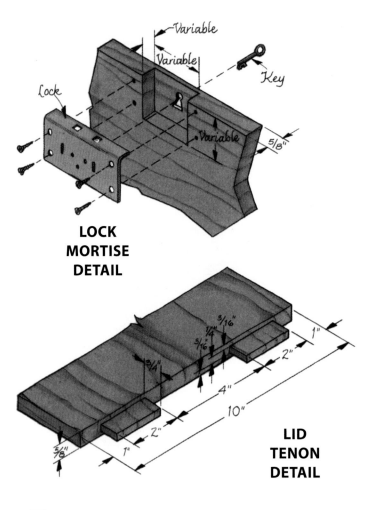

**LOCK
MORTISE
DETAIL**

**LID
TENON
DETAIL**

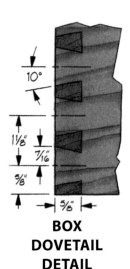

**BOX
DOVETAIL
DETAIL**

9

Cut the front lid molding and the breadboards to fit the lid.

10

Cut ¼"-wide, 2"-long mortises in the breadboards to fit over the lid tenons.

11

Finish sand the lid. Glue the front lid molding and the breadboards to the lid. (Apply glue along the edge of the lid and to the tenons, but not to the ends.)

12

When the glue dries, sand molding and breadboard joints clean and flush. Shape the front lid molding and the breadboards as shown in the *Lid Molding Profile.*

13

Shape the edge of the bottom molding stock, as shown in the *Bottom Molding Profile.* Rip the bottom molding from the stock.

14

Finish sand the bottom molding and cut it to length, mitering the adjoining ends at 45°. Glue the molding to the box.

15

Round the bottom portion of the pegs, as shown in the *Peg Detail.*

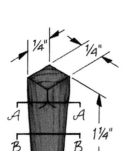

PEG DETAIL
(Make from **very** hard wood.)

 SECTION A

 SECTION B

 SECTION C

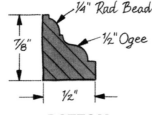

BOTTOM MOLDING PROFILE

¼" Rad Bead
½" Ogee

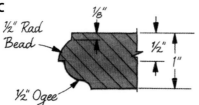

LID MOLDING PROFILE

½" Rad Bead
½" Ogee

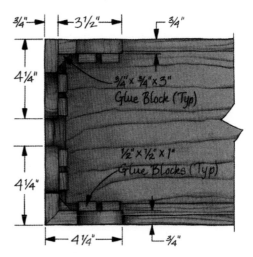

BOTTOM DETAIL

¾" x ¾" x 3"
Glue Block (Typ)

½" x ½" x 1"
Glue Blocks (Typ)

Plan of Procedure

16

Drill a ¼"-diameter hole through each mortise-and-tenon joint in the breadboards, then drive pegs through the holes from the top. Cut the pegs flush with the bottom surface of the breadboards.

17

Drill ¼"-diameter, 1¼"-deep holes through the front lid molding and the bottom moldings, where shown in the *Front View* and *Side View*. Drive pegs in the holes.

18

Cut the back feet to length, then shape the remaining stock to the profile shown in the *Foot Pattern*.

19

Cut the front and side feet to length, mitering the adjoining ends.

20

Lay out the front and side bracket feet on the stock, as shown in the *Foot Pattern*, then cut the shapes of the feet. Sand the sawed edges.

21

Assemble the feet with glue, reinforcing the joints with the long glue blocks. When the glue dries, sand the joints clean and flush. Finish sand the outside surfaces of the feet.

22

Glue the feet to the box, and reinforce the joints with short glue blocks.

23

Cut the dovetails that join the front, back, and sides of the tray, as shown in the *Tray Dovetail Detail*.

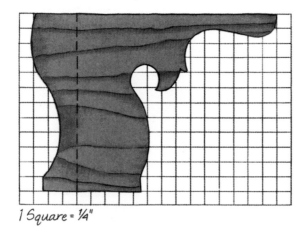

1 Square = ¼"

FOOT PATTERN

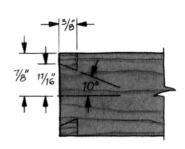

**TRAY
DOVETAIL DETAIL**

24

Make the handle cutout in the tray divider. Sand the sawed edges.

25

Finish sand the parts of the tray and assemble them with glue and wire brads. *Don't* glue the ends of the tray bottom to the tray sides — just attach the parts with brads. Set the heads of the brads.

26

Finish sand the cleats. Attach them to the inside surfaces of the box side with glue and brads. Set the brads.

27

Place the tray on the cleats to check the fit. Install the latch in the lid and mount the lid back on the box to check the fit and the action of the latch. If necessary, adjust the fit of the tray or the lid.

28

Disassemble the box, removing the tray, lid, and all the hardware. Set the hardware aside and apply a finish to the box. If you wish, paint an escutcheon around the keyhole, as shown in the *Front View*. When the finish dries, reassemble the box.

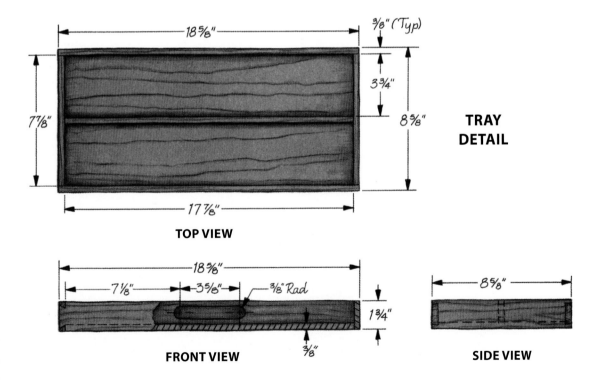

TOP VIEW

TRAY DETAIL

FRONT VIEW

SIDE VIEW

PENCIL-POST BED

In winters gone by, bedrooms were cold places after the fire had died down. Folks hung heavy canopies over and around their beds, warding off drafts and creating tents that could be warmed by their own body heat. In warmer weather, lighter hangings protected them from insects. Winter or summer, the canopies provided privacy. Several people — sometimes whole families — slept in the same room.

At first, these canopies were suspended from the ceiling. Around 1550, English craftsmen began to extend the bedposts to support "testers," wooden frames over which the canopies were draped. The posts of these early "tent" beds were massive and often richly carved. As styles changed, the posts narrowed. By the early eighteenth century, both English and American craftsmen were making slender, graceful bedposts. Among country folks, octagonal "pencil posts" were particularly popular, because they could make these without using a large, expensive lathe.

The pencil-post bed is a versatile design. As shown, the bed supports a standard queen-size mattress and box springs. You can easily change its size to fit almost any mattress — just alter the length of the rails and canopy. If you eliminate the support brackets, you can build the frame to surround a water bed. Hang a dust ruffle from the bed rails to hide the supporting platform. The pencil posts will support either a straight or Queen Anne (arched) canopy. The plans show straight testers. These were the most common; country folks rarely made arched testers. However, if you wish to arch them, shorten the bedposts. You can also change the shape of the headboard, or add a footboard, to suit your taste.

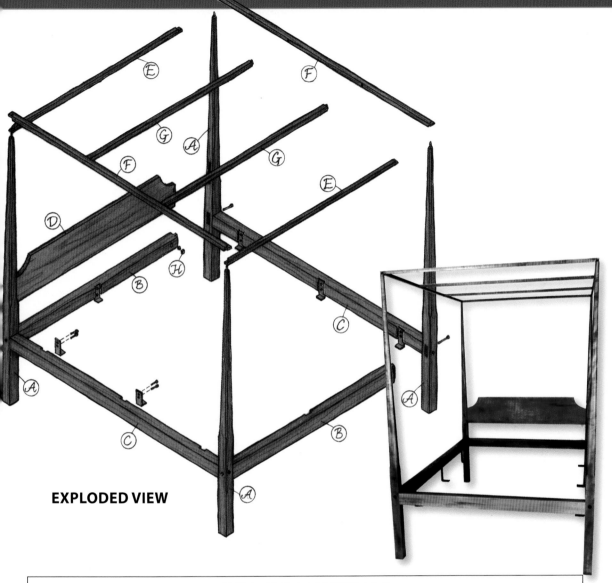

EXPLODED VIEW

BILL OF MATERIALS

WOODEN PARTS/_FINISHED DIMENSIONS_

A. Posts (4) $2\frac{1}{2}$" × $2\frac{1}{2}$" × $81\frac{1}{8}$"
B. End bed rails (2) $2\frac{1}{2}$" × $3\frac{1}{2}$" × $62\frac{1}{2}$"
C. Side bed rails (2) $2\frac{1}{2}$" × $3\frac{1}{2}$" × $82\frac{1}{2}$"
D. Headboard $\frac{3}{4}$" × 12" × $62\frac{1}{2}$"
E. End tester rails (2) $\frac{7}{8}$" × 1" × $64\frac{1}{2}$"
F. Side tester rails (2) $\frac{7}{8}$" × 1" × $84\frac{1}{2}$"
G. Tester stretchers (2) $\frac{7}{8}$" × 1" × $64\frac{1}{2}$"
H. Nut caps (8) $\frac{1}{2}$" × $\frac{3}{4}$" × $\frac{3}{4}$"

HARDWARE

$\frac{1}{2}$" × $4\frac{1}{2}$" Bed bolts, flat washers, and nuts (8)
Box springs support brackets and mounting
  screws (6–8)
$\frac{1}{4}$"-dia. × 2" Metal pins (4)

PLAN OF PROCEDURE

1

Plane, rip, and cut the parts to the sizes shown in the Bill of Materials, except for the nut caps. Cut these about $1/16$" thicker and wider than specified.

2

Cut the joinery needed to assemble the bed:

- $3/4$"-wide, $3/4$"-deep, $3\frac{1}{2}$"-long mortises in the inside surfaces of the bedposts, as shown in the *Bedpost Layout,* to hold the rails

- $3/4$"-wide, $3/4$"-long tenons on the ends of the rails, as shown in the *End Rail Layout* and *Side Rail Layout,* to fit the bedpost mortises

- $3/4$"-wide, $3/4$"-long, $1\frac{5}{8}$"-deep mortises in the inside surfaces of the rails, as shown in the *Rail and Headboard Joinery Detail,* to hold the nuts and washers that secure the rails to the posts

- $3/4$"-wide, $3/4$"-deep, 7"-long mortises in the inside surfaces of the head bedposts, as shown in the *Bedpost Layout/Inside Side View,* to hold the headboard

- 2"-wide, $3/8$"-deep dadoes in all four rails, as shown in the *Side Rail Layout/Side View* and *End View,* to hold the box spring support brackets

- 1"-wide, $7/16$"-deep rabbets in the ends of the tester rails, as shown in the *Tester Joinery Detail,* so the rails will overlap at the corners

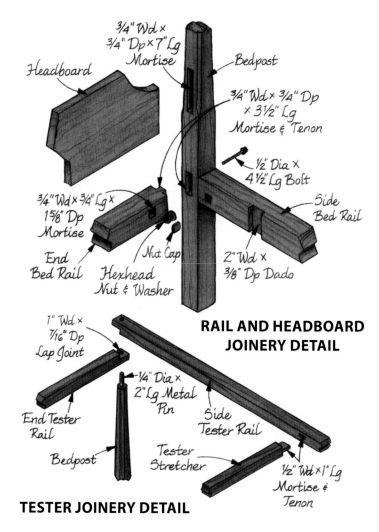

RAIL AND HEADBOARD JOINERY DETAIL

TESTER JOINERY DETAIL

- ½"-wide, 1"-long mortises through the inside surface of the side tester rails to hold the tester stretchers
- ½"-wide, 1"-long tenons in the ends of the tester stretchers to fit the mortises

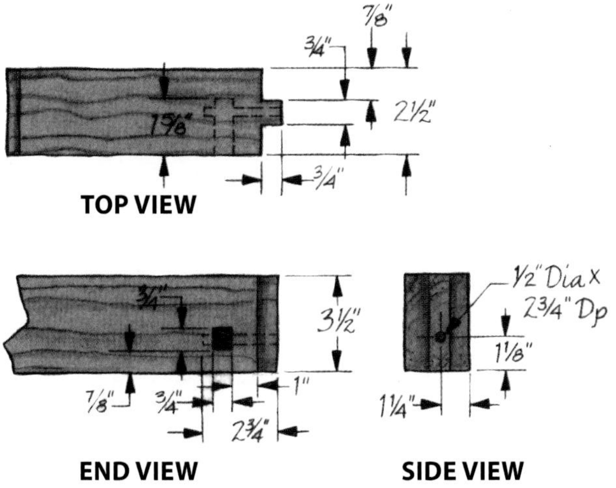

7/8"
3/4"
2½"
1⅝"
3/4"
TOP VIEW
3/4"
3½"
7/8"
3/4"
1"
2¾"
½" Dia x 2¾" Dp
1⅛"
1¼"
END VIEW
SIDE VIEW

END RAIL LAYOUT

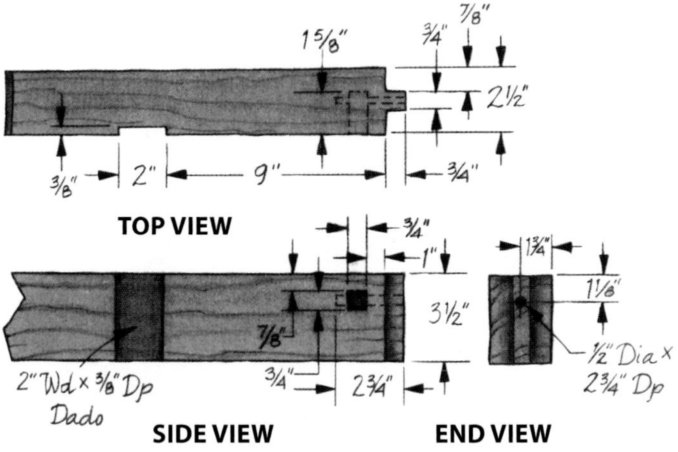

1⅝"
3/4"
7/8"
2½"
3/8"
2"
9"
3/4"
TOP VIEW
3/4"
1"
1¾"
1⅛"
3½"
7/8"
3/4"
2¾"
½" Dia x 2¾" Dp
2" Wd x 3/8" Dp Dado
SIDE VIEW
END VIEW

SIDE RAIL LAYOUT

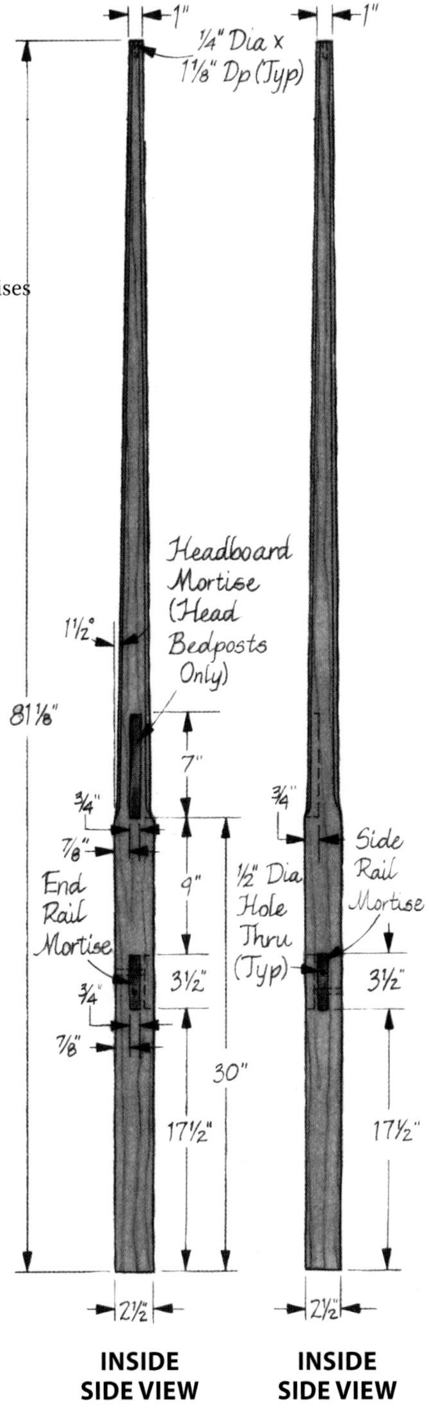

1"
1"
¼" Dia x 1⅛" Dp (Typ)
Headboard Mortise (Head Bedposts Only)
1½°
81⅛"
7"
3/4"
3/4"
7/8"
9"
End Rail Mortise
½" Dia Hole Thru (Typ)
Side Rail Mortise
3½"
3½"
3/4"
7/8"
30"
17½"
17½"
2½"
2½"
INSIDE SIDE VIEW
INSIDE SIDE VIEW

BEDPOST LAYOUTS

PLAN OF PROCEDURE

3

Drill the holes needed:

- ½"-diameter holes through the bedposts, as shown in the *Bedpost Bolt Hole Layout,* for the bed bolts

- ½"-diameter, 2¾"-deep holes in the ends of the rails, as shown in the *End Rail Layout* and *Side Rail Layout,* for the bed bolts

- ¼"-diameter, 1⅛"-deep holes in the top ends of the bedposts, as shown in the *Bedpost Layout,* to hold the tester pins

- ¼"-diameter holes through the tester rails, near the ends, as shown in the *Tester Joinery Detail,* to fit over the tester pins

4

Cut the octagonal tapers in the upper portions of the bedposts, as shown in the *Bedpost Layout* and explained in Making Pencil Posts on page 117.

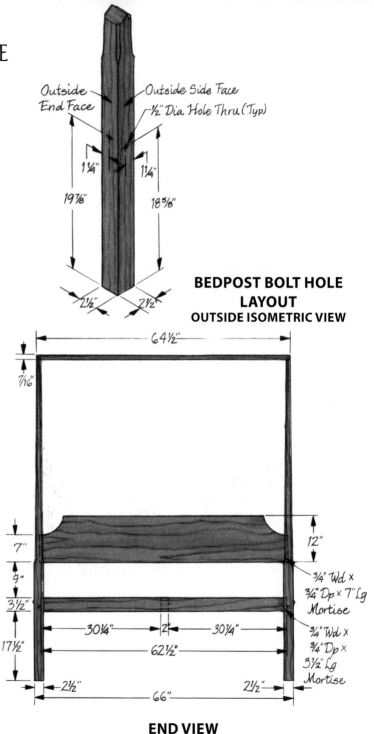

Outside End Face

Outside Side Face

½" Dia Hole Thru (Typ)

1¼" 1¼"

19⅞" 18⅝"

2½" 2½"

**BEDPOST BOLT HOLE
LAYOUT
OUTSIDE ISOMETRIC VIEW**

64½"

7⁄16"

7"

9"

3½"

17½"

30¼" 2" 30¼"

62½"

2½" 2½"

66"

12"

¾" Wd × ¾" Dp × 7" Lg Mortise

¾" Wd × ¾" Dp × 3½" Lg Mortise

END VIEW

5

Cut the shape of the headboard, as shown in the *Headboard Layout.* Sand the sawed edges.

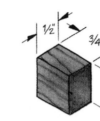

½"

¾"

¾"

¾"

NUT CAP DETAIL

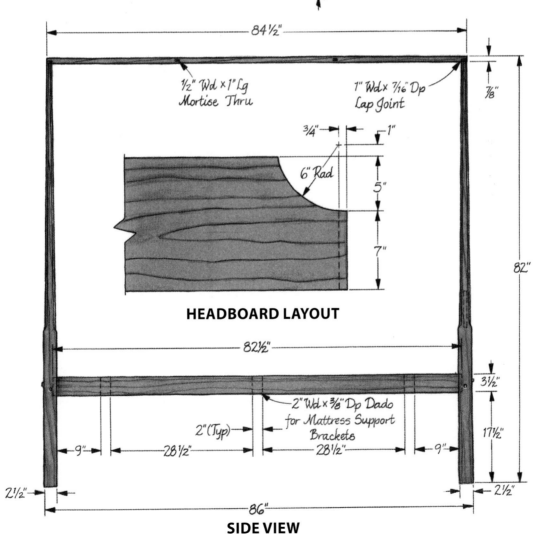

84½"

½" Wd × 1" Lg
Mortise Thru

1" Wd × ⁷⁄₁₆" Dp
Lap Joint

⅞"

¾"

1"

6" Rad

5"

7"

82"

HEADBOARD LAYOUT

82½"

3½"

2" Wd × ⅜" Dp Dado
for Mattress Support
Brackets

2" (Typ)

28½"

28½"

17½"

9"

9"

2½"

2½"

86"

SIDE VIEW

PLAN OF PROCEDURE

6

Finish sand all the parts of the bed and assemble them to test the fit of the joints. Using hot glue or epoxy, glue the nuts and washers in place, inside the bed rails. Be careful not to get any glue on the bolt threads. When you take the bed apart, the nuts and bolts should remain in their mortises.

7

Sand the nut caps, slightly tapering the ends and sides, so they fit the nut mortises like plugs. With the bed bolts, nuts, and washers in place, glue the caps in place. Sand them flush with the surface of the rails.

8

Attach the box spring support brackets to the rails.

9

Disassemble the bed and remove all the hardware (except for the nuts and washers inside the rails). Do any necessary touch-up sanding and apply a finish to the completed project.

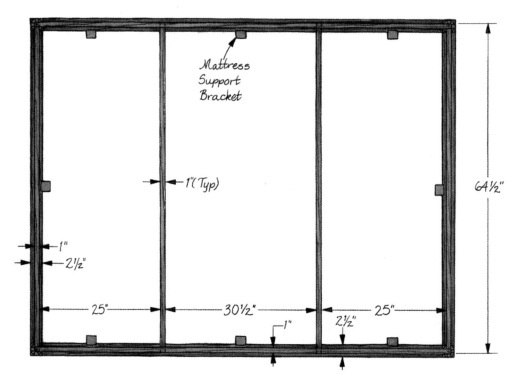

TOP VIEW

COUNTRY CRAFTSMAN'S KNOW-HOW:
MAKING PENCIL POSTS

Country craftsmen cut the octagonal tapers in long pencil posts with simple hand tools — a drawknife, a plane, chisels, and scrapers. These are still the best tools for the job, although you can save some time by roughing out the tapers with a band saw.

1 To shape each post, you must make *eight* tapers — four *face* tapers and four *corner* tapers. To begin, mark two tapers for *opposing* faces, using a long straightedge.

2 Rough-cut the first two tapers on a band saw, cutting a little wide of the lines.

3 Using a hand plane, smooth the tapers. Carefully cut down to the lines, but no *farther!*

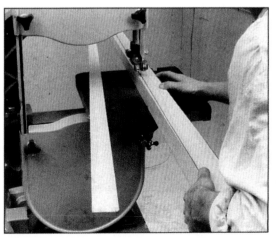

4 Repeat Steps 1, 2, and 3 for the two remaining face tapers. When you're finished, the post should taper on all four sides.

COUNTRY CRAFTSMAN'S KNOW-HOW:
MAKING PENCIL POSTS—*CONTINUED*

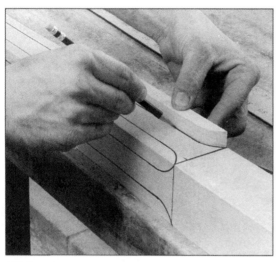

5 Scribe all four of the corner tapers. The shoulders of these tapers (where the octagonal, tapered portion of the post ends and the square, straight portion begins) are rounded. Use a template to mark these so they're all precisely the same.

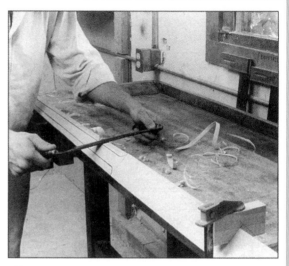

6 Clamp the post in two or more V-blocks so one of the corners faces up. Using a drawknife or spoke-shave, remove stock down to the lines.

7 Cut the rounded shoulder with a chisel. Then repeat Steps 6 and 7 for each corner taper.

8 Smooth all the tapers with a hand scraper and sandpaper. Use a sanding block so you preserve the hard edges of the octagonal shape.

CHEST OF DRAWERS

Chests have been popular storage pieces since Egyptian times, but they have always presented the same problem: How do you retrieve an item on the bottom of the chest without disturbing everything piled on top of it? You couldn't, until the late sixteenth century when English Renaissance joiners introduced the *mule chest* — a chest with a single *drawing box* or *till* (as a drawer was then called) at the bottom. This finally solved the problem.

This chest with drawer grew increasingly popular in the seventeenth century. Gradually, English craftsmen added more drawers until the chest portion was just a shallow bin at the top of the piece. At first, the makers hid the drawers behind paneled doors so the piece retained the same appearance as a traditional chest. By the second half of the century, however, they began to omit these doors. Finally, about mid-century, the craftsmen completely filled the chest with drawers, made it much taller than previously, and fixed the lid in place. This was the beginning of the *chest of drawers* as we know it.

American craftsmen began to make chests of drawers about the same time and continued through the eighteenth and nineteenth centuries. They were fond of tall chests and made them long after they had gone out of style in England — perhaps to provide their clients

with more storage and make better use of the available space. This tall six-drawer chest is a copy of an early nineteenth-century piece made by a Shaker craftsman at the Union Village community near Lebanon, Ohio.

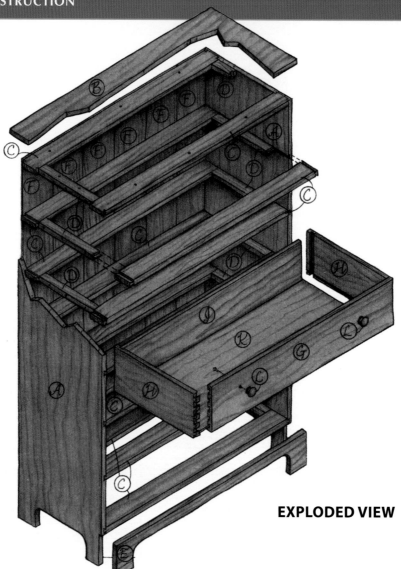

EXPLODED VIEW

BILL OF MATERIALS

WOODEN PARTS/*FINISHED DIMENSIONS*

A.	Sides (2)	¾" × 18" × 62"
B.	Top	¾" × 19" × 42"
C.	Web frame rails (14)	¾" × 3" × 39½"
D.	Web frame stiles (14)	¾" × 1¼" × 12¼"
E.	Baseboard	¾" × 5¾" × 40"
F.	Backboards (5–6)	½" × (variable) × 56¼"
G.	Drawer fronts (6)	¾" × 8⁷/₁₆" × 38⅜"
H.	Drawer sides (12)	¾" × 8⁷/₁₆" × 17⅛"

J.	Drawer backs (6)	¾" × 7¹⁵/₁₆" × 37⅝"
K.	Drawer bottoms (6)	½" × 17⅛" × 37⁹/₁₆"
L.	Drawer pulls (12)	1¼" dia. × 1"

HARDWARE

6d Square-cut nails (40–48)
1¼" Wire or headless brads (36–40)
#10 × 1¼" Flathead wood screws (10)
#10 × 1½" Flathead wood screws (12)

PLAN OF PROCEDURE

1

If necessary, glue up stock to make the sides and top. Plane, rip, and cut the parts to the sizes shown in the Bill of Materials, except the backboards and drawer parts. Rip the backboards so they will form a single panel 39¼" wide, with a ¹/₁₆" gap between each board. Make the drawer fronts, sides, backs, and bottoms about ¹/₁₆" wider and longer than specified. Cut two pieces 1½" × 1½" × 10" to make the turning stock for the pulls.

2

Cut the joinery needed to assemble the case:

- ½"-wide, ¾"-deep, 2¼"-long dovetail sockets in the top ends of the sides to hold the top web frame rails, as shown in the *Top Web Frame Joinery Detail*

- 2¼"-wide, ½"-long dovetails in the ends of the top web frame rails

- ½"-wide, ½"-deep, 3"-long dovetail grooves in the sides to hold the remaining web frame rails, as shown in the *Side Layout*

- ½"-thick, ½"-long dovetail tenons in the ends of the remaining web frame rails, as shown in the *Web Frame Joinery Detail*

- ½"-wide, ⅜"-deep, 56¼"-long blind rabbets in the sides to hold the backboards

- ¼"-wide, ⅜"-deep, 1¾"-long grooves in the inside edges of all web frame rails to hold the web frame stiles

- ¼"-thick, ⅜"-long tenons in the ends of the web frame stiles

3

Drill and countersink ³/₁₆"-diameter pilot holes through the top web frame rails and stiles. Make the countersinks on the bottom faces of these parts. Make three to four pilot holes in each rail, and two pilot holes in each stile. The positions of these holes are not critical, but they should be centered in the boards and evenly spaced.

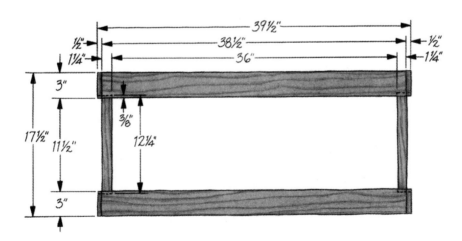

WEB FRAME LAYOUT

PLAN OF PROCEDURE

4

Drill ⅛" pilot holes (for nails) through the web frame stiles, from edge to edge. Make three holes in each stile. Once again, the positions aren't critical, but they should be evenly spaced.

5

Lay out and cut the shapes of the feet in the baseboard and sides, as shown in the *Front View* and *Side Layout*. Sand the sawed edges.

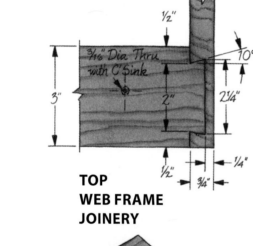

TOP WEB FRAME JOINERY

¾₁₆" Dia Thru with C'Sink

½"

3"

2"

2¼"

10°

½"

¾"

¼"

¼" Wd × ⅜" Dp ×1¾" Lg Groove

Web Frame Rail

Web Frame Stile

¼" Wd × ⅜" Lg Tenon

½"

3"

¼"

½"

¼"

1¼"

¼"

WEB FRAME JOINERY DETAIL

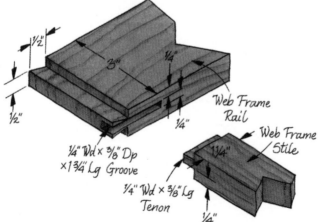

3" — 11½" — 3"

½" Wd × ⅜" Dp Rabbet

½" Wd × ½" Dp Dovetail Groove (Typ)

Nail Drawer Guides Here

⁵⁄₁₆"

¾"

9¼" O.C. (Typ)

6⅛" O.C.

5¾"

2" Rad

2¾" — 11" — 3½"

¾"

18"

SIDE LAYOUT

6

Lay out and cut the notches that hold the baseboard in the front edges of the sides.

7

Finish sand the parts of the case and assemble them in the following order:

- Set the sides on a flat surface with the bottom edge down. Glue the top web frame rails and the baseboard in place. Reinforce the baseboard with nails.

- Glue the remaining front web frame rails in the dovetail grooves in the sides.

- Turn the assembly over so the sides rest on their front edges. Glue the web frame stiles to the front web frame rails, inserting the tenons in the grooves.

- Apply glue to the back tenons on the web frame stiles. Slide the back web frame rails into their dovetails. As you do so, insert the stile tenons in the grooves.

- Nail the stiles to the sides, driving the nails through the ⅛"-diameter pilot holes. Do *not* glue the stiles to the sides.

- Place the case on its feet. Attach the top with #10 × 1 ¼" flathead wood screws, driving the screws through the top web frame rails and stiles. Do *not* glue the top in place.

- Using wire or headless brads, attach the backboards to the sides and back web frame rail. Do *not* glue the backboards in place.

Sand all joints clean and flush as you work. After the case is assembled, set the heads of the nails slightly below the surface. If you wish cover the heads of the baseboard nails with putty.

8

Turn the drawer pulls on a lathe. Turn six pulls from each piece of turning stock, and finish sand them on the lathe. Cut them apart with a band saw and do any necessary touch up sanding to remove the saw marks.

9

Cut the joinery needed to assemble the drawers:

- ¾"-wide, ⅜"-deep dadoes in the sides, to hold the backs, as shown in the *Drawer/ Top View*

- ¼"-wide, ⅜"-deep grooves in the front and the sides to hold the bottom

- Half-blind dovetails that fasten the sides to the fronts, as shown in the *Dovetail Layout*

For more information for cutting these dovetails, refer to Making Hand-Cut Dovetails on page 48.

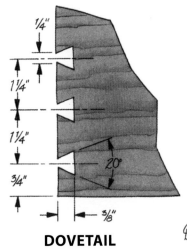

DOVETAIL LAYOUT

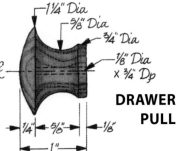

DRAWER PULL

PLAN OF PROCEDURE

10

Drill and countersink $3/16$"-diameter holes through the drawer fronts where you wish to mount the pulls.

11

Finish sand the drawer parts, then assemble them in the following order:

- Assemble fronts, sides, and backs with glue.

- Reinforce the side-to-back joints with nails and set the heads.

- Slide the drawer bottoms into their grooves. Drive one or two headless brads through the bottoms and into the backs. Do *not* glue the bottoms in place.

- Mount the drawer pulls to the drawer fronts with #10 × ½" flathead wood screws.

12

Fit the drawers to the case. If necessary, plane a little stock from the assemblies until they slide in and out of the case easily.

13

Remove the drawers from the case and do any necessary touch-up sanding. Apply a finish to the drawer fronts and *all* sides of the case — inside and outside. Do *not* finish the drawer sides, backs, or bottoms.

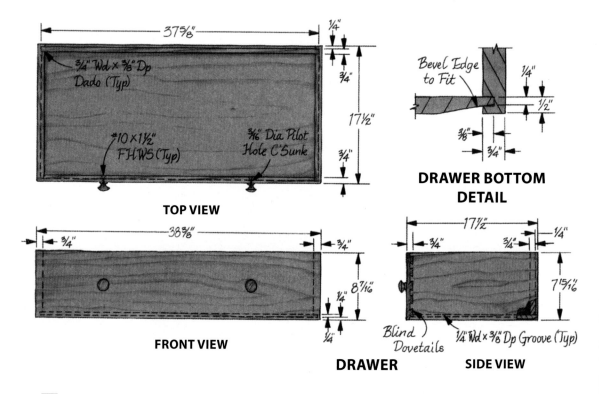

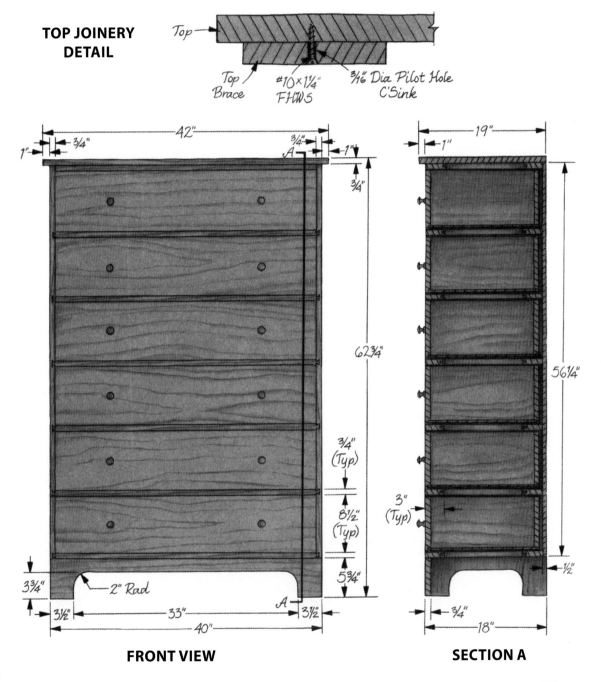

TOP JOINERY DETAIL

Top

Top Brace

#10 × 1¼" FHWS

³⁄₁₆" Dia Pilot Hole C'Sink

42"

¾"

1"

¾"

A

1"

¾"

62¾"

¾" (Typ)

8½" (Typ)

5¾"

3¾"

2" Rad

3½"

33"

A

3½"

40"

FRONT VIEW

19"

1"

56¼"

3" (Typ)

½"

¾"

18"

SECTION A

SHAKER CRADLE

Although the Shakers practiced celibacy, they sometimes accepted whole families, including the children, into their communities. They also took in unwed mothers, foundlings, and orphans. Consequently, there were often infants — and cradles — in the Shaker nurseries. The cradle shown is a copy of one now on display in the Shaker Museum in Old Chatham, New York. It was made by Shaker craftsmen early in the nineteenth century, although its community of origin is not clear.

The design is typical of many country cradles made during this period. The headboard and the sides are raised to protect the uncovered head of the infant from drafts. The rockers are extended far beyond the sides not only for stability, but so the mother could rock the infant while she attended to other chores. She would sit next to the cradle with a pile of clothes to mend or beans to shell and place a foot on the knobbed end of one rocker. As she worked, she'd push gently on the knob, rocking the cradle.

EXPLODED VIEW

BILL OF MATERIALS

WOODEN PARTS/_FINISHED DIMENSIONS_

A.	Sides (2)	¾" × 16" × 39¼"
B.	Headboard	¾" × 17" × 17½"
C.	Footboard	¾" × 14¼" × 15½"
D.	Bottom	¾" × 9⅞" × 31⅞"
E.	Rockers (2)	⅞" × 4⅝" × 22⅞"
F.	Stretcher	¾" × 1¼" × 25⅜"
G.	Wedges (2)	⁵⁄₁₆" × ⁷⁄₁₆" × 2"

HARDWARE

#8 × 1½" Flathead wood screws (4)
4d Square-cut nails

PLAN OF PROCEDURE

1

Glue up stock to make the wide boards needed for the headboard, footboard, sides, and bottom. Plane the parts to the thicknesses needed, then rip and cut the stretcher and wedges to the sizes shown in the Bill of Materials. Cut the other parts about ½" wider and longer than specified.

2

Compound-miter the ends of the headboard, footboard, and sides with the miter gauge angled at 79¼° and the saw blade tilted to 2°. When assembled, all four parts will slope at 11°.

3

Lay out and cut the dovetails. Lay out the baselines (bottoms) of the tails and pins parallel to the *ends* of the headboard, footboard, and sides. Then lay out the tails on the sides, as shown in the *Dovetail Layout/ Side View*. Note that the centerline of these tails is parallel to the *bottom edge* of each board. Transfer the layout lines across the end grains so that they will be parallel to the bottom edge of the headboard or footboard, as shown in the *Dovetail Layout/End View*.

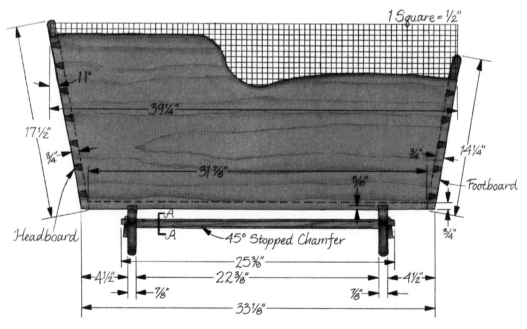

SIDE VIEW

Cut the sides of the tails with a dovetail saw, then remove the waste with a chisel. Chisel along each baseline, cutting halfway through the board. Then flip the board over and chisel from the other side. Trim the bases (the spaces between each tail) so they're parallel to the end of the board.

Position the finished tails over the end grain of the adjoining headboard or footboard. Trace around the tails with an awl to lay out the ends of the pins. Connect the ends of the pins to the baselines. Remember, the pins must be parallel to the bottom edges of the boards. Cut and chisel out the pins. For further instructions, see Making Hand-Cut Dovetails on page 48.

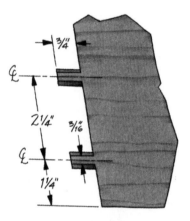

END VIEW

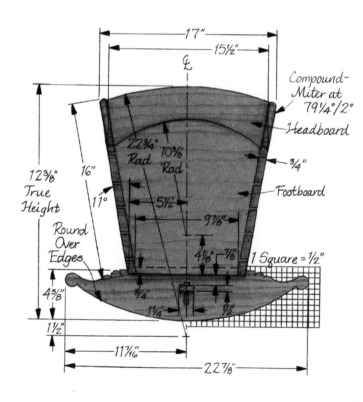

END VIEW

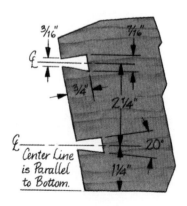

SIDE VIEW
DOVETAIL LAYOUT

PLAN OF PROCEDURE

4

Dry assemble the headboard, footboard, and sides. Fit the bottom to the assembly, beveling the edges and ends at 11°.

5

Cut the joinery needed to assemble the rockers and stretcher:

- ½"-wide, 1¼"-long mortise through the rocker stock, as shown in the *End View*

- ⁵/₁₆"-wide, ⁵/₁₆"-long mortises through the ends of the stretcher, as shown in the *Stretcher Joinery Detail*

- ½"-thick tenons on the ends of the stretcher, as shown in the *Stretcher Tenon Detail*

6

Cut tapers and bevels in the wedges, as shown in the *Stretcher Joinery Detail*.

7

Lay out and cut the shapes of the headboard, footboard, sides, and rockers. Sand the sawed edges.

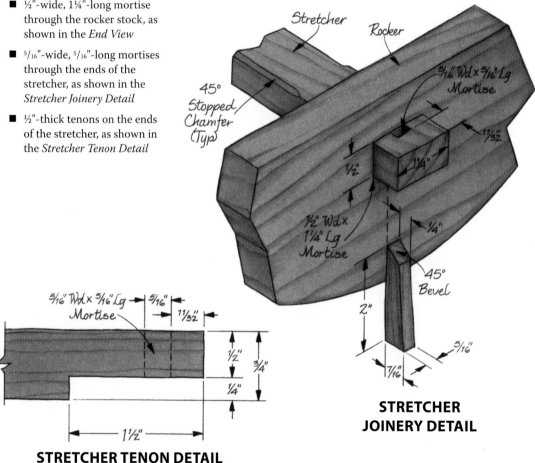

STRETCHER TENON DETAIL

STRETCHER JOINERY DETAIL

8

Cut a stopped chamfer in all four corners of the stretcher, as shown in the *Side View* and *Section A*.

9

Round over the top edges of the headboard, footboard, and sides with a ⅜" quarter-round bit. Round over the bottom of the rockers with the same bit.

10

Finish sand all the parts of the cradle. Glue the headboard, footboard, and sides together. Then attach the bottom with nails, driving the nails through the headboard, footboard, and sides. Do *not* glue the bottom in place. Sand the joints clean and flush.

11

Set the nails and, if you wish, cover the heads with putty.

12

Assemble the rockers and stretchers with glue. Before the glue dries, press the wedges into the ends of the stretcher to pin the parts together.

13

Attach the rocker assembly to the cradle with flathead wood screws. Do *not* glue the rockers to the bottom. Countersink the heads of the screws.

14

Do any necessary touch-up sanding, then apply a finish to the cradle.

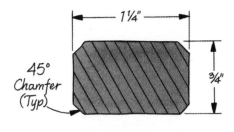

SECTION A

Six-Board Chest

The simple chest — a box with a lid — is probably the oldest form of furniture. Since prehistoric times, people have hollowed logs and fitted them with lids of rived wood or animal skins to store and transport their possessions. Dug-out chests or *trunks* were used in Western Europe through the Middle Ages.

In the thirteenth century, joiners began to nail boards together to form plank chests. These usually consisted of just six major parts — the four sides, the top, and the bottom. At first, these chests rested on short tables or stands to keep them off the damp earth. Then craftsmen lengthened the side boards, creating a built-in stand.

This simple six-board design proved so practical that it was used by country folks in Europe, and then in America,

for hundreds of years. Depending on the prevailing fashion at the time, the planks might be gaily painted, covered with intricate ironwork, or decorated with moldings and chip carvings. The basic design, however, remained the same. The six-board chest shown is typical of many built by the early settlers in New England.

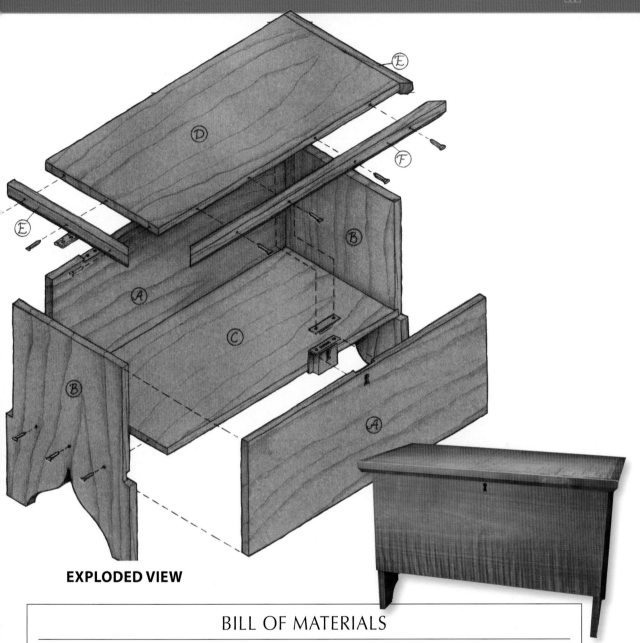

EXPLODED VIEW

BILL OF MATERIALS

WOODEN PARTS/*FINISHED DIMENSIONS*

A.	Front/back (2)	¾" × 11½" × 28¾"
B.	Sides (2)	¾" × 14½" × 19"
C.	Bottom	¾" × 13" × 28"
D.	Lid	¾" × 14⁹/₁₆" × 28⅞"
E.	Side trim (2)	¾" × 1" × 15⁵/₁₆"
F.	Front trim	¾" × 1" × 30⅜"

HARDWARE

6d Square-cut nails (16)

1½" × 3" Butt hinges and mounting screws (1 pair)

Chest lock, latch, and mounting screws

PLAN OF PROCEDURE

1

If necessary, glue up the stock to make the front, back, sides, bottom, and lid. Plane, rip, and cut the parts to the sizes shown in the Bill of Materials, except the side and front trim. Cut these ½"–1" longer than specified.

2

Rout or cut a ¾"-wide, ⅜"-deep dado in the inside surface of each side, as shown in the *Side Layout*.

3

Cut a ¾"-deep, 11½"-long notch in the front and back edges of each side, as shown in the *Side Layout*.

4

Lay out the shape of the feet on the sides, as shown in the *Side Layout*, and cut them with a band saw or saber saw. Sand the sawed edges.

5

Cut a mortise in the inside face of the front for the lock. With a drill and a file, create a hole for the key.

6

Finish sand the parts you have made, then join the bottom and sides, gluing the bottom into the dadoes. Reinforce the glue joints with square-cut nails.

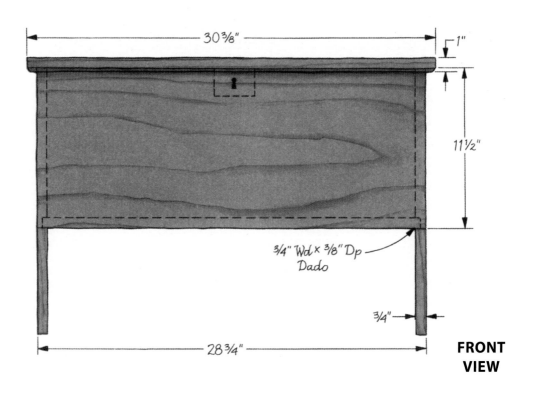

FRONT VIEW

7

Join the front and back to the sides and bottom. Glue the front and back to the bottom, but *not* the sides. If you glue the front and back to the sides, the long, horizontal parts won't be able to expand and contract properly. The glue joints will eventually pop, and the wood may warp, cup, or split. Instead, nail the front and back to the sides and set the heads. The nails will give slightly when the wood moves.

8

Fit the trim to the lid, mitering the adjoining ends. Glue the front trim to the front edge of the lid and reinforce it with nails. Then nail (but do *not* glue) the side trim to the ends of the lid.

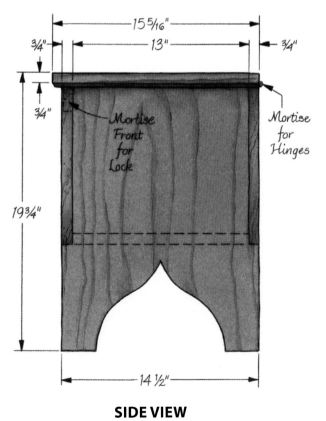

SIDE VIEW

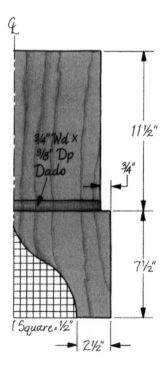

SIDE LAYOUT

PLAN OF PROCEDURE

9

Using a handplane, cut a 45° chamfer in the bottom outside corner of the three trim parts, as shown in the *Trim Profile*.

10

Set all the nails, and cover the heads with putty.

11

Mortise the lid and the back for hinges, then mount the lid on the chest. The trim must fit over the front and sides.

12

Install the lock in the front. Mark the location of the latch on the bottom face of the lid, then remove the lid from the chest and cut a mortise for the latch.

13

Remove all the hardware from the chest. Do any necessary touch-up sanding, then apply a finish to the *outside* wooden surfaces. Leave the inside of the chest unfinished. When the finish dries, reassemble the lid to the chest. Replace the lock and the latch.

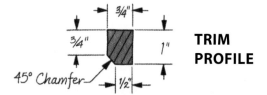

TRIM PROFILE

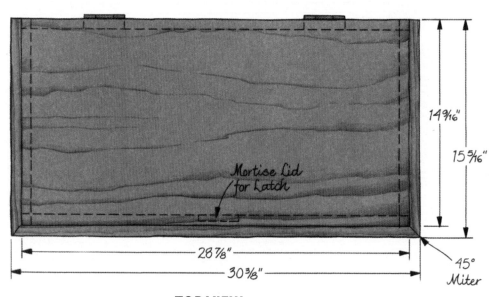

TOP VIEW

FRETWORK MIRROR

Country mirrors were framed in many ways, but one of the most popular was an ornate fretwork frame. The intricate shapes were copied in the mid-eighteenth century from Japanese "cloud forms." Cabinetmakers first saw these forms on furniture imported from the Orient. The English architect and designer, Thomas Chippendale, and others began to use them on their furniture, and soon fretwork was all the rage. As American craftsmen imitated their English counterparts, the style became popular on both sides of the Atlantic. Complex, veneered fretwork mirrors appeared in American cities. Country craftsmen copied these, making simpler, solid-wood versions.

Although the frame looks difficult, it's actually simple to make. The basic frame is made like any other, using ordinary miter joints reinforced with splines. The fretwork is cut from thin stock, then glued to the frame and backed up with glue blocks.

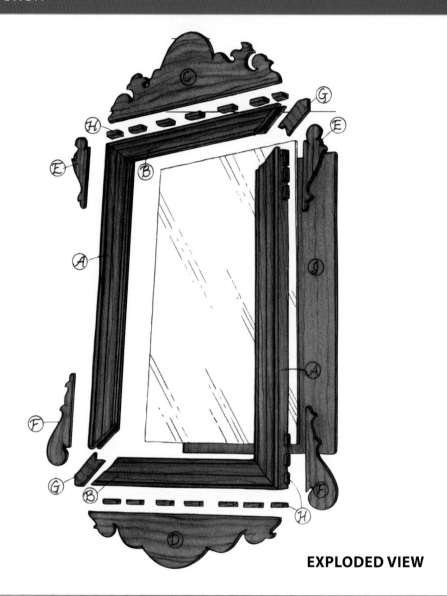

EXPLODED VIEW

BILL OF MATERIALS

WOODEN PARTS/*FINISHED DIMENSIONS*

A.	Side stretchers (2)	⅞" × 1⅜" × 19"
B.	Top/bottom stretchers (2)	⅞" × 1⅜" × 12½"
C.	Top fretwork	¼" × 5" × 12½"
D.	Bottom fretwork	¼" × 2¾" × 12½"
E.	Top side fretwork (2)	¼" × 1½" × 5"
F.	Bottom side fretwork (2)	¼" × 1¾" × 4¾"
G.	Splines (4)	⅛" × 1" × 2¼"

H.	Glue blocks (26)	¼" × ¼" × 1"
J.	Mirror back	¼" × 10¼" × 16¾"

HARDWARE
10³/₁₆" × 16¹/₁₆" Mirror
⅞" Wire or headless brads (6–8)
¼" Eye screws (2)
Picture-hanging wire (16")

PLAN OF PROCEDURE

1

Plane the stock to the thicknesses specified in the Bill of Materials. Rip the stretcher and spline stock to the proper width, but don't cut them to length yet. Cut the fretwork stock into rectangles about ¼" wider and longer than specified. Cut the glue blocks and mirror back to the sizes specified.

2

Cut or rout the shape of the stretchers, as shown in the *Stretcher Profile*. Make this shape in three separate passes, cutting a portion of the shape with each pass:

- Cut a ⅝"-diameter bead in the outside corner.
- Cut a 1"-radius cove in the inside corner. (You can create large coves on your table saw by making a *cove cut*.)
- Cut a ¼"-radius cove inside the larger cove.

3

Cut or rout a ¼"-wide, ⅜"-deep rabbet in the back inside edge of the stretcher stock.

4

Cut the stretcher stock to the proper length, mitering the ends at 45°.

5

Using a table saw blade that cuts a ⅛"-wide kerf, cut ⅛"-wide, ½"-deep spline grooves in the mitered ends of the stretchers.

6

Cut the splines to the proper length and shape them to look like small feathers, as shown in the *Spline Layout*. Pay careful attention to the grain direction of the splines. It must run side to side, across the *width* of the parts, not the length.

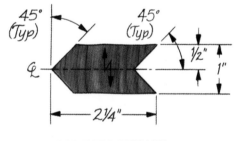

SPLINE LAYOUT

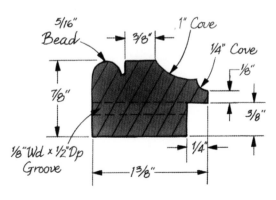

STRETCHER PROFILE

PLAN OF PROCEDURE

7

Dry assemble the stretchers and splines to check the fit of the joints. Finish sand the stretcher parts, then assemble the stretcher frame with glue. As you assemble the frame, fit the splines in the grooves, as shown in the *Stretcher Joinery Detail*.

8

When the glue dries, sand the joints clean and flush.

9

Lay out the fretwork patterns on the fretwork stock. Once again, pay careful attention to the grain direction, as indicated in the pattern drawings. Cut the shapes of the fretwork and sand the sawed edges.

10

Finish sand the fretwork, then glue it to the frame, reinforcing the joints with glue blocks, as shown in the *Side View*.

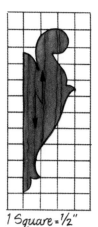

1 Square = ½"

TOP SIDE FRETWORK

1 Square = ½"

BOTTOM SIDE FRETWORK

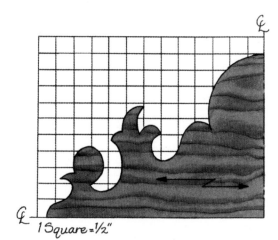

1 Square = ½"

TOP FRETWORK

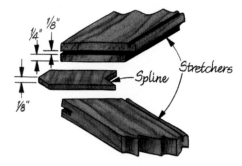

STRETCHER JOINERY DETAIL

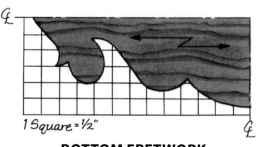

1 Square = ½"

BOTTOM FRETWORK

11

Do any necessary touch-up sanding, then paint or finish the completed frame.

12

Install the mirror and mirror back in the frame, securing them with 1" wire brads.

13

Install eye screws in the back of the frame, one on either side, toward the top. Stretch picture-hanging wire between them.

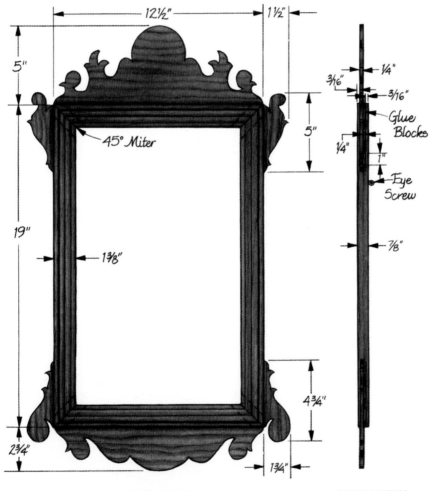

FRONT VIEW   **SIDE VIEW**

TURNED-POST BED

Beds were in short supply in the American wilderness. When families first arrived, they often slept huddled together on the floors of their hastily built cabins. Later, as they settled the land and had time to attend to their own comfort, they began to build simple beds, similar to the one shown. The posts were thick and heavy, usually turned, and often had large, round finials on the ends. Later, these were nicknamed "cannonball" beds.

These early bedsteads were short by our standards, and always had a wide headboard at one end. From the seventeenth until well into the nineteenth century, folks customarily slept sitting up, with their shoulders and head resting against the headboard. (They believed that if they slept lying down, their lungs would fill with fluid and they might suffocate.) The mattresses were supported by ropes woven between the stretchers.

Although the turned posts of this bed are copied from an early nineteenth-century antique, the remainder of the project has been updated in two important ways. First, it's been lengthened to accommodate a standard-size twin mattress — you can sleep lying down. Second, the traditional ropes have been eliminated. Instead, metal brackets support a contemporary box spring.

EXPLODED VIEW

BILL OF MATERIALS

WOODEN PARTS/_FINISHED DIMENSIONS_

A.	Head bedposts (2)	3¼" × 3¼" × 34"
B.	Foot bedposts (2)	3¼" × 3¼" × 26"
C.	End rails (2)	2½" × 3½" × 41½"
D.	Side rails (2)	2½" × 3½" × 77½"
E.	Headboard	¾" × 12" × 41½"
F.	Nut caps (8)	½" × ¾" × ¾"

HARDWARE

½" × 5" Bed bolts, flat washers, and nuts (8)
Box springs support brackets and mounting
   screws (8)

PLAN OF PROCEDURE

1

Plane, rip, and cut the parts to the sizes shown in the Bill of Materials, except for the nut caps. Cut these to the thickness specified, but make them about $1/16$" longer and wider than shown.

2

Cut the joinery needed to assemble the bed:

- $3/4$"-wide, $3/4$"-deep, $3\,1/2$"-long mortises in the inside surfaces of the bedposts, as shown in the *Head Bedpost Layout* and *Foot Bedpost Layout,* to hold the rails

- $3/4$"-wide, $3/4$"-long tenons on the ends of the rails, as shown in the *End Rail Layout* and *Side Rail Layout,* to fit the bedpost mortises

- $3/4$"-wide, $3/4$"-long, $1\,5/8$"-deep mortises in the inside surfaces of the rails to hold the nuts and washers that secure the rails to the posts

- $3/4$"-wide, $3/4$"-deep, $4\,3/4$"-long mortises in the inside surfaces of the head bedposts, as shown in the *Head Bedpost Layout,* to hold the headboard

- 2"-wide, $3/4$"-deep dadoes in all four rails, as shown in the *Top View,* to hold the box spring support brackets

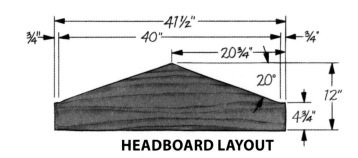

HEADBOARD LAYOUT

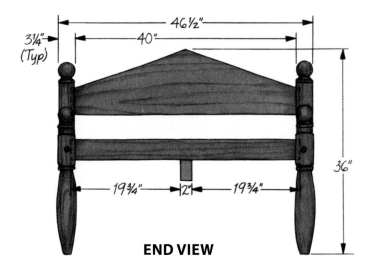

END VIEW

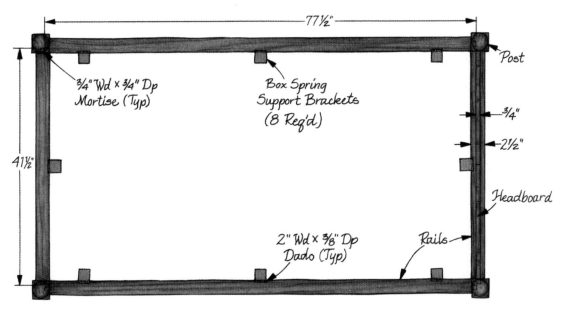

TOP VIEW

77½"

¾" Wd × ¾" Dp
Mortise (Typ)

Box Spring
Support Brackets
(8 Req'd)

Post

¾"

2½"

41½"

Headboard

2" Wd × ⅜" Dp
Dado (Typ)

Rails

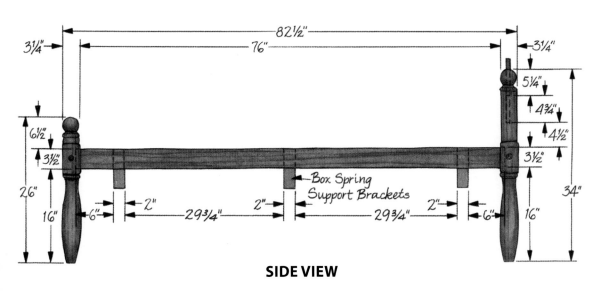

SIDE VIEW

82½"

76"

3¼"

3¼"

5¼"

4¾"

4½"

6½"

3½"

3½"

26"

Box Spring
Support Brackets

34"

16"

6"

2"

29¾"

2"

2"

29¾"

2"

6"

16"

Plan of Procedure

3

Drill the holes needed:

- ½"-diameter holes through the bedposts, as shown in the *Bedpost Bolt Hole Layout*, for the bed bolts

- ½"-diameter, 2¾"-deep holes in the ends of the rails, as shown in the *End Rail Layout* and *Side Rail Layout*, for the bed bolts

4

Turn the shapes of the bedposts, as shown in the *Head Bedpost Layout* and *Foot Bedpost Layout*.

5

Cut the shape of the headboard, as shown in the *Headboard Layout*. Sand the sawed edges.

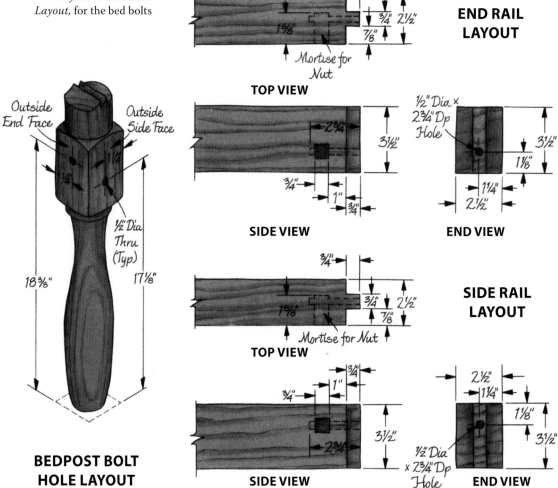

END RAIL LAYOUT

SIDE RAIL LAYOUT

BEDPOST BOLT HOLE LAYOUT

6

Finish sand all the parts of the bed and assemble them to test the fit of the joints. Put the bed bolts and nuts in place. Using hot glue or epoxy, glue the nuts and washers in place, inside the bed rails. Be careful not to get any glue on the bolts' threads. When you take the bed apart, the nuts and bolts should remain in their mortises.

7

Sand the nut caps, slightly tapering the ends and sides, so they fit the nut mortises like plugs. With the bed bolts, nuts, and washers in place, glue the caps in place. Sand them flush with the surface of the rails.

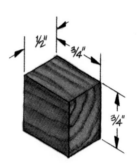

NUT CAP DETAIL

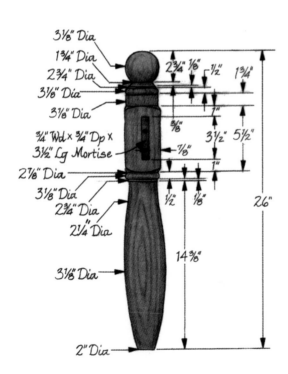

FOOT BEDPOST LAYOUT

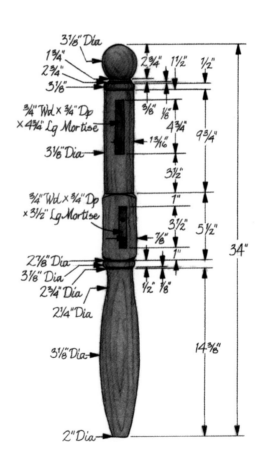

HEAD BEDPOST LAYOUT

PLAN OF PROCEDURE

8

Attach the box spring support brackets to the rails.

9

Disassemble the bed and remove all the hardware (except for the nuts and washers inside the rails). Do any necessary touch-up sanding and apply a finish to the completed project. When the finish dries, reassemble the bed.

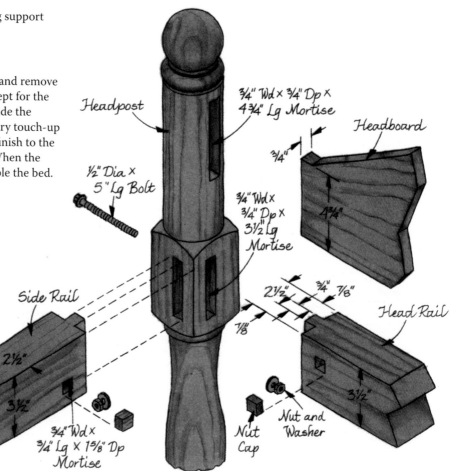

Headpost

¾" Wd × ¾" Dp × 4¾" Lg Mortise

Headboard

¾"

½" Dia × 5" Lg Bolt

¾" Wd × ¾" Dp × 3½" Lg Mortise

4¾"

Side Rail

2½"

3½"

2½"

¾" 7/8"

7/8"

Head Rail

3½"

¾" Wd × ¾" Lg × 1⅝" Dp Mortise

Nut Cap

Nut and Washer

**POST-TO-RAIL
JOINERY DETAIL**

FOR SITTING
& REFLECTING

LADDER-BACK CHAIR

The ladder-back chair was a popular furniture design throughout Europe long before America was discovered. In the American A colonies, English immigrants began to make ladder-back chairs in the late seventeenth century, and the Germans, shortly after that. These early American ladder-backs were fairly heavy and intricately turned — not much different than their European predecessors. Then in the late eighteenth century, an obscure religious sect modified this chair to produce one of America's most-admired country furniture designs.

In 1789, the United Society of Believers in Christ's Second Appearing (better known as the Shakers) began making these chairs for use in their community dwellings. Because they believed in the virtues of utility and simplicity, Shaker craftsmen avoided unnecessary ornament in their furniture. They stripped the ladder-back design to its barest essentials, creating a light, austere chair that was surprisingly elegant and durable.

The Shakers also believed that their love of God was expressed in the integrity of their work and, therefore, quickly earned a reputation for excellent workmanship. By the early nineteenth century, outsiders were asking to buy Shaker furniture. At first, the Shakers simply sold their excess chairs to the "world's people." By the 1820s, they increased production and began to actively market ladder-back chairs and rockers.

In 1852, they standardized their designs, and in 1873 built a chair factory at their community in New Lebanon, New York. This factory continued to produce the distinctive Shaker chairs until 1935.

This ladder-back armchair is copied from one made in the early nineteenth century, before Shaker chair designs were standardized. Although its community of origin is not certain, it was probably built at Union Village, Ohio.

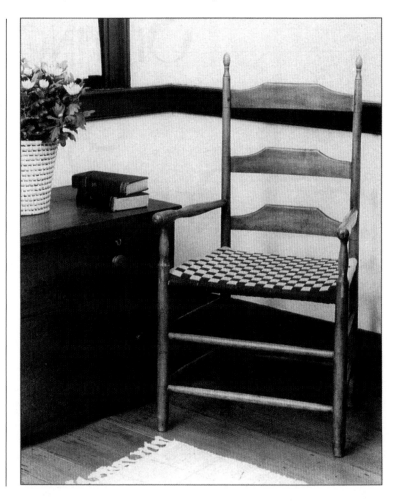

EXPLODED VIEW

BILL OF MATERIALS

WOODEN PARTS/*FINISHED DIMENSIONS*

A.	Back legs (2)	1⅜" dia. × 41½"
B.	Front legs (2)	1⅜" dia. × 24¼"
C.	Front rungs/stretchers (3)	1" dia. × 20"
D.	Side rungs/stretchers (6)	1" dia. × 15⅞"
E.	Back rungs/stretchers (2)	1" dia. × 16"
F.	Top/middle slats (2)	¼" × 3" × 16⅞"
G.	Bottom slat	¼" × 2¾" × 16⅞"
H.	Arms (2)	1⅜" dia. × 18¼"
J.	Pegs (2)	¼" dia. × ⅝"

HARDWARE

Tape or rush (sufficient to weave the seat)
- A tape seat requires 30 yards of 1"-wide tape
- A rush seat requires 2–3 lbs. of ⁵/₃₂" fiber cord.

You may also need small tacks, cotton batting, or foam rubber, depending on the type of seat you weave.

PLAN OF PROCEDURE

1

Plane, rip, and cut the parts to the sizes shown in the Bill of Materials, except for the turned parts — legs, arms, stretchers, and rungs. Make these about 9"–2" longer than specified.

2

Turn the legs, arms, stretchers, and rungs to the shapes shown. Turn ⁵/₈"-diameter, ³/₄"-long tenons on both ends of the rungs and stretchers, on the top end of each front leg, and on the back end of each arm.

Lay out the mortises by scoring the pieces with a skew as they turn, as shown in the *Back Leg Layout* and *Front Leg Layout*. Finish sand the turnings on the lathe.

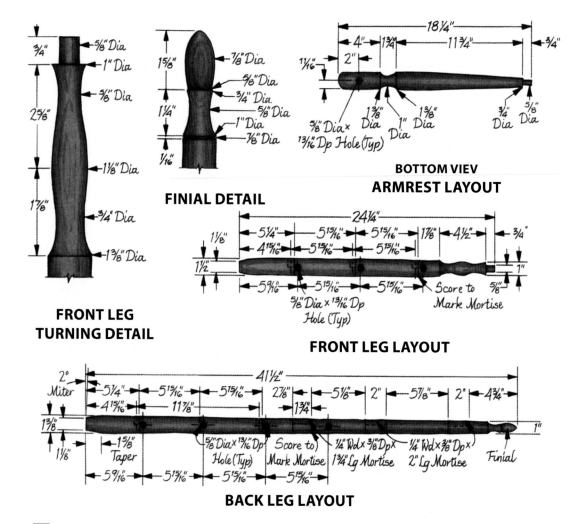

FRONT LEG TURNING DETAIL

FINIAL DETAIL

BOTTOM VIEW ARMREST LAYOUT

FRONT LEG LAYOUT

BACK LEG LAYOUT

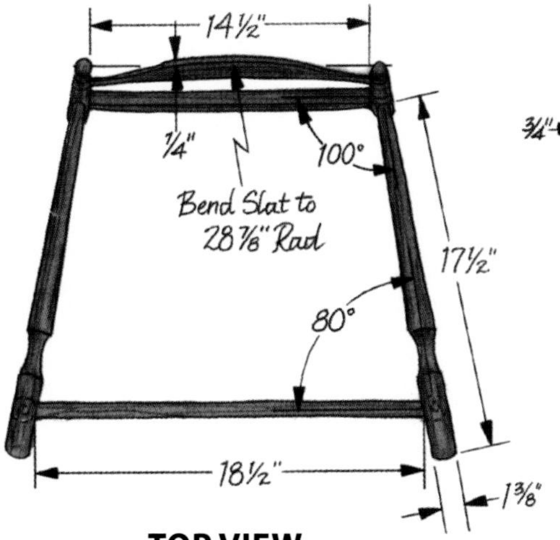
14 1/2"
1/4"
100°
Bend Slat to 28 7/8" Rad
17 1/2"
80°
18 1/2"
1 3/8"

TOP VIEW

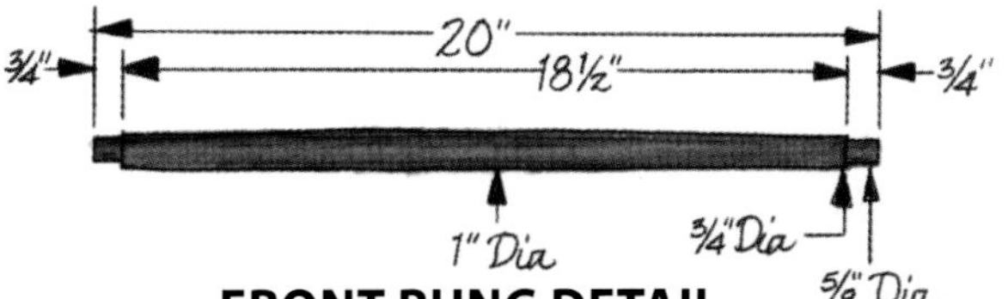
20"
3/4"
18 1/2"
3/4"
1" Dia
3/4" Dia
5/8" Dia

FRONT RUNG DETAIL

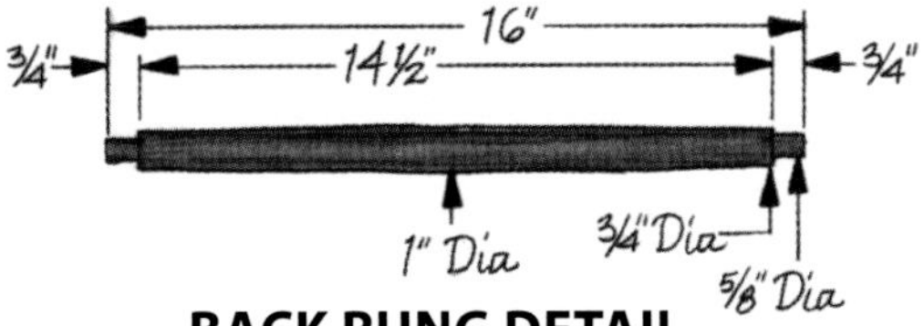
16"
3/4"
14 1/2"
3/4"
1" Dia
3/4" Dia
5/8" Dia

BACK RUNG DETAIL

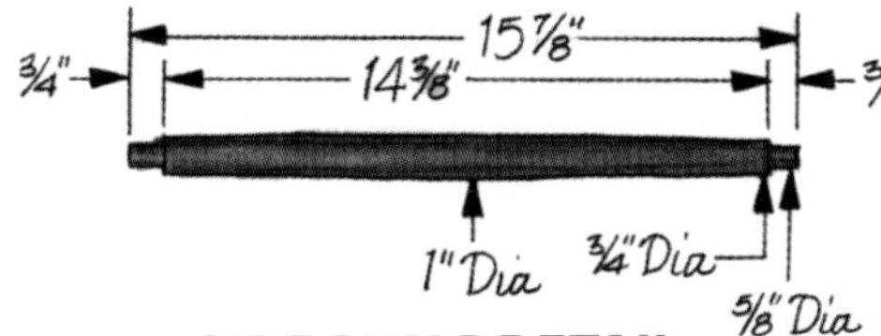
15 7/8"
3/4"
14 3/8"
3/4"
1" Dia
3/4" Dia
5/8" Dia

SIDE RUNG DETAIL

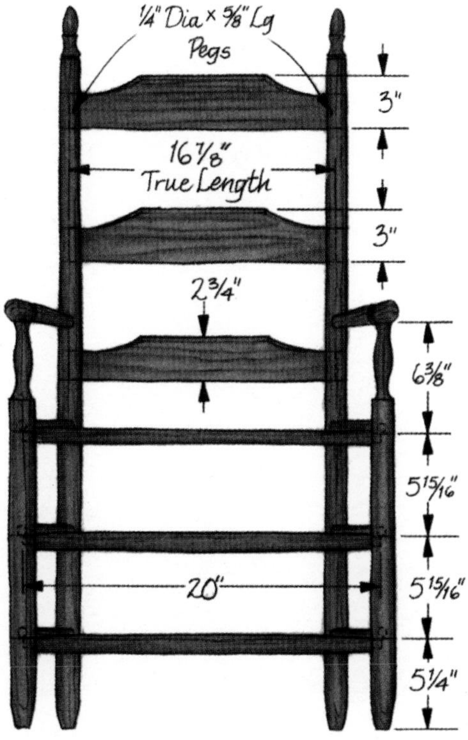
1/4" Dia × 5/8" Lg Pegs
3"
16 7/8" True Length
3"
2 3/4"
6 3/8"
5 15/16"
20"
5 15/16"
5 1/4"

FRONT VIEW

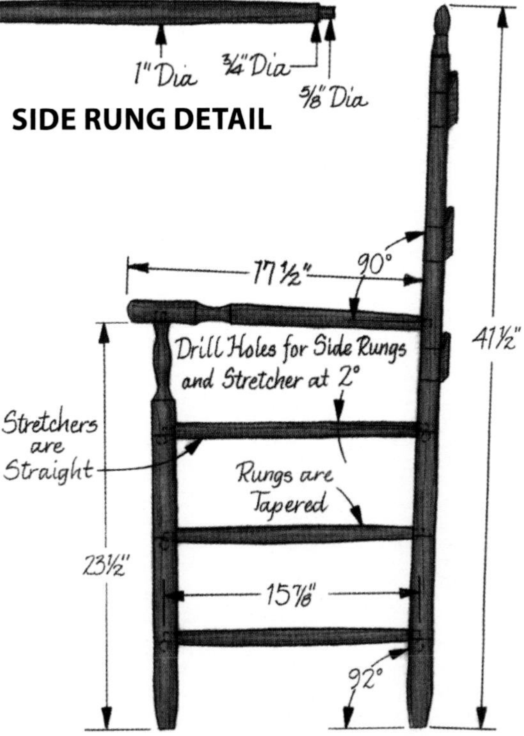
17 1/2"
90°
41 1/2"
Drill Holes for Side Rungs and Stretcher at 2°
Stretchers are Straight
Rungs are Tapered
23 1/2"
15 7/8"
92°

SIDE VIEW

PLAN OF PROCEDURE

3

Drill ⅝"-diameter, ¹³/₁₆"-deep mortises in the legs to hold the rungs and stretchers. Note that the back leg mortises for the side rungs and stretcher must be drilled 2° off perpendicular, as shown in the *Side View*. Also drill mortises in the arms to fit the front leg tenons.

4

Rout ¼"-wide, ¾"-deep, 2"-long mortises in the back legs to hold the top and middle slats, and ¼"-wide, ¾"-deep, 1¾"-long mortises to hold the bottom slat.

5

Miter the bottom ends of the back legs at 92°, as shown in the *Side View*.

6

Cut the shapes of the slat, as shown in the *Slat Layout and Pattern*. Chamfer the top edge of each slat. Sand the sawed edges.

7

Using heat, hot water, or steam, bend the slats to a 28⅞" radius, as shown in the *Top View*. If you use water or steam, make a bending form from a 3"-thick block of hardwood or glued up particleboard. The parts will spring back partially when you remove them from the bending form, losing about 20 percent of their curve. To compensate, make the bending form with a 22" radius. Steam or boil the slats for 45–60 minutes, then place them in the form. Clamp the two halves of the form together, bending the slats. Let them dry in the jig for at least two weeks.

8

Finish sand the slats. Dry assemble all the parts of the chair to be sure of the fit, then assemble the parts with glue.

9

From the front of the chair assembly, drill ¼"-diameter, ¹¹/₁₆"-deep holes near the top end of each back leg, through the mortise that holds the top slat. Glue a peg in each hole, letting the ends protrude slightly. Round over the ends of the pins with sandpaper, but don't sand them completely flush.

10

Do any necessary touch-up sanding, and paint or finish the chair frame. Then weave a tape or rush seat onto the stretchers.

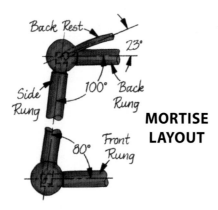

MORTISE LAYOUT

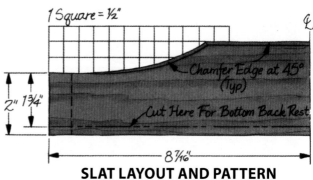

SLAT LAYOUT AND PATTERN

COUNTRY CRAFTSMAN'S KNOW-HOW:
WEAVING A TAPE SEAT

Tape chair seats first appeared in the early nineteenth century. They were rare until the Shakers began to cover the seats of the chairs they sold to the "world's people" with cloth tape or "listing," as it was called then. As Shaker chairs became more popular, so did the tape seats. By the twentieth century, tape was as common as rush or reed.

Cloth tape comes in two common widths — ⅝" and 1". The wider tape is the most popular and the easiest to work with, especially if you're weaving a simple checkerboard pattern. More complex patterns are best woven from ⅝"-wide tape. The tape also comes in a variety of colors. Most seat weavers prefer to mix two colors, using one color for the warp (front-to-back tape) and another for the woof (side-to-side tape).

Tape normally comes in 5- and 10-yard rolls. A typical chair seat requires 30 yards of tape — 15 yards of each color, if you're weaving a two-color seat. In addition to the tape, you'll also need:

- 20–24 small upholstery tacks and a tack hammer to secure the tape to the chair frame
- A needle and thread to splice the tape
- A 1"-thick foam rubber pad to make a seat cushion
- Scissors, to cut and trim the tape
- A metal spoon, to help adjust the weave

You can purchase the tape and other supplies from:
The Connecticut Cane and Reed Company
P.O. Box 1276
Manchester, CT 06040

Shaker Workshops
P.O. Box 1028
Concord, MA 01742

1 Before you begin, decide what pattern you want to weave. The two most common are the *checkerboard* and *herringbone* patterns shown.

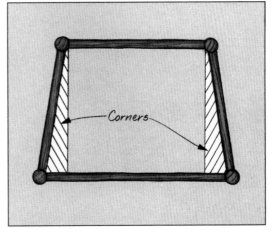

2 Chair seats are, more often than not, trapezoid-shaped when you look at them from the top. The warp and woof are square to each other — the weave forms a rectangle. When you impose a rectangle on top of a trapezoid, it leaves two "corners" on either side. Find these corners with a square and mark them on the front stretcher. Later on, you'll fill in these corners with short lengths of tape.

(Continued)

COUNTRY CRAFTSMAN'S KNOW-HOW:
WEAVING A TAPE SEAT —CONTINUED

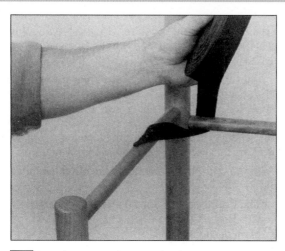

3 Begin by weaving the warp. If you're using two colors of tape, use the *darker* color for the warp. Because the warp covers the front stretcher, the dirt will show less. Tack the end of a roll of cloth tape to the left side stretcher, near the back stretcher.

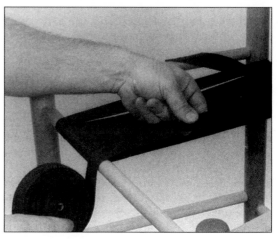

4 Stretch the warp tape under, then back over the back stretcher. Bring it forward, over, and under the front stretcher, then back under and over the back stretcher. Do *not* fill in the corners at this time; leave them open. Continue wrapping the tape onto the stretchers until you've covered the back stretcher. Tack the warp tape to the right side stretcher and cut it off.

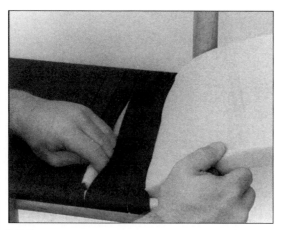

5 The top and bottom warps will have a space between them. Cut a 1"-thick foam rubber pad to the trapezoid shape of the seat, and stuff it into this space.

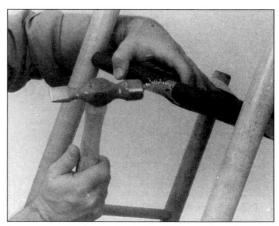

6 Next, weave the woofs into the warps. Insert the end of a roll of tape into the space between the warps, near the back stretcher. Temporarily spread the warps on the back stretcher apart and tack the woof tape to the left stretcher near the back leg.

7 Stretch the woof tape under the left side stretcher, bring it over the stretcher, then begin weaving the tape over and under the warps as needed to achieve the pattern. Go over and under the right side stretcher, then continue weaving on the bottom of the seat. (The pattern of both the seat bottom and top should be identical.) Repeat, alternating the weave at the beginning of each new row as needed to create the pattern.

8 Every two or three rows, stop weaving and "comb" the woof tapes with your fingers, as shown. Even them out so the woofs and warps are square to one another.

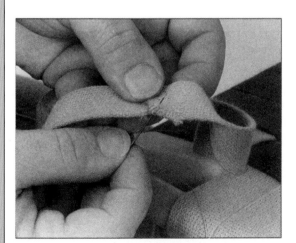

9 If the roll of tape runs out in the middle of the warps or woofs, splice another roll onto the end of the first. Overlap the ends and sew them together. Make these splices on the *bottom* of the seat where they won't show.

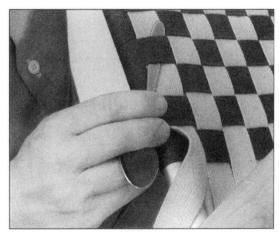

10 As you finish up the woofs, the weaving wil become tighter and more difficult. During the last few rows, you may not be able to weave with your fingers. Instead, use the handle of a spoon to push the woofs between the warps. You can also use the spoon to comb the tape.

COUNTRY CRAFTSMAN'S KNOW-HOW:
WEAVING A TAPE SEAT —CONTINUED

11 When you've covered the side stretchers with woofs, tack the tape to the underside of the front stretcher and cut it off.

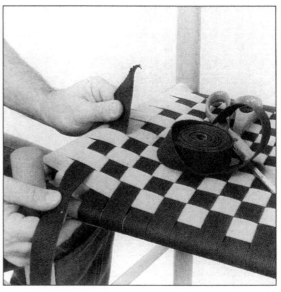

12 Fill in the corners with short lengths of warp tape, completely covering the front stretcher. Weave these short warps over and under the woofs, following your pattern.

13 When you've completely covered the front stretcher, spread the woof tapes apart and tack the ends of the short warp tapes to the side stretchers. Put the woof back in place so you can't see where the warps are attached. Comb the weave so it's even, and trim any loose tape ends or threads that may be hanging out.

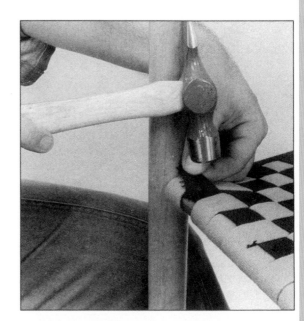

SPLAY-LEG SIDE TABLE

Small "side" tables first appeared in country homes in the seventeenth century. As the name suggests, they were used beside chairs, beds, and larger furniture to hold candles, needlework, serving bowls, and pitchers.

This particular side table is typical of the early nineteenth century. Like so many country designs, this one is a blend of styles. The slender, tapered legs echo the Hepplewhite style, while the fretwork aprons and heart cutouts show the influence of the German and Scandinavian immigrants. Practically speaking, the small size and simple, lightweight construction made the table easy to move. The splayed legs helped to steady the small surface, keeping it from becoming top-heavy.

EXPLODED VIEW

BILL OF MATERIALS

WOODEN PARTS/*FINISHED DIMENSIONS*

A.	Tabletop	¾" × 15" × 15"
B.	Aprons (4)	¾" × 5½" × 11⅛"
C.	Legs (4)	1¼" × 1¼" × 27³/₁₆"
D.	Pegs(12)	⅜" × ⅜" × 1¼"

HARDWARE
#8 × 1¼" Flathead wood screws (8)

PLAN OF PROCEDURE

1

Plane, rip, and cut the parts to the sizes shown in the Bill of Materials. As you cut the parts to size, bevel the edges of the aprons at 86° and compound-miter the ends of the legs at 4°.

2

Cut two ¼"-wide, ¾"-deep, 1⅝"-long mortises in each inside surface of each leg, as shown in the *Leg Mortise Layout*. These mortises meet in the center of each leg, as shown in the *Leg-to-Apron Joinery Detail.*

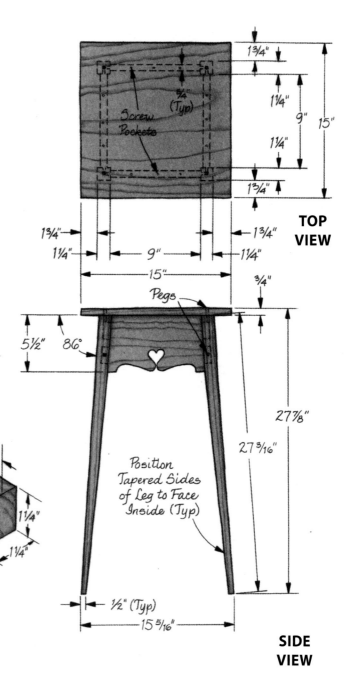

TOP VIEW

SIDE VIEW

LEG MORTISE LAYOUT

PLAN OF PROCEDURE

3

Cut a 2° taper in each inside surface of each leg, as shown in the *Leg Layout.*

4

Miter the ends of the aprons at 94°, then bevel them at 45°. The 45° bevel will allow the tenons to meet inside the leg mortises.

5

Cut ¼"-wide, ¾"-long tenons in both ends of each apron. Notch each tenon, as shown in the *Apron Layout,* to make two split tenons, each 1⅝" long.

6

Drill two screw pockets in the top edge of each apron as shown in the *Top-to-Apron Joinery Detail.*

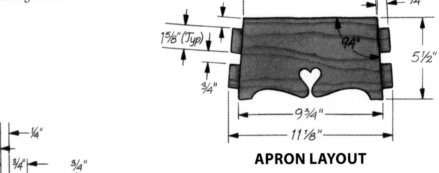

APRON LAYOUT

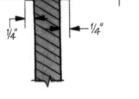

LEG-TO-APRON JOINERY DETAIL

TOP-TO-APRON JOINERY DETAIL

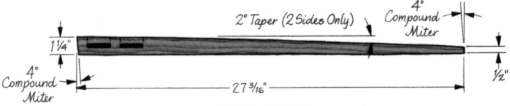

LEG LAYOUT

7

Lay out and cut the *Apron Pattern* in the bottom edge of each apron. Sand the sawed edges.

8

Dry assemble the legs and aprons to check the fit of the joints. Make any necessary adjustments. Finish sand all the parts of the table, then assemble the legs and aprons with glue.

9

Round the bottom portion of the pegs, as shown in the *Peg Detail*.

10

Drill a ⅜"-diameter, 1¼"-deep hole through the *bottom* mortise-and-tenon joints in each leg, then drive the pegs into the holes from the outside.

11

Put the top upside down on the workbench and attach the top to the aprons with #8 × 1¼" roundhead wood screws and flat washers. Drive the screws through the screw pockets and into the underside of the top, as shown in the *Top-to-Apron Joinery Detail.*

12

Turn the table right side up and drill a ⅜"-diameter, 1¼"-deep hole through the tabletop and into the end of each leg. Drive pegs into the holes, as shown in the *Top-to-Leg Joinery Detail.*

13

Do any necessary touch-up sanding on the table. Then apply a finish to the completed project.

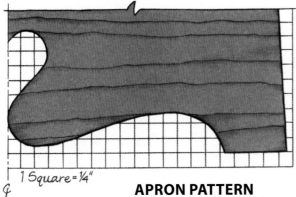

1 Square = ¼"

APRON PATTERN

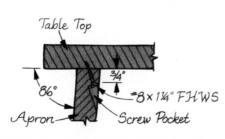

Table Top

86°

¾"

#8 × 1¼" FHWS

Apron

Screw Pocket

TOP-TO-LEG JOINERY DETAIL

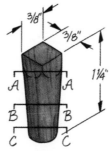

⅜"

⅜"

1¼"

A   A

B   B

C   C

PEG DETAIL

SECTION A

SECTION B

SECTION C

(**Make from *very* hard wood.**)

POUTING CHAIR

Although this looks like a child's chair, it wasn't originally. The German immigrants who settled in Pennsylvania in the eighteenth and nineteenth centuries often made stepstools with high backs. The back served as a handle, letting them move the stool around easily, without having to bend over and pick it up. These high-back stools proved indispensable in country kitchens, helping the cooks reach the high shelves in the pantry and cupboards.

When not in use, the stool was often kept in an out-of-the-way corner — probably the same corner where naughty children were banished from time to time. The children would sit on the stool while they contemplated their misdeeds. Consequently, the high-back stool acquired a whimsical nickname — the "pouting chair."

Today, the pouting chair remains as useful as it ever was — for *both* its applications. The chair shown is built from planks, in the same manner as a settle. The sides have been extended to add a bit of decoration and make the stool look like a miniature wing-and-arm chair.

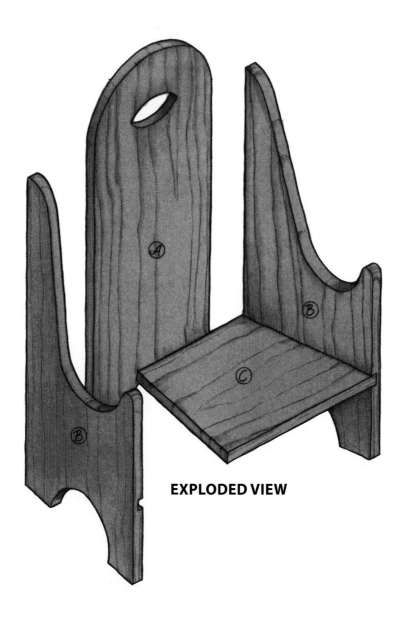

EXPLODED VIEW

BILL OF MATERIALS

WOODEN PARTS/*FINISHED DIMENSIONS*

A. Back   ⅝" × 9" × 23 ¾"
B. Sides (2)   ⅝" × 10⅜" × 21 ¾"
C. Seat   ⅝" × 8⅞" × 12"

HARDWARE
4d Square-cut nails

PLAN OF PROCEDURE

1

Plane, rip, and cut the parts to the sizes shown in the Bill of Materials, except the seat. Cut this ¼"–½" longer than specified. When you rip the part, cut the following bevels:

- Both edges of the back at 10°
- The back edges of the sides at 10°
- Both edges of the seat at 3½°
- The bottom end of the back at 3½°

2

Rout a ⅝"-wide, ⁵⁄₁₆"-deep dado in each side, on the inside face, as shown in the *Side Pattern*.

3

Enlarge the *Side Pattern* and *Back Pattern* and trace them on the stock. Cut the shapes of the back and sides, then sand the sawed edges.

4

Miter the ends of the seat at 10° and fit it to the back and sides. Leave the seat a little long when you first miter it, then shave it down a little bit at a time until it fits properly.

5

Finish sand all the pats, then assemble them with glue and nails. Sand all the joints clean and flush.

⁵⁄₈" Wd × ⁵⁄₁₆" Dp Dado

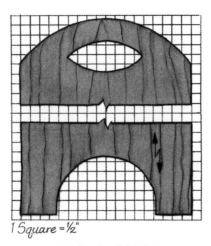

1 Square = ½"

BACK PATTERN

1 Square = ½"

SIDE PATTERN

6

Set the heads of the nails and cover them with putty.

7

Do any necessary touch-up sanding, then apply a finish to the completed pouting chair.

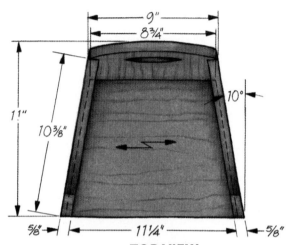

TOP VIEW

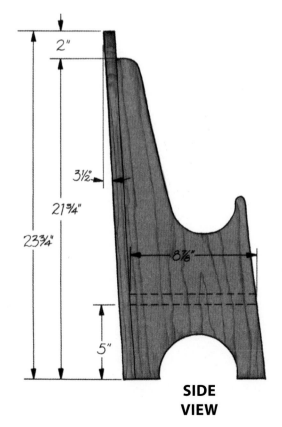

SIDE VIEW

FRONT VIEW

SOFA TABLE

The invention of the sofa table is usually credited to the English draftsman and teacher, Thomas Sheraton. In his collection of patterns, *The Cabinet-Maker and Upholsterer's Drawing Book,* published between 1791 and 1794, he included a design for a table "to take a useful place before the sofa." The idea appealed to folks on both sides of the Atlantic, and both English and American cabinetmakers built sofa tables well into the nineteenth century.

True sofa tables were rare in the country, since country folks rarely had sofas. While sofas and sofa tables were more common among the stylish upper class, country folks did have tables that resembled sofa tables. However, these had an entirely different purpose. They were long, narrow, waist-high sideboards, used for cooking, serving, and (occasionally) eating. The sofa table shown is copied from these simple sideboards.

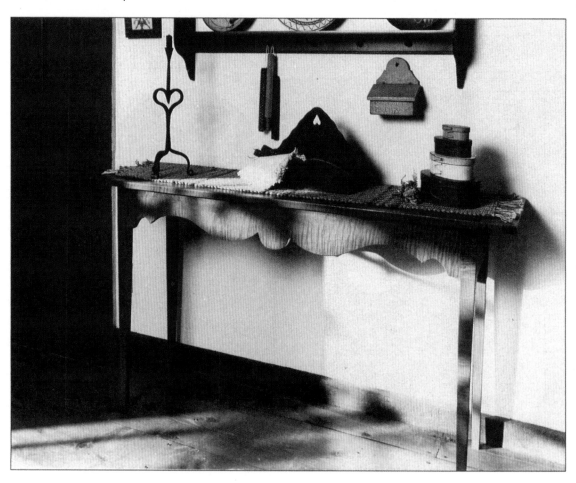

EXPLODED VIEW

BILL OF MATERIALS

WOODEN PARTS/_FINISHED DIMENSIONS_

A.	Top	¾" × 15" × 50"
B.	Breadboards (2)	¾" × 1 ¼" × 15"
C.	Plugs (6)	⅜" × ½" × 1 ¼"
D.	Legs (4)	1 ½" × 1 ½" × 28 ¼"
E.	Front/back aprons (2)	¾" × 5" × 41 ½"
F.	Side aprons (2)	¾" × 5" × 11 ½"
G.	Pegs (16)	⅜" × ⅜" × 1"

HARDWARE

#12 × 1 ½" Roundhead wood screws (6)
#12 Flat washers (6)
#8 × 1 ¼" Flathead wood screws (10)
#8 Flat washers (10)

PLAN OF PROCEDURE

1

If necessary, glue up stock for the 15"-wide top. Then plane, rip, and cut the parts to the sizes shown in the Bill of Materials.

2

Cut three ⅜"-wide, ¾"-deep, 1¼" long mortises in the outside edge of each breadboard. Then drill a 3/16"-wide, ½"-long slot, centered in each mortise, as shown in the *Breadboard Joinery Detail*.

3

Fasten the breadboards to the tabletop, driving #12 × 1½" roundhead wood screws (with washers) through the slots and into the pilot holes in the ends of the top. Do *not* glue the breadboard to the top.

4

Glue plugs in the breadboard mortises, covering the heads of the screws. The *end grain* of each plug must face out, so it appears to be a tenon. Sand the plugs flush with the outside edges of the breadboards.

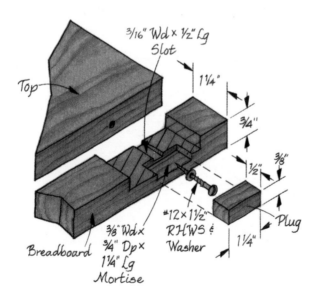

**BREADBOARD
JOINERY DETAIL**

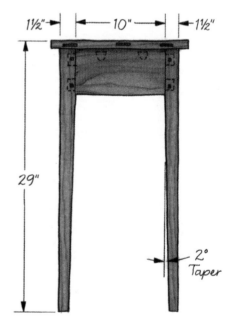

SIDE VIEW

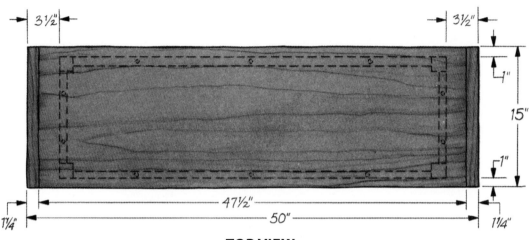

TOP VIEW

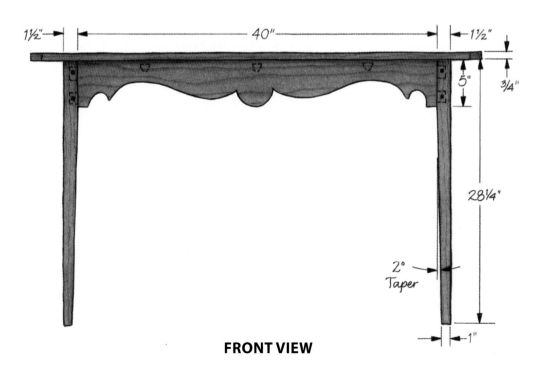

FRONT VIEW

PLAN OF PROCEDURE

5

Cut two ³⁄₈"-wide, ¾"-deep, 1½"-long mortises in the inside surfaces of each leg, as shown in the *Leg Layout*.

6

Cut a 2° taper in the inside surfaces of each leg, as shown in the *Front View* and *Side View*.

7

Cut ³⁄₈"-wide, ¾"-long tenons in the ends of each apron. Notch each tenon, as shown in the *Front/Back Apron Layout*, to make two "split tenons," each 1½" wide.

8

Drill two screw pockets in the top edge of each side apron, as shown in the *Top-to-Apron Joinery Detail*. Drill three screw pockets in the top edges of the front and back aprons.

9

Lay out and cut the shapes in the bottom edges of the front and back aprons, as shown in the *Front/Back Apron Layout*. Sand the sawed edges.

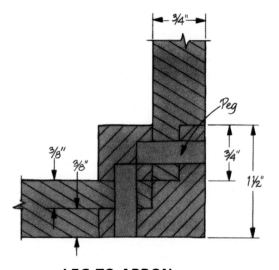

**LEG-TO-APRON
JOINERY DETAIL**

**FRONT VIEW
FRONT/BACK APRON LAYOUT**

**END
VIEW**

1 Square = 1"

10

Dry assemble the legs and aprons to check the fit of the joints. Finish sand all the parts of the table, then assemble the legs and aprons with glue.

11

Round the bottom portion of the pegs, as shown in the *Peg Detail*.

12

Drill a $3/8$"-diameter, 1 ¼"-deep hole through the mortise-and-tenon joints in each leg, then drive the pegs into the holes from the outside. Leave about $1/16$" of the peg protruding.

13

Turn the table upside down on the top and attach the top to the aprons with #8 × 1 ¼" flathead wood screws. Drive the screws through the screw pockets and into the top, as shown in the *Top-to-Apron Joinery Detail*.

14

Do any necessary touch-up sanding on the table. Then apply a finish to the completed project.

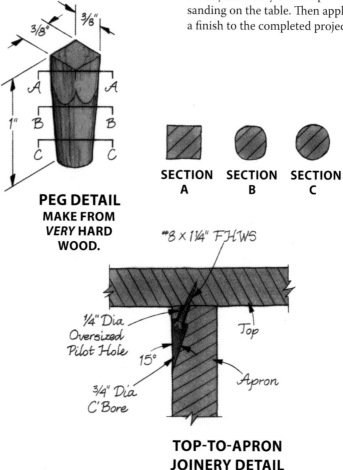

PEG DETAIL
MAKE FROM *VERY* HARD WOOD.

SECTION A   SECTION B   SECTION C

#8 × 1¼" FHWS

¼" Dia Oversized Pilot Hole

Top

15°

Apron

¾" Dia C'Bore

TOP-TO-APRON JOINERY DETAIL

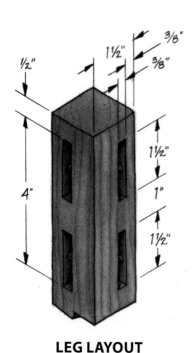

LEG LAYOUT

WING-AND-ARM CHAIR

Country chairs evolved from two different medieval woodworking traditions. Most familiar to us is the "turner's" chair, which was assembled of parts "thrown" on a lathe. The Shaker ladder-back chair and Sheraton step-down chair are examples of the turner's tradition.

"Joiner's" chairs are less familiar. The parts were ordinary planks and boards, assembled in the same manner as a chest or a cabinet. The five-board bench, the table/chair, and similar kinds of country seating descended from the joiner's tradition. This tradition survives today in upholstered armchairs and sofas. Springs, webbing, and batting have replaced the broad wooden planks, but many of the furniture forms remain the same.

The chair shown is typical of the joiner's tradition. This form first appeared in the seventeenth century as a shortened version of the settle and was sometimes called a settle chair. Later, joiners replaced the side planks with shaped wings and arms, calling it a "wing-and-arm" chair. This was the forerunner of the upholstered wing chair.

While the wings are strictly decorative today, they once added to the warmth and comfort of the folks who sat in these chairs. When facing the fire, the broad surfaces reflect heat onto the person sitting in the chair. The wings also protect them from cold drafts.

A wing-and-arm chair, like any chair built of flat planks, is hard. Their owners often padded them with rugs, cushions, or small pillows. You can make your own cushions and stuff them with down, horsehair, or shredded foam. With a little padding, the chair will be surprisingly comfortable.

EXPLODED VIEW

BILL OF MATERIALS

WOODEN PARTS/*FINISHED DIMENSIONS*

A.	Back	¾" × 20" × 53¾"
B.	Sides (2)	¾" × 30" × 48¾"
C.	Seat	¾" × 22½" × 23½"
D.	Apron	¾" × 4" × 25"
E.	Back seat support*	¾" × 3¼" × 18½"
F.	Side seat supports*	¾" × 3" × 21"

HARDWARE

8d Square-cut nails (¼ lb.)
#10 × 1¼" Roundhead wood screws (9)
#10 Flat washers (9)
4d Finishing nails (4–6)

*These parts must be hand-fitted. The lengths are approximate.

PLAN OF PROCEDURE

1

Plane, rip, and cut the parts to the sizes shown in the Bill of Materials, except the supports — cut these slightly longer than specified. While you're cutting the parts to size, bevel the following ends and edges:

- Both edges of the back at 5°
- Back edges of the sides at 5°
- Both ends of the apron at 5°
- Bottom end of the back at 10°
- Top edge of the back seat support at 10°
- Back edge of the seat at 10°

2

Lay out the *Side Pattern* and *Back Patterns* on the stock, then cut the shapes. Sand the sawed edges.

3

Finish sand the sides, back, and apron, then assemble them with glue and square-cut nails. Set the heads of the nails.

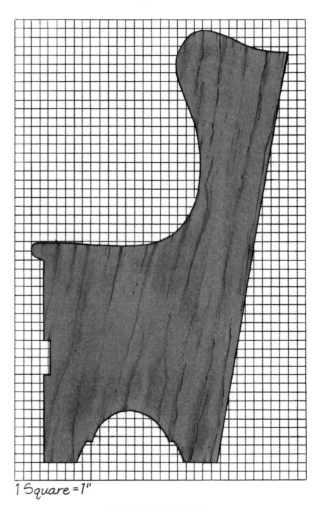

1 Square = 1"

SIDE PATTERN

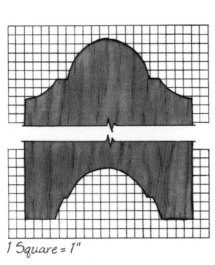

1 Square = 1"

BACK PATTERN

4

Cut the side seat supports to fit in the chair assembly. Bevel the front ends of the supports at 5°. Compound-miter the back ends, setting the blade at 5° and the miter gauge at 10°. Tack the supports in place with finishing nails, but don't drive them all the way home.

5

Fit the back seat support in the same manner as the side support, beveling the ends at 5°.

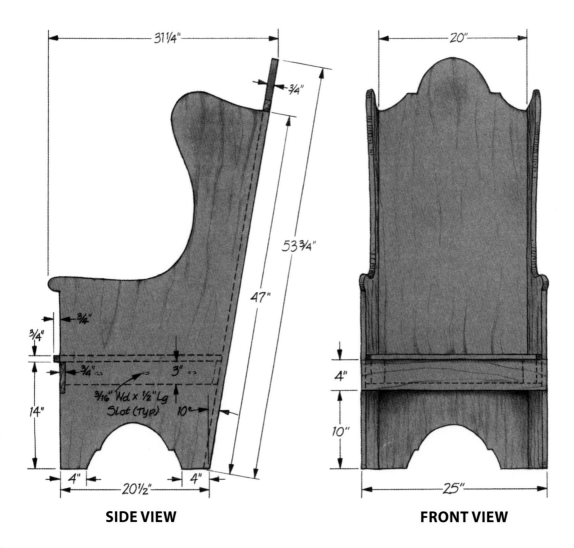

SIDE VIEW

31¼"

¾"

53¾"

47"

¾"

¾"

3"

⅜"

¾"

³⁄₁₆" Wd x ½" Lg
Slot (Typ)

10°

14"

4"

20½"

4"

FRONT VIEW

20"

4"

10"

25"

Plan of Procedure

6

Pull the finishing nails out of the side seat supports and discard them. Remove the supports from the chair. Drill a series of holes to make $3/16$"-wide, $\frac{1}{2}$"-long slots in both the side and back supports, as shown in the *Support Slot Detail*.

7

Attach the supports to the sides and back with #10 × 1 $\frac{1}{4}$" roundhead wood screws and flat washers, driving the screws through the slots. *Don't* glue these parts in place. The screws and slots in the supports will allow the sides and back to expand and contract.

8

Cut the shape of the seat as shown in the *Top View*, mitering the sides at 85°. Chamfer the front corners at 45°. Fit the seat to the chair.

9

Finish sand the seat. Attach it to the sides, back, back support, and apron with glue and square-cut nails. To secure the edges of the seat, drive the nails down through them into

the apron and back seat support. To secure the ends, drive nails horizontally through the sides and into the seat. Set the heads of the nails. *Don't* glue or nail the seat to the side seat supports — just let it rest on them.

10

Do any necessary touch-up sanding and apply a finish to the project.

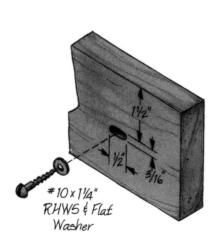

SUPPORT SLOT DETAIL

$1\frac{1}{2}$"

$\frac{1}{2}$"

$3/16$"

#10 x 1¼"
RHWS & Flat
Washer

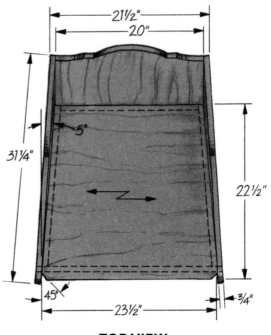

TOP VIEW

21½"

20"

5°

31¼"

22½"

45°

¾"

23½"

FIVE-BOARD BENCH

Benches are among the oldest and most versatile furniture designs. Originally, common folks used them for working as well as sitting. The surface was long and flat to hold a craftsman's tools and materials while he straddled the bench. (This is the origin of the word *workbench*.) Over thousands of years, various cultures have adapted the bench to make seats, beds, and low tables.

The traditional American five-board bench is descended from the medieval *form,* a backless stool that was used throughout Europe in the Middle Ages. A form was made much like a trestle table — the plank seat was supported by two vertical slabs and stabilized by one or more horizontal rails. To minimize ground contact — and help prevent rot — the bottom end of each supporting slab was shaped, creating two "feet." The rails were often scalloped or pierced with designs to add decoration to the otherwise utilitarian form.

This simple design proved so serviceable that it has been used up through the present day, without modification. The five-board bench shown is typical of many built in colonial America for sitting and working. You can build it almost any length, depending on the available space and how you want to use it. You shouldn't make it any longer than 78", however, without adding additional legs or brace work or the bench may start to sag.

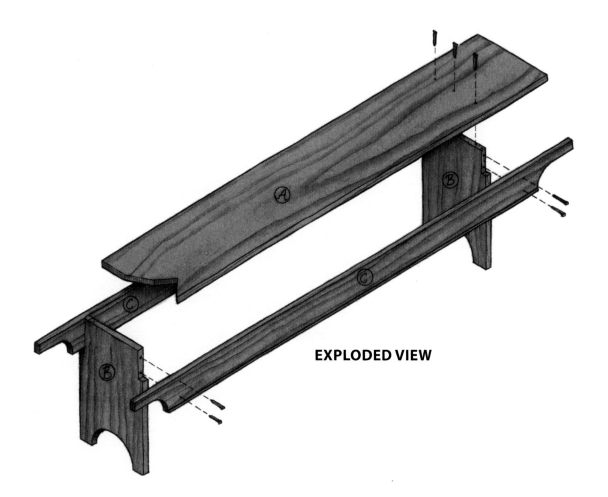

EXPLODED VIEW

BILL OF MATERIALS

WOODEN PARTS/*FINISHED DIMENSIONS*

A. Top $\frac{7}{8}$" × 1 $\frac{1}{2}$" × (variable)
B. Legs (2) $\frac{7}{8}$" × 10 $\frac{1}{2}$" × 17 $\frac{1}{8}$"
C. Rails (2) $\frac{7}{8}$" × 4" × (variable)

HARDWARE
6d Square-cut nails (14–16)

PLAN OF PROCEDURE

1

If necessary, glue up stock for the legs and seat. Plane, rip, and cut the parts to the sizes shown in the Bill of Materials.

2

Lay out and cut the shape of the legs, creating the feet, as shown in the *End View*. Sand the sawed edges. Notch the edges of the legs, near the top ends, to hold the rails.

3

Rout or cut beads in the front face of the rails, near the bottom edges, as shown in the *Rail Profile*.

4

Lay out and cut the shapes of the rails, as shown in the *Front View*. Sand the sawed edges.

5

Finish sand the parts of the bench and dry assemble them to check the fit. Reassemble the parts with glue and square-cut nails. Set the nails and cover the heads with putty.

6

Do any necessary touch-up sanding and apply a finish to the completed project.

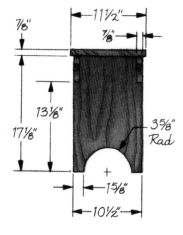

END VIEW

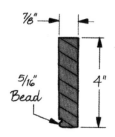

RAIL PROFILE

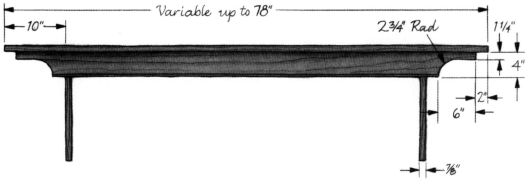

FRONT VIEW

OCCASIONAL TABLES

Because floor space was at a premium, country folks often designed their furniture to fill a particular space. These occasional tables are tailored for two common household spaces. The triangular table fits in a corner, and the half-round table sits against a wall.

Like so much country furniture, the designs are strictly utilitarian — although they have been influenced by other styles, both classic and traditional. The half-round table echoes the lines of bow-front side tables and sideboards that were popular during the Federal period. The corner table is reminiscent of three-legged "cricket" tables that were used in English taverns during the seventeenth and eighteenth centuries. In both cases, however, their beauty derives mainly from their simplicity.

Both tables are built in exactly the same manner, except the shapes of the tops. Each top rests on three tapered legs, joined by a T-shaped apron.

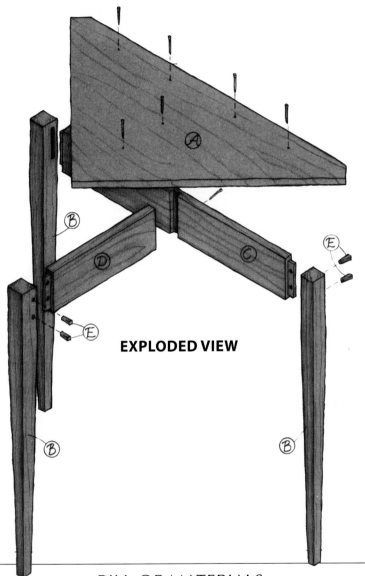

EXPLODED VIEW

BILL OF MATERIALS

WOODEN PARTS/*FINISHED DIMENSIONS*

A.	Corner tabletop	¾" × 17¼" × 31¹¹⁄₁₆"
	Half-round tabletop	¾" × 16" × 32"
B.	Legs (3)	1½" × 1½" × 27"
C.	Long apron	¾" × 4" × 26½"
D.	Short apron	¾" × 4" × 12½"
E.	Pegs (6)	⅜" × ⅜" × 1¼"

HARDWARE
8d Square-cut nails (6–8)

PLAN OF PROCEDURE

1

If necessary, glue up the stock to make the tabletop. Then plane, rip, and cut the parts to the sizes shown in the Bill of Materials.

2

Cut a ¼"-wide, ¾"-deep, 3"-long mortise in the inside surface of each leg, as shown in the *Leg Mortise Layouts*. Note that the position of the mortise in each back leg is different from that in the front leg.

3

Cut a 1° taper in all four surfaces of each leg, as shown in the *Front View*.

4

Cut ¼"-wide, ¾"-long tenons in *both* ends of the long apron and in one end of the short apron. Notch the tenons, as shown in the *Tenon Layout*, so they are 3" from edge to edge.

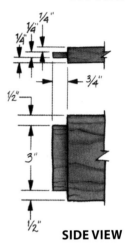

TOP VIEW

SIDE VIEW

TENON LAYOUT

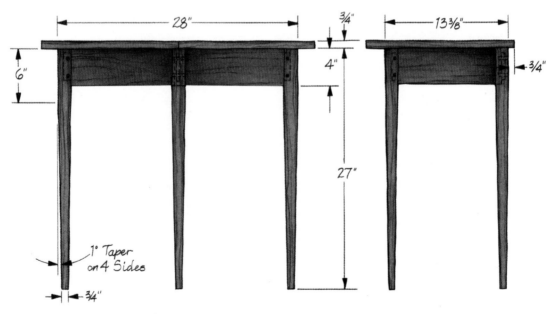

FRONT VIEW

SIDE VIEW

5

Cut a ¾"-wide, ⅜"-deep dado, centered in the inside face of the long apron, as shown in the *Base Layout/Top View*.

6

Lay out and cut the shape of the top, as shown in the *Half-Round Table/Top View* or *Corner Table/Top View*. Sand the sawed edges.

7

Dry assemble the legs and aprons to check the fit of the joints. Finish sand all the parts of the table, then assemble the legs and aprons with glue.

8

Reinforce the dado joint connecting the long and short aprons with square-cut nails.

9

Round the bottom portion of the pegs, as shown in the *Peg Detail*.

10

Drill two ⅜"-diameter, 1¼"-deep holes through the mortise-and-tenon joint in each leg, then drive the pegs into the holes from the outside. Leave about ¹/₁₆" of each peg protruding.

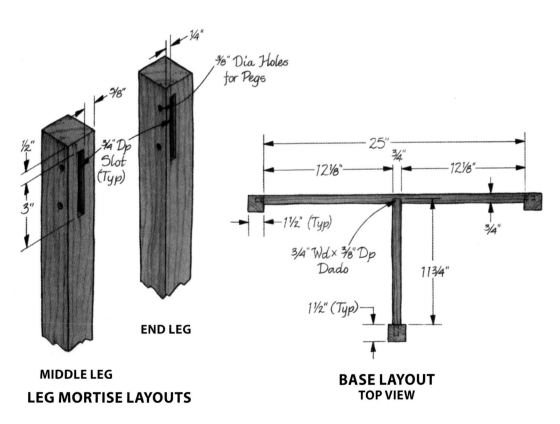

LEG MORTISE LAYOUTS

MIDDLE LEG

END LEG

BASE LAYOUT
TOP VIEW

PLAN OF PROCEDURE

11

Attach the top to the aprons with square-cut nails. When the top expands and contracts, the nails will give slightly. Do *not* glue the top to the aprons or legs; this would restrict the wood movement.

12

Set all nails, then cover the heads with putty.

13

Do any necessary touch-up sanding on the table. Then apply a finish to the completed project.

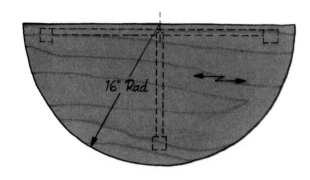

16" Rad

HALF-ROUND TABLE/TOP VIEW

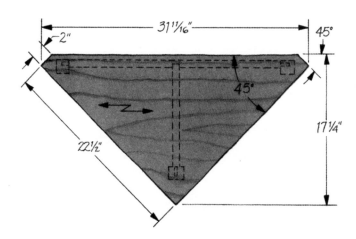

31¹¹⁄₁₆"

2"

45°

45°

17¼"

22½"

CORNER TABLE/TOP VIEW

³⁄₈"

³⁄₈"

A   A

B   B

C   C

1¼"

PEG DETAIL
(MAKE FROM *VERY* HARD WOOD.)

 SECTION A

 SECTION B

 SECTION C

FOR COOKING & BAKING

BUCKET BENCH

When America was first settled, every cabin had a "bucket bench" just outside the back door. This bench held two or three buckets of water ready for drinking, cooking, and washing. As a bucket emptied, it was quickly refilled so the cook always had fresh water.

The settlers built bucket benches in all shapes and sizes. Some had several shelves to help organize buckets and other materials. On the bench shown, the drinking water was probably kept on the bottom shelf. The middle shelf prevented debris from falling into the drinking water buckets. The middle shelf also held wash water, supporting the buckets at a comfortable height to wash dishes, clothes, or your hands and face. The small top shelf held soap, wash-rags, dippers, and cups.

These simple (but indispensable) pieces quickly developed into more convenient forms. Craftsmen added work surfaces and splashboards, making pieces like the Water Bench. Later, they enclosed the shelves, brought the unit inside, and called it a *dry sink*. The old bucket benches began to serve other purposes. Today, they are useful shelving and display units.

The design shown is a copy of a late eighteenth-century bucket bench, possibly built by a pioneer in the Northwest Territory (now Ohio, Michigan, Indiana, and Illinois).

EXPLODED VIEW

BILL OF MATERIALS

WOODEN PARTS/_FINISHED DIMENSIONS_

A. Sides (2)   ¾" × 12" × 44"
B. Top shelf   ¾" × 8" × 36"
C. Lower shelves (2)   ¾" × 12" × 35¼"

HARDWARE
6d Square-cut nails (16)

PLAN OF PROCEDURE

1

Plane, rip, and cut the parts to the sizes shown in the Bill of Materials.

2

Cut ¾"-wide, ⅜"-deep dadoes in the sides, as shown in the *Side View.*

3

Lay out and cut the shape of the sides, as shown in the *Side View.*

4

Cut a ¾"-wide, 6"-long dovetail notch in the top ends of the sides, and cut matching dovetail tenons on both ends of the top shelf, as shown in the *Top Shelf Layout.*

5

Finish sand the parts of the bucket bench and dry assemble them to check the fit of the joints. Reassemble the parts with glue and square-cut nails. Set the heads of the nails.

6

Do any necessary touch-up sanding and apply a finish to the completed project.

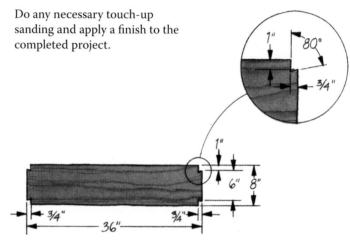

TOP SHELF LAYOUT

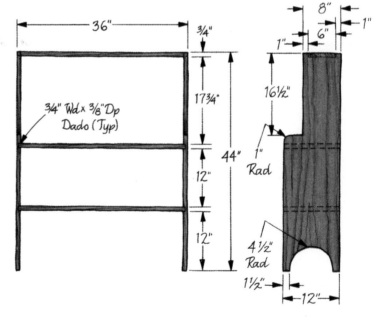

FRONT VIEW   **SIDE VIEW**

PIE SAFE

Late in medieval times, joiners began to enclose the shelves on which cooks stored food. They found that they needed to ventilate these enclosures, or the food in them quickly developed molds. Throughout the centuries that followed, these ventilated cupboards were known by many names — aumbries, hutches, livery cupboards, and food presses, to list a few.

There were also many different ways to ventilate these cupboards. Some had woven reed or lattice panels; others used frame doors with close-set slats or spindle turnings. One of the most popular ventilation methods was to pierce a wooden panel with many small holes. These holes usually formed a design.

In the early nineteenth century, advances in metallurgy made thin sheets of metal cheaper and more abundant. American craftsmen began to use pierced metal panels to ventilate food cupboards. Perhaps

because these cupboards were partially made of metal, they reminded folks of a bank safe. Their makers gave them a whimsical nickname that has stuck to this day: *pie safe*.

**CABINET
EXPLODED VIEW**

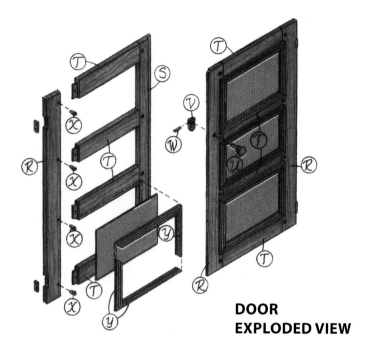

**DOOR
EXPLODED VIEW**

BILL OF MATERIALS

WOODEN PARTS/*FINISHED DIMENSIONS*

A.	Legs (4)	2" × 2" × 68¾"
B.	Top front rail	¾" × 6" × 40"
C.	Bottom front rail	¾" × 4" × 40"
D.	Top side rails (2)	¾" × 9" × 15¼"
E.	Middle side rails (4)	¾" × 3" × 15¼"
F.	Bottom side rails (2)	¾" × 7" × 15¼"
G.	Top/middle back rails (2)	¾" × 3" × 40"
H.	Bottom back rail	¾" × 7" × 40"
J.	Back panels (2)	½" × 18⅞" × 38⅝"
K.	Shelves (3)	¾" × 15¾" × 41¼"
L.	Top	½" × 21" × 49½"
M.	Front cove molding	¾" × 4⅝" × 48½"
N.	Side cove moldings (2)	¾" × 4⅝" × 20½"
P.	Front bead molding	¾" × 1" × 44"
Q.	Side bead moldings (2)	¾" × 1" × 18¼"

R.	Door stiles (3)	¾" × 3" × 39⅜"
S.	Left inside door stile	¾" × 3½" × 39⅜"
T.	Door rails (8)	¾" × 3" × 14¹⁵⁄₁₆"
U.	Door pull	1¼" dia. × 2⅝"
V.	Door latch	⅝" × 1" × 2⅛"
W.	Pin	¼" dia. × 1"
X.	Pegs (46)	¼" × ¼" × 1¼"*
Y.	Three-bead molding (total)	⁵⁄₁₆" × ¾" × 640"

*Make the pegs at least this long, then — if necessary —
cut them to length after installing them.*

HARDWARE

1½" × 2" Butt hinges and mounting screws (2 pairs)
10" × 14¼" Tin panels, 24 gauge (12)
1" Wire or headless brads (160–180)
6d Square-cut nails (16–24)

PLAN OF PROCEDURE

1

If necessary, glue up stock to make the wide parts — the shelves and back panels. Plane, rip, and cut the parts to the sizes shown in the Bill of Materials, except the moldings and door parts. Don't cut the door parts or the three-bead moldings yet; wait until you've built the case. Cut the cove moldings 1"–2" longer than specified.

2

Cut ¼"-wide, ⅜"-deep grooves in the inside edges of the back rails and the back legs, as shown in the *Back Layout Detail* and *Left Back Leg Layout*. These grooves will hold the back panels.

3

Cut the ¼"-wide, 1"-deep mortises in the inside faces of the legs, as shown in the *Left Front Leg Layout* and *Left Back Leg Layout*.

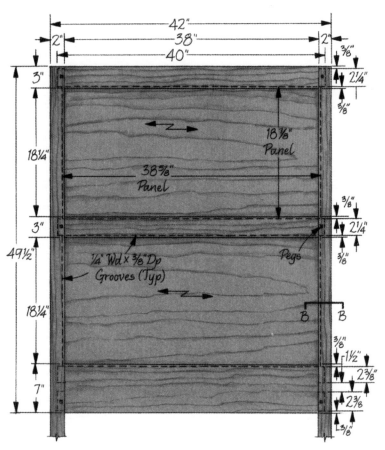

BACK LAYOUT DETAIL

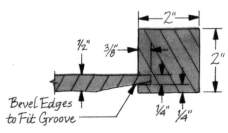

SECTION B

4

Cut ¼"-wide, 1"-long tenons on the ends of the case rails. Notch the shoulders of these tenons to fit the leg mortises, as shown in the *Top Front Rail Layout, Bottom Front Rail Layout, Top Side Rail Layout, Middle Side Rail Layout, Bottom Side Rail Layout,* and *Back Layout Detail*.

5

Cut ¾"-wide, ⅜"-deep dadoes in the inside faces of the middle and bottom side rails, as shown in the *Middle Side Rail Layout* and *Bottom Side Rail Layout*.

6

Lay out and cut the shapes of the shelves, as shown in the *Shelf Layout*. Also bevel the back panels as shown in *Section B*.

7

Cut a ⅜"-wide, ⅜"-deep, 1¾"-long mortise in the top shelf, as shown in the *Shelf Layout*. This mortise will hold the door catch.

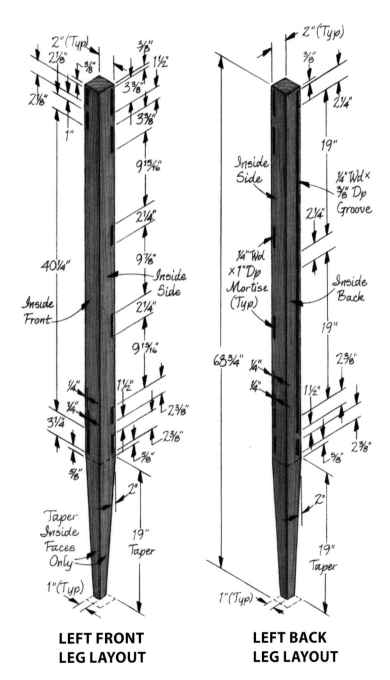

LEFT FRONT LEG LAYOUT

LEFT BACK LEG LAYOUT

PLAN OF PROCEDURE

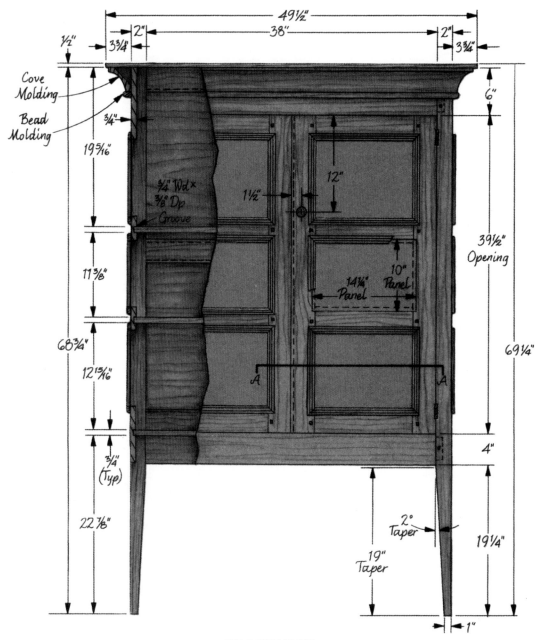

Cove Molding

Bead Molding

49½"

38"

2"

3¾"

½"

2"

3¾"

6"

¾"

19⁵⁄₁₆"

¾" Wd ×
⅜" Dp
Groove

1½"

12"

39½"
Opening

11⅜"

68¾"

14¼"
Panel

10"
Panel

69¼"

12¹⁵⁄₁₆"

A

A

¾"
(Typ)

4"

22⅞"

2°
Taper

19"
Taper

19¼"

1"

FRONT VIEW

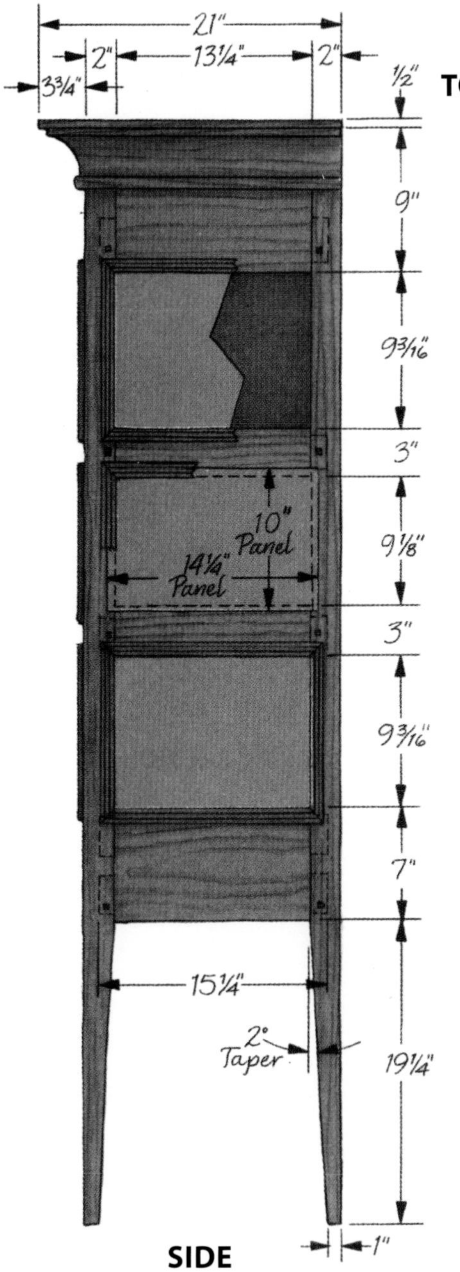
21"
2"
13¼"
2"
3¾"
½"
9"
9³⁄₁₆"
3"
9⅛"
10" Panel
14¼" Panel
3"
9³⁄₁₆"
7"
15¼"
2° Taper
19¼"
1"

SIDE VIEW

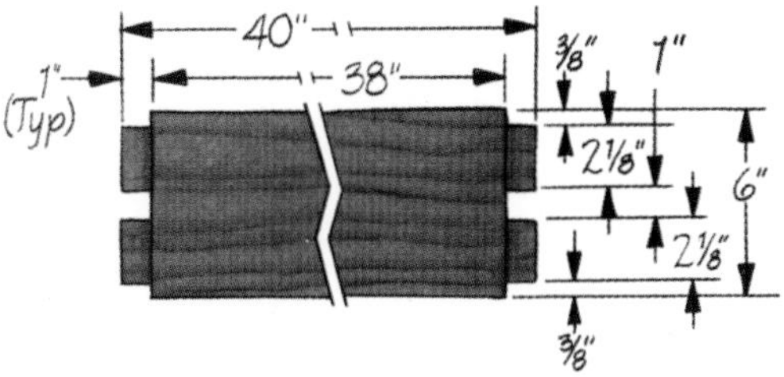
40"
38"
1" (Typ)
⅜"
1"
2⅛"
2⅛"
6"
⅜"

TOP FRONT RAIL LAYOUT

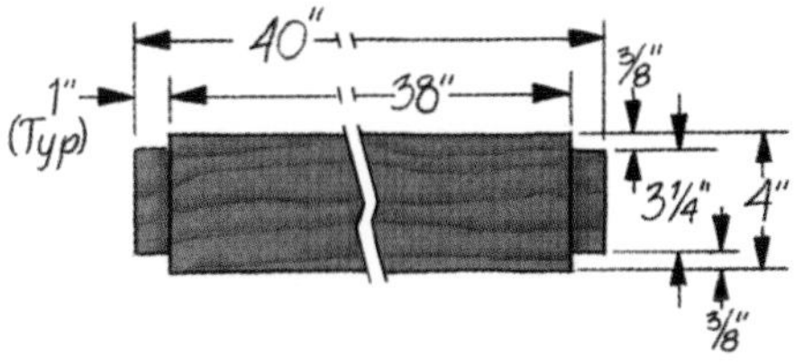
40"
38"
1" (Typ)
⅜"
3¼"
4"
⅜"

BOTTOM FRONT RAIL LAYOUT

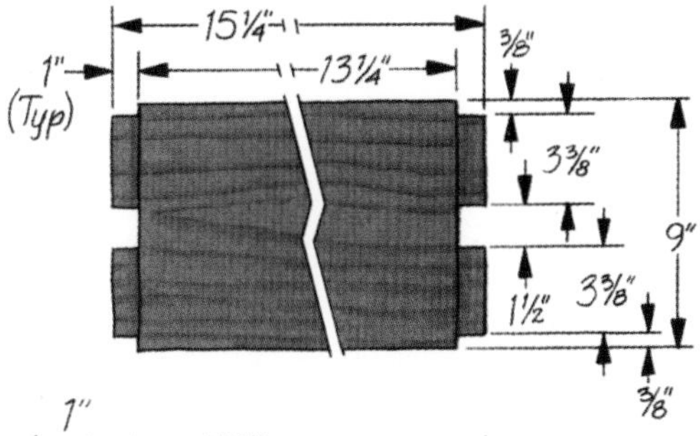
15¼"
13¼"
1" (Typ)
⅜"
3⅜"
9"
1½"
3⅜"
⅜"

TOP SIDE RAIL LAYOUT

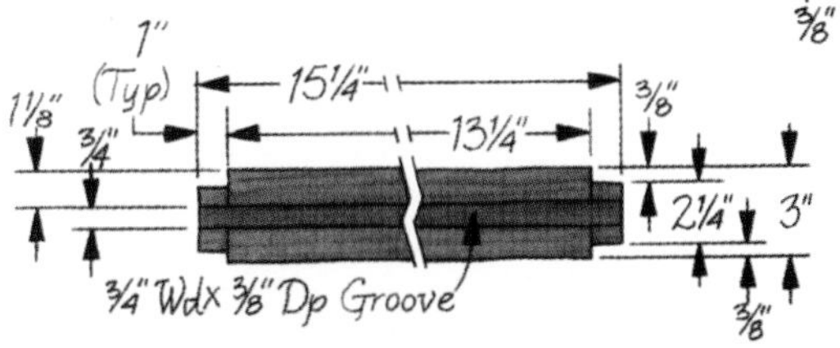
1" (Typ)
15¼"
13¼"
1⅛"
¾"
⅜"
2¼"
3"
⅜"
¾" Wd x ⅜" Dp Groove

MIDDLE SIDE RAIL LAYOUT

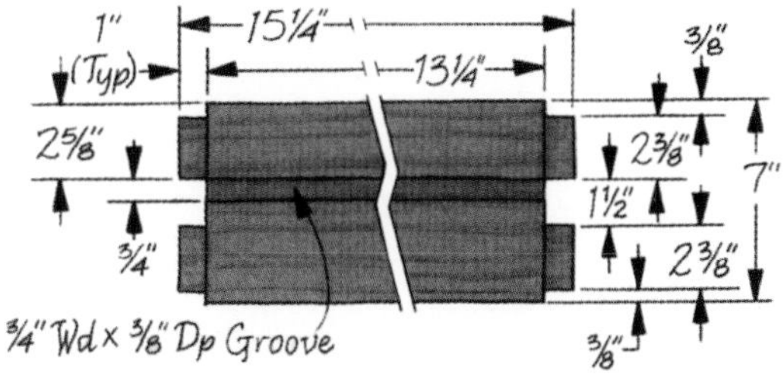
1" (Typ)
15¼"
13¼"
⅜"
2⅝"
¾"
2⅜"
1½"
7"
2⅜"
⅜"
¾" Wd x ⅜" Dp Groove

BOTTOM SIDE RAIL LAYOUT

PLAN OF PROCEDURE

8

Finish sand the legs, rails, panels, and shelves. Assemble the parts of the case as follows:

- Glue the legs and side rails together, inserting the tenons in the mortises, and let the glue dry. This will make two side assemblies.

- Glue the front and back rails in the left side assembly.

- Before the glue dries, slide the back panels into the grooves in the back rails, but do *not* glue them in place. They must float in the grooves.

- Place the shelves in the dadoes in the left middle and bottom side rails. Again, this must be done before the glue on the rails dries, but do *not* glue the shelves in place.

- Glue the right side assembly to the front and back rails. Once again, do *not* glue the panels or shelves; let them float. Clamp the assembly together; make sure it's square, and let the glue dry.

9

Round the bottom portion of the pegs, as shown in the *Peg Detail*.

10

Drill a ¼"-diameter, 1¼"-deep hole through each mortise-and-tenon joint in the case. Drive a peg into each hole to secure the tenon in the mortise, letting the peg protrude slightly.

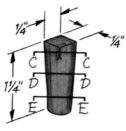

PEG DETAIL

(MAKE FROM *VERY* HARD WOOD.)

 SECTION C

 SECTION D

 SECTION E

11

Finish sand the top. Attach the top to the legs and top rails with nails. Don't drive these nails all the way in, in case you have to shift the position of the top when you attach the moldings.

12

Cut the coves in the cove moldings, then miter the edges at 45°, as shown in the *Top Molding Profile*.

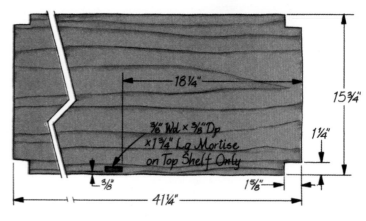

18¼"

15¾"

⅜" Wd × ⅜"Dp × 1¾" Lg Mortise on Top Shelf Only

1¼"

⅜"

1⅝"

41¼"

SHELF LAYOUT

13

Round over the front edges of the bead moldings.

14

Fit the top moldings to the case, compound-mitering the adjoining ends at 45°.

15

Finish sand the cove moldings and attach them to the case with glue and nails. If necessary, shift the position of the top to center it over the moldings. Nail the top to the moldings, but do *not* glue it in place.

16

Fit the bead moldings, mitering the adjoining ends. Attach them to the case just below the cove moldings, using glue and nails.

17

Set the nails and cover the heads with putty.

18

Measure the door opening and make any necessary changes in the dimensions of the door parts. Cut the door parts to size, then cut the joinery needed to assemble the doors:

- ½"-wide, ⅜"-deep rabbets in the adjoining edges of the inside door stiles

- ¼"-wide, 1"-deep, 2¼"-long mortises in the inside edges of the door stiles, as shown in the *Door Joinery Detail*

- ¼"-thick, 1"-long tenons on the ends of the door rails

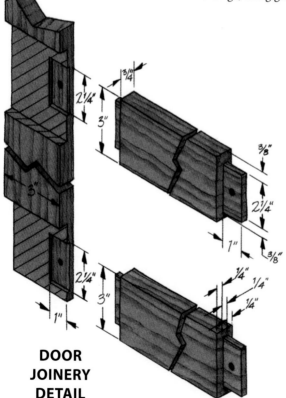

DOOR JOINERY DETAIL

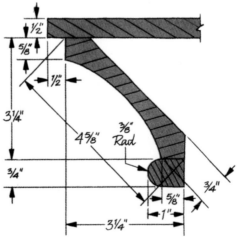

TOP MOLDING PROFILE

PLAN OF PROCEDURE

19

Notch the tenons in the rails as shown in the *Door Joinery Detail,* fitting each tenon to its mortise.

20

Drill a ⁹⁄₁₆"-diameter hole through the right inside door stile, as shown in the *Door Layout.* This hole will hold the door pull.

21

Finish sand the door parts and assemble the rails and stiles with glue.

22

Reinforce the mortise-and-tenon joints in the door frames with pegs, as you did on the face frame. Cut the pegs off flush with the back surfaces of the frames.

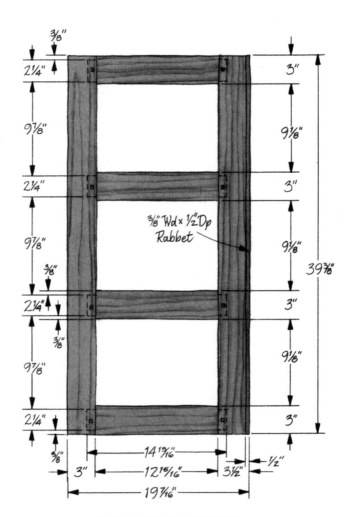

LEFT DOOR LAYOUT

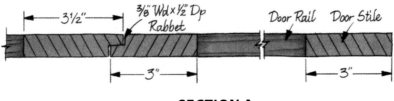

SECTION A

23

Mortise the door stiles and case for hinges, then mount the doors to the case.

24

Turn the shape of the door pull, as shown in the *Door Pull Layout.*

25

Cut the 60° taper in the door catch, as shown in the *Door Latch Detail,* and drill a ½"-diameter hole near one end.

26

Insert the door pull through the hole in the right door stile. Press the catch on the pull shaft to check the locking action. The door pull and the catch should turn together. When the catch is vertical, the tapered end must rest in the mortise in the top shelf.

27

Remove the doors and the hardware from the case. Also, disassemble the door pull and catch. Do any necessary touch-up sanding, then apply a finish to the pie safe. Finish *all* sides of the project — inside and out, top and bottom.

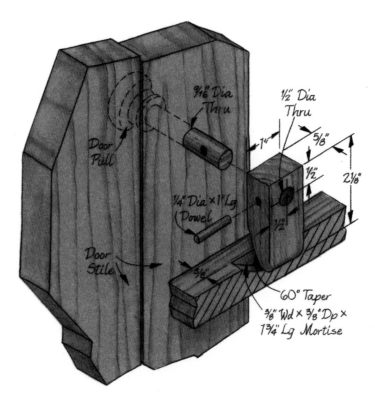

**DOOR PULL
LAYOUT**

DOOR LATCH DETAIL

PLAN OF PROCEDURE

28

Lay out the design on the tin panels, as shown in the *Tin Panel Pattern*. Punch the design with a nail set or large nail, then finish the panels. For more detailed information, see Making Tin Panels on page 203.

29

Cut the beads in the bead molding stock, as shown in the *Bead Molding Profile.*

30

Tack the tin panels over the openings in the case and door frames with the dimples facing *out*. (Country cabinetmakers believed this made it harder for insects to find their way into the pie safe.) Fit bead moldings around the perimeter of each panel, mitering the adjoining corners of the molding.

31

Finish sand the moldings and apply a finish to them. Nail (but do *not* glue) the moldings to the case and door frames. Set the heads of the nails.

32

Touch up the finish on the panels and three-bead moldings wherever necessary. Then replace the doors on the cabinet.

33

Replace the door pull in the right door and glue the catch onto the door pull shaft. Don't press the catch too tightly on the shaft — the pull and catch must turn freely. Drill a ¼"-diameter hole through the catch and pull shaft; glue the pin in the hole.

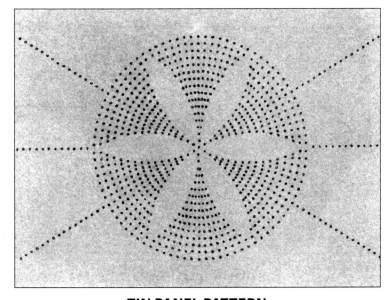

TIN PANEL PATTERN

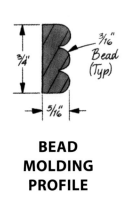

BEAD MOLDING PROFILE

COUNTRY CRAFTSMAN'S KNOW-HOW:
MAKING TIN PANELS

Each tin panel on the Pie Safe is decorated with a six-pointed star or *rosette*. This is an ancient symbol, dating back to the Dark Ages. In the eighth and ninth centuries, the Germanic peoples of the Rhine Valley in Europe developed a system of religious and superstitious symbols, combining designs from the newly adopted Christian faith and their pagan heritage. They painted these symbols on their furniture, doors, fireplaces, houses, and barns. When the Germans began to settle in America, they still used many of these symbols to decorate their homes and furnishings.

Over the centuries, however, the symbols had lost their significance. By the time the German immigrants arrived in America, these symbols were more traditional than meaningful. It's now difficult to establish the original purpose of any one symbol, but the rosette may have once prevented bad fortune. It's thought that medieval Germans used it to keep the devil out of a building or cupboard on which it was displayed. If this is so, it makes good sense to decorate a pie safe with rosettes.

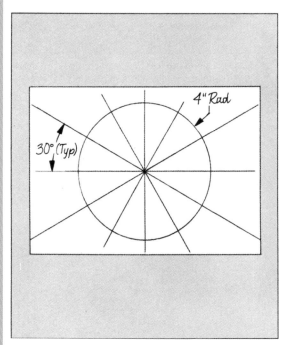

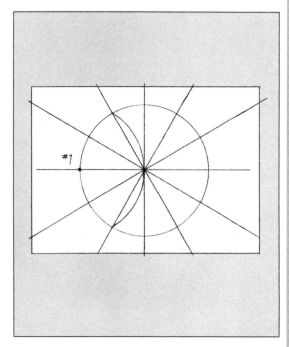

1 To lay out the rosettes for the pie safe, cut a piece of paper the same size as the tin panels — 10" × 14¼". Divide the paper into equal quadrants by drawing two perpendicular lines. Scribe a 4"-radius circle, using the point where the two lines intersect as the center. Then draw four more lines through the center, every 30°, dividing the circle into 12 wedge-shaped sections.

2 Without changing the setting of the compass, place the pivot on a point where the line through the long dimension of the paper intersects the circle. Draw a 4" radius arc from one side of the circle to the other. This arc should intersect the circle at the center and two points where other radial lines intersect it.

COUNTRY CRAFTSMAN'S KNOW-HOW:
MAKING TIN PANELS — CONTINUED

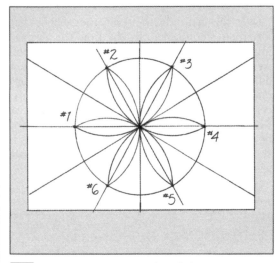

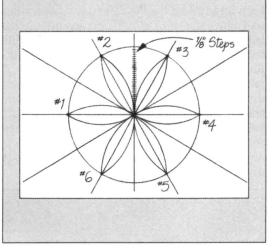

3 Move the pivot to a point where the last arc intersected the circle and draw another arc. Repeat until you've scribed six arcs — one every 60°. These arcs should meet at the center and the circumference of the circle, forming a rosette.

4 Measure along the line that runs through the short dimension of the paper, and mark every ⅛" out from the center.

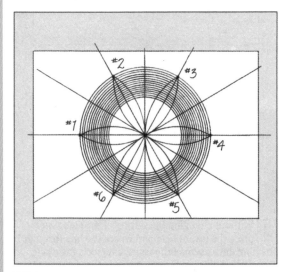

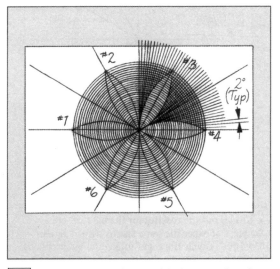

5 Place the compass pivot at the center of the circle and scribe concentric circles through the marks on the short line. The radius of each successive circle should be ⅛" larger or smaller than the one preceding.

6 Measure the circumference of the largest circle with a protractor, marking it every 2°. Draw radial lines from these marks to the center of the circle. Do *not* draw these radial lines inside the "leaves" of the rosette.

7 Make 12 photocopies of the pattern. Using spray adhesive, adhere a copy to each tin panel.

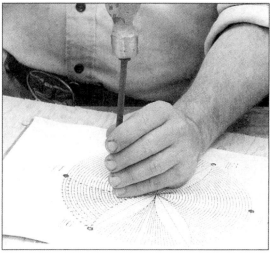

8 Temporarily tack each panel to a scrap of plywood with the pattern facing up. Grind a nail set or a 40d nail to a sharp, tapered point. Using a hammer to drive the tool through the tin, make a hole about $1/32$"–$1/16$" in diameter.

9 Use the grid as a *guide* to help space the holes evenly, every ¼" or so. (Don't try to punch holes everywhere the radial lines intersect the circles — the holes will be too close together, especially toward the center of the pattern.) Also, punch holes about every ¼" from the circumference of the largest circle to the edge of the panel along the three longest lines shown.

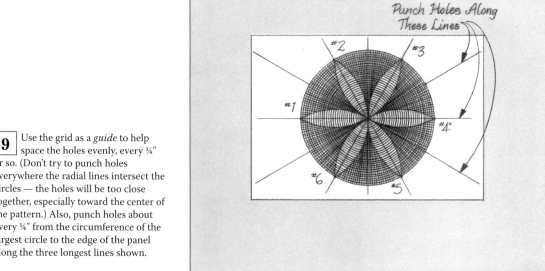

WATER BENCH

The water bench was an important step in the evolution of the kitchen sink. Before country homes had indoor plumbing, most folks fetched their water from a well outside. They brought the water up to the house in buckets and set the buckets on the back porch until they needed the water. They often built a special *bucket bench* to hold the buckets and added a top shelf at waist level to hold a basin and a pitcher for washing up.

Soon, the bucket bench moved inside — it was more convenient to have the water *inside* the house, especially on cold days. Craftsmen put splashguards around the top shelf to prevent the water from sloshing on the floor, and the bucket bench became a *water bench*.

The water bench shown is a simple, traditional design, with a high splashguard in back, and a lower one in front. A single, narrow shelf, running along the back splashguard, once held soap and other small wash-day items.

EXPLODED VIEW

BILL OF MATERIALS

WOODEN PARTS/*FINISHED DIMENSIONS*

A.	Sides (2)	⅝" × 16¼" × 43"
B.	Bottom shelf	⅝" × 16¼" × 29½"
C.	Top shelf	⅝" × 15" × 29½"
D.	Front splashguard	⅝" × 5¾" × 30"
E.	Back splashguard	⅝" × 13¾" × 30"
F.	Soap shelf	⅝" × 3½" × 28¾"
G.	Cleats (2)	⅝" × ⅝" × 3½"

HARDWARE

6d Square-cut nails (¼ lb.)
4d Square-cut nails (6–8)

PLAN OF PROCEDURE

1

Plane, rip, and cut the parts to the sizes shown in the Bill of Materials.

2

Miter the ends of the cleats at 45°, as shown in the *Cleat Layout*.

3

Cut the joinery in the sides:

- ⅝"-wide, ⅜"-deep dadoes in the side stock, as shown in the *Side Layout*
- ⅝"-wide, 11¼"-long notches in both edges of the side stock, near the top*

*When you cut the shape of the side, the front notch will be shortened to 5¾".

4

Lay out and cut the shape of the back splashguard and sides, as shown in the *Front View* and *Side View*.

5

Rout or cut a $5/16$"-diameter bead in the bottom edge of the front splashguard, as shown in the *Front Splashguard Profile*.

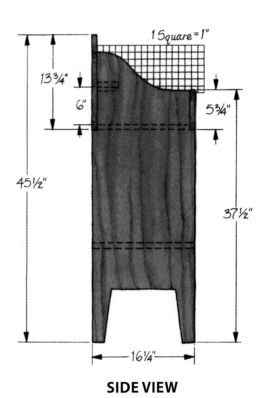

SIDE VIEW

SIDE LAYOUT

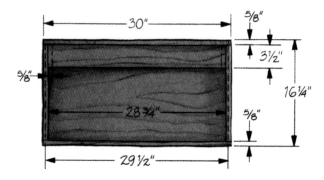

TOP VIEW

30"

5/8"

3½"

16¼"

5/8"

5/8"

28¾"

29½"

5/8"

FRONT VIEW

30"

42" Rad

43"

5/8" Wd × 3/8" Dp
Dado

5/8" (Typ)

**FRONT SPLASH-
GUARD PROFILE**

5/8"

5¾"

5/16"
Bead

CLEAT LAYOUT

3½"

5/8"

45°

6

Finish sand the parts of the water
bench and dry assemble them
to check the fit of the joints.
Reassemble the parts — except
the cleats and soap shelf — with
glue and 6d square-cut nails. Set
the heads of the nails.

7

Attach the cleats to the sides
with glue and 4d square-cut
nails. Once again, set the heads.
Then lay the soap shelf across
the cleats — do not attach it with
glue or nails. The soap shelf on
water benches and dry sinks was
often left loose. Oftentimes, it
was removed to make room for a
large tub of water.

8

Do any necessary touch-up
sanding and apply a finish to the
completed project.

HERB CUPBOARD

lthough the United Society of Believers in Christ's Second Appearing — the Shakers — are best remembered for their simple, elegant furniture designs, they also excelled in many other industries. Among them was growing and curing herbs and spices. In fact, the Shakers of Sabbathday Lake, Maine (the last functional Shaker community), still sell their spices and teas worldwide.

This "herb cupboard" was designed to assist in the spice trade at the Pleasant Hill Shaker community in Kentucky. It was adapted from a common washstand design. The unter of the old

washstand originally held buckets of water; the pegs (or *hangers*), towels and washcloths; the cupboard, soap and fresh linen. For this new application, the craftsman added more pegs and enlarged the counter. This provided a bigger work surface on which to process and package the spices. The pegs probably held bundles of cured herbs, waiting to be cut and cleaned. The cupboard may have held tins, boxes, and tools.

Today, it makes a useful addition to a kitchen, particularly if you spend a lot of time there. The top is well below normal counter height, and provides a comfortable sit-down work area.

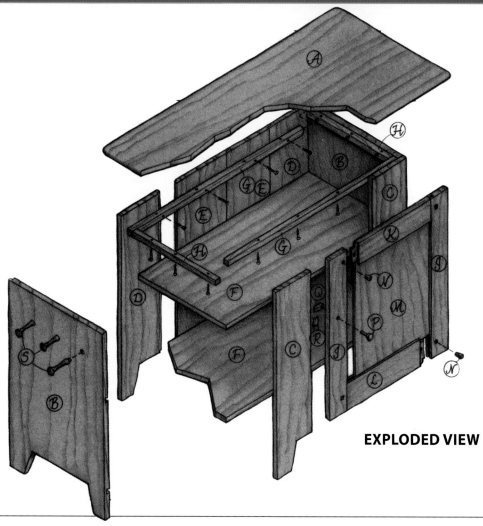

EXPLODED VIEW

BILL OF MATERIALS

WOODEN PARTS/*FINISHED DIMENSIONS*

A.	Top	¾" × 19½" × 41"
B.	Sides (2)	¾" × 16¼" × 27¼"
C.	Front stiles (2)	¾" × 6" × 27¼"
D.	Right/left backboards (2)	½" × 7⅞" × 27¼"
E.	Middle backboards (2)	½" × 7⅞" × 23½"
F.	Shelves (2)	¾" × 15¾" × 30"
G.	Front/back cleats (2)	¾" × ¾" × 29½"
H.	Side cleats (2)	¾" × ¾" × 14¼"
J.	Door stiles (2)	¾" × 3" × 23⁷/₁₆"
K.	Top door rail	¾" × 3" × 14⅞"
L.	Bottom door rail	¾" × 4" × 14⅞"
M.	Door panel	½" × 13⅜" × 17⅛"

N.	Pegs (4)	⁵/₁₆" × ⁵/₁₆" × 1¼"*
P.	Door pull	1¼" dia. × 2⁷/₁₆"
Q.	Door latch	½" × ⅞" × 2¼"
R.	Wedge	¼" × 1¼" × 1¼"
S.	Hangers (6)	1" dia. × 3⅜"

*Make the pegs at least this long, then cut them to length after you install them.

HARDWARE

1½" × 2" Butt hinges and mounting screws (1 pair)
4d Square-cut nails (24–30)
#8 × 1¼" Flathead wood screws (32)
#8 × 1" Flathead wood screws (4)

PLAN OF PROCEDURE

1

Glue up stock for the sides, top, shelves, and door panel. Plane, rip, and cut the parts to the sizes shown in the Bill of Materials, except the door parts and hangers. Wait to cut the door parts until after you've assembled the case. Cut the stock for the hangers ⅛"–¼" thicker and wider than the specified diameter and ½"–1" longer.

Note: You can substitute commercially made Shaker pegs for the hangers, if you wish.

2

Cut the joinery needed to assemble the case:

- ¾"-wide, ¼"-deep dadoes in the sides to hold the shelves, as shown in the *Front View*

- ½"-wide, ¼"-deep rabbets in the back edges of the sides to hold the backboards, as shown in the *Top View*

- ½"-wide, ¼"-deep rabbets in the *adjoining* edges of the backboards, to overlap them

3

Drill the holes needed to assemble the case:

- ½"-diameter, ⅝"-deep holes in the sides to hold the hangers, as shown in the *Top View* and *Side View*

- 3/16"-diameter pilot holes in the cleats for the screws, as shown in the *Top Joinery Detail*

Drill the pilot holes in the cleats both side to side and top to bottom, so you can attach the top to the case. Countersink the holes on the *inside* surfaces for the heads of the screws. These pilot holes are slightly larger than the shafts of the screws. This will allow the wood to which the cleats are attached to expand and contract.

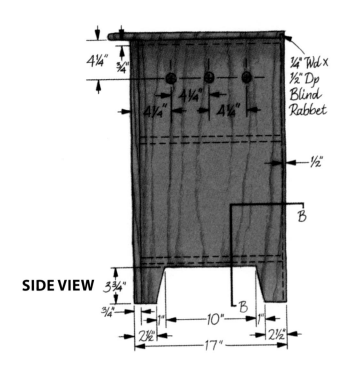

SIDE VIEW

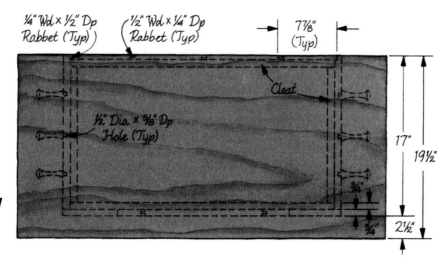

TOP VIEW

¼" Wd × ½" Dp
Rabbet (Typ)

½" Wd × ¼" Dp
Rabbet (Typ)

7⅞"
(Typ)

Cleat

½" Dia × ⅝" Dp
Hole (Typ)

17"

19½"

¾"

2½"

¾"

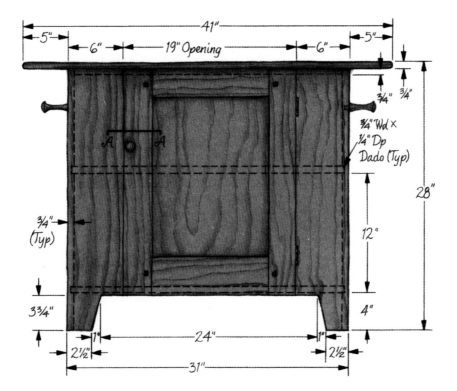

**FRONT
VIEW**

41"

5"

6"

19" Opening

6"

5"

¾"   ¾"

¾" Wd ×
¼" Dp
Dado (Typ)

28"

A   A

¾"
(Typ)

12"

3¾"

4"

1"

24"

1"

2½"

2½"

31"

PLAN OF PROCEDURE

4

Lay out the feet on the front stiles, sides, right backboard, and left backboard. Cut the shapes of the feet and sand the sawed edges.

5

If you're making the hangers (rather than buying commercially made pegs), turn them to the shape shown in the *Hanger Layout*. Finish sand the hanger on the lathe.

6

Finish sand the parts you've made so far. Assemble them in the following order:

- Fasten the sides to the shelves with glue and nails.

- Fasten the front stiles to the sides with glue and nails. Also, nail the stiles to the shelves, but do *not* glue these parts together.

- Nail the backboards to the assembly — do *not* glue them.

- Fasten the cleats to the front stiles and sides with 1¼"-long flathead wood screws. Fasten a cleat to the backboards with 1"-long screws — do *not* glue the cleats to the assembly.

- Fasten the top to the cleats with 1¼"-long screws — do *not* glue the top to the assembly.

- Glue the hangers in the holes in the sides. Sand all the joints clean and flush.

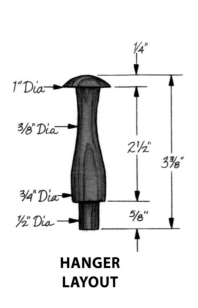

HANGER LAYOUT

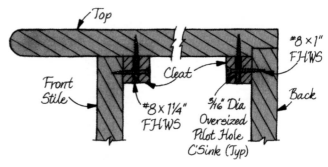

TOP JOINERY DETAIL

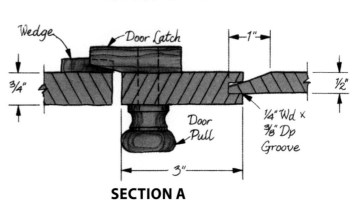

SECTION A

7

Set all the heads of the nails and cover them with putty.

8

Measure the door opening, and — if necessary — adjust the dimensions of the door parts. Cut the door parts to size, except the door pull. Cut the stock for the pull ⅛"–¼" thicker and wider than the specified diameter and ½"–1" longer.

Note: You can make the door pull out of a wooden knob and a short length of ½"-diameter dowel, if you wish.

9

Cut the joinery needed to assemble the door, as shown in the *Door Assembly Detail:*

- ¼"-wide, ⅜"-deep grooves centered in the inside edges of the rails and stiles

- ¼"-wide, 1"- deep, 2⅛"-long mortises in the upper ends of the stiles

- ¼"-wide, 1"- deep, 3⅛"-long mortises in the lower ends of the stiles

- 1"-long, ¼"-thick tenons in the ends of both rails; cut a ⅜"-wide, ⅝"-long notch or *haunch* in the tenons to fit the tenons to the mortises

10

Raise the door panel as shown in *Section A.*

DOOR ASSEMBLY DETAIL

Top Rail

Bottom Rail

¼" Wd × ⅜" Dp Groove (Typ)

3"

1"

⅝"

2⅛"

3⅛"

¼"

½"

2⅛"

2⅝"

¼"

1"

3⅛"

3⅝"

¼"

½"

PLAN OF PROCEDURE

11

Drill the holes needed to assemble the door:

- $^9/_{16}$"-diameter hole through the left door stile, as shown in the *Door Layout,* for the door pull

- ½"-diameter hole through the door latch, as shown in the *Door Latch Detail,* to attach the pull

12

If you're making the door pull, turn it to the shape shown in the *Door Pull Layout.* Finish sand the pull on the lathe.

13

Cut tapers in the wedge and door latch, as shown in the *Wedge Detail* and *Door Latch Detail.*

14

Finish sand the door parts. Assemble the door stiles and rails with glue. Slide the panel in place, raised face toward the inside. Do *not* glue it to the rails or stiles. Let the panel float in the grooves.

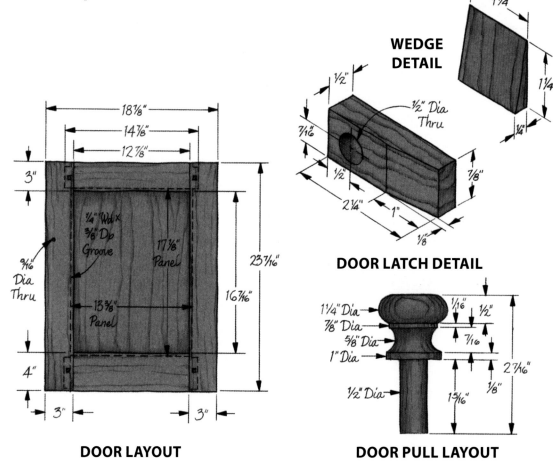

WEDGE DETAIL

DOOR LATCH DETAIL

DOOR LAYOUT

DOOR PULL LAYOUT

15

Round the bottom portion of the pegs, as shown in the *Peg Detail*.

16

Drill a ⁵⁄₁₆"-diameter hole through each mortise-and-tenon joint, then drive the pegs through the holes from the outside. Cut the pegs off flush with the inside surface of the door frame.

17

Cut hinge mortises in the door frame and right front stile, then mount the door in the case.

18

Insert the door pull through the hole in the door frame, and glue the latch to it. Be careful not to press the pull too far into the hole in the latch or get any glue on the door frame. The pull and latch must rotate easily in the door frame.

19

Glue the wedge inside the left front stile, opposite the door pull and about ¼" below it. The wedge should be flush with the inside edge of the stile, as shown in *Section A*.

20

Remove the door from the case and the hinges from the door. Do any necessary touch-up sanding, then apply a finish to the completed cupboard. When the finish dries, replace the hinges and the door.

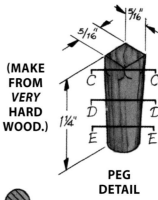

(MAKE FROM *VERY HARD* WOOD.)

PEG DETAIL

SECTION C   **SECTION D**   **SECTION E**

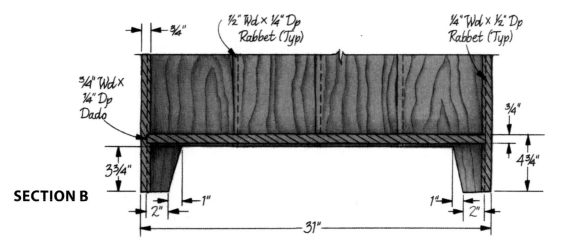

¾"

½" Wd × ¼" Dp Rabbet (Typ)

¼" Wd × ½" Dp Rabbet (Typ)

¾" Wd × ¼" Dp Dado

¾"

3¾"

4¾"

SECTION B

2"   1"

1"   2"

31"

DRY SINK

This distinctive cupboard was once as much a fixture in American country kitchens as the kitchen sink is now. Over the span of the eighteenth and nineteenth centuries, the dry sink became a country institution.

It evolved from a simple bench that once sat outside the back door of a cabin and held buckets of water. As the land became more settled, craftsmen found the time to refine this bench. First, they added a shelf above the first to hold the water while they washed. Then they enclosed this upper shelf with splash-guards to keep the water from dripping on the floor, creating a "sink." They extended the side to hold a third, smaller shelf above the sink. This held soap, dippers, brushes, and similar items. Finally, they enclosed the bottom shelf with doors to keep dirt from settling in the buckets of water.

In a few lucky cases, folks built their kitchens directly over wells. They installed cabinets similar to these over the well and mounted a pump on them. These were "wet sinks" — using the pump, the cook could draw water directly into the sink. Most people, however, weren't that fortunate. They had "dry sinks" and continued to haul water from an outside well and store it inside the cupboard.

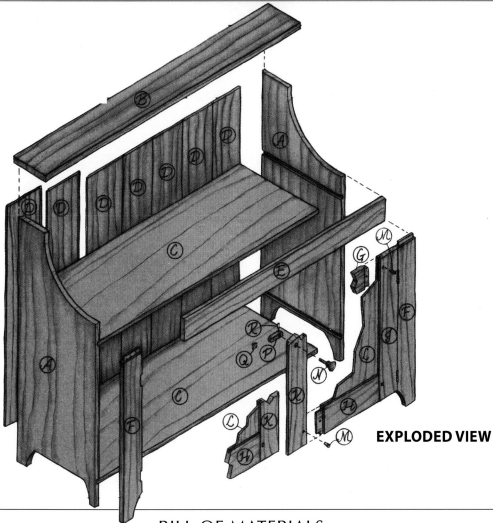

EXPLODED VIEW

BILL OF MATERIALS

WOODEN PARTS/*FINISHED DIMENSIONS*

A.	Sides (2)	$\frac{3}{4}$" × 17 $\frac{1}{4}$" × 45 $\frac{1}{8}$"
B.	Top	$\frac{7}{8}$" × 7" × 50"
C.	Shelves (2)	$\frac{3}{4}$" × 16 $\frac{3}{4}$" × 47 $\frac{1}{4}$"
D,	Backboards (7)	$\frac{1}{2}$" × 7 $\frac{5}{32}$" × 41 $\frac{1}{2}$"
E.	Face frame rail	$\frac{3}{4}$" × 4" × 48"
F.	Face frame stiles (2)	$\frac{3}{4}$" × 4" × 31"
G.	Top door rails (2)	$\frac{3}{4}$" × 4" × 13 $\frac{7}{8}$"
H.	Bottom door rails (2)	$\frac{3}{4}$" × 5" × 13 $\frac{7}{8}$"
J.	Outside door stiles (2)	$\frac{3}{4}$" × 4" × 25 $\frac{15}{16}$"
K.	Inside door stiles (2)	$\frac{3}{4}$" × 4 $\frac{1}{2}$" × 25 $\frac{15}{16}$"
L.	Door panels (2)	$\frac{1}{2}$" × 12 $\frac{3}{8}$" × 17 $\frac{5}{8}$"
M.	Pegs (8)	$\frac{5}{16}$" × $\frac{5}{16}$" × 1 $\frac{1}{4}$"*

N.	Door pull	1 $\frac{1}{4}$" dia. × 2 $\frac{5}{8}$"
P.	Door latch	$\frac{5}{8}$" × 1" × 2 $\frac{5}{8}$"
Q.	Wedge	$\frac{1}{4}$" × 1" × 1 $\frac{1}{2}$"
R.	Pin	$\frac{1}{4}$" dia. × 1"

Make the pegs at least this long, then cut them to length after you install them.

HARDWARE
1 $\frac{1}{2}$" × 2" Butt hinges and mounting screws (2 pair)
Small door catch and mounting screws
6d Square-cut nails (24–30)
1 $\frac{1}{4}$" Wire or headless brads (30–36)

PLAN OF PROCEDURE

1

If necessary, glue up stock to make the wide parts — sides, shelves, and door panels. Plane, rip, and cut the parts to the sizes shown in the Bill of Materials, except for the pegs. Cut the pegs about ¼" longer than specified.

BOTTOM VIEW
TOP LAYOUT

2

Cut the joinery needed to assemble the case:

- ¾"-wide, ⅜"-deep dadoes in the sides to hold the shelves, as shown in the *Side Layout*

- ½"-wide, ⅜"-deep, 41⅛"-long blind rabbets in the back edges of the sides

- ½"-wide, ⅜"-deep, 47¼"-long double-blind rabbet in the back edge of the top, as shown in the *Top Layout/ Bottom View*

- ½"-wide, ¼"-deep rabbets in *both* edges of the middle backboards and *one* edge of the right and left backboards, as shown in the *Top View*

- ¼"-wide, 1"-deep, 3¼"-long mortises in the bottom edge of the face frame rail, as shown in the *Face Frame Assembly Detail*

- ¼"-thick, 1"-long, 3¼"-wide tenons on the top ends of the face frame stiles

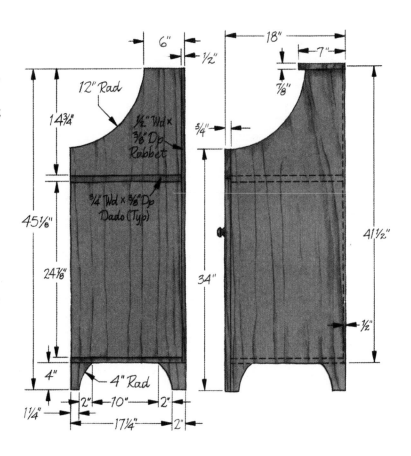

SIDE LAYOUT   **SIDE VIEW**

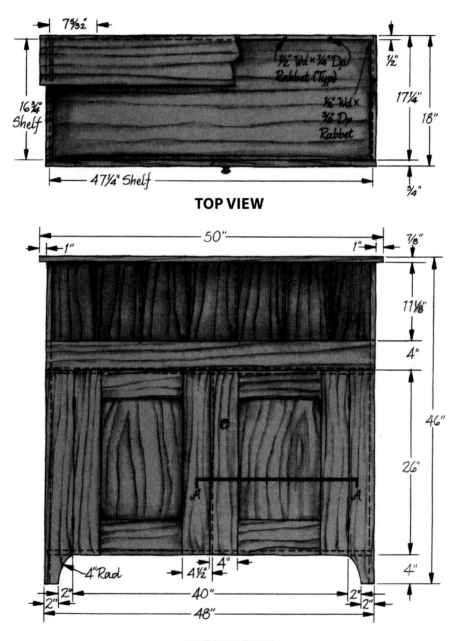

7⁹⁄₃₂"

½" Wd × ¾" Dp
Rabbet (Typ)

½" Wd ×
⅜" Dp
Rabbet

16¾"
Shelf

½"

17¼"

18"

47¼" Shelf

¾"

TOP VIEW

50"

1"

1"

⅞"

11⅛"

4"

46"

26"

A

A

4"Rad

4½"

4"

4"

2"

2"

40"

2"

2"

48"

FRONT VIEW

PLAN OF PROCEDURE

3

Lay out and cut the shapes of the sides and face frame stiles, as shown in the *Side Layout* and *Front View*. Sand the sawed edges.

4

Stain the rabbets in the backboards a dark brown or black.

5

Finish sand the parts of the case and assemble them in the following order:

- Glue the shelves to the sides and reinforce the joints with square-cut nails.

- Glue the face frame stiles to the face frame rail, inserting the tenons in the mortises.

- Glue the assembled face frame to the case and reinforce it with nails.

- Attach the top to the sides with nails.

- Nail the backboards to the sides, top, and shelves with brads. Do *not* glue the backboards in place.

As you work, sand all joints clean and flush. Set the heads of the nails. If you wish, cover the heads of the nails in the sides and front with putty.

6

Cut the joinery needed to assemble the doors:

- ½"-wide, ⅜"-deep rabbets in the adjoining edges of the inside door stiles, as shown in *Section A*

- ¼"-wide, ⅜"-deep grooves in the inside edges of all door rails and stiles, as shown in the *Door Assembly Detail*

- ¼"-wide, 1"-deep, 3¼"-long mortises in the inside edges of the door stiles, ⅜" from the top ends

- ¼"-wide, 1"-deep, 4¼"-long mortises in the inside edges of the door stiles, ⅜" from the bottom ends

- ¼"-wide, 1"-long tenons on the ends of the door rails

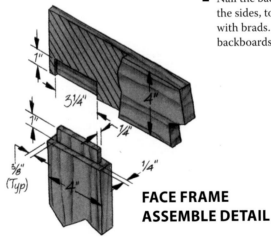

FACE FRAME ASSEMBLE DETAIL

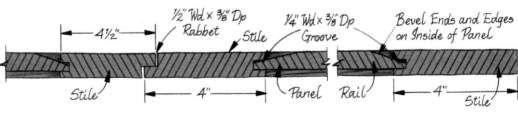

SECTION A

Notch the tenons in the rails as shown in the *Door Assembly Detail*, creating a haunch in each tenon and fitting it to its mortise.

7

Raise the door panels, beveling the edges and ends to fit the grooves in the rails and stiles, as shown in *Section A*.

8

Drill a $^9/_{16}$"-diameter hole in the right inside door stile for the door latch assembly, as shown in the *Front View*.

9

Finish sand the door parts and assemble the rails and stiles with glue. Put the panels in place as you glue up the door frames, but do not apply glue to them. The panels must float in the grooves.

10

Round the bottom portion of the pegs, as shown in the *Peg Detail*.

11

Drill a $^5/_{16}$"-diameter hole through each mortise and tenon in the door frames. Drive a peg into each hole to secure the tenon in the mortise, then cut off the peg flush with the inside surface of the door frame.

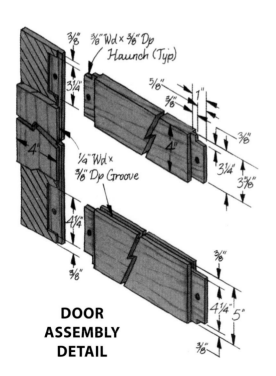

DOOR ASSEMBLY DETAIL

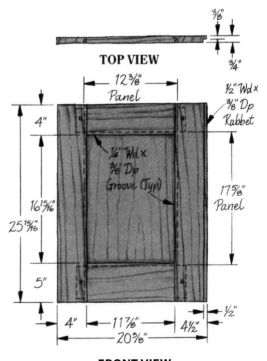

TOP VIEW

FRONT VIEW LEFT DOOR LAYOUT

PLAN OF PROCEDURE

12

Mortise the door stiles and face frame stiles for hinges, then mount the doors to the case.

13

Turn the door pull as shown in the *Door Pull Layout*. Finish sand the pull on the lathe.

14

Drill a ½"-diameter hole through the door latch, ½" from one end, as shown in the *Door Latch Assembly Detail*.

15

Bevel the end of the latch opposite the hole you just drilled. Also, cut a taper in the wedge.

16

Insert the door pull through the hole in the right inside stile. Glue the latch on the pull shaft. Don't press the latch too tightly on the shaft — the pull must turn freely. Drill a ¼"-diameter hole through the latch and pull; glue the pin in the hole.

17

Experiment with the position of the wedge on the left inside door stile. When you turn the pull counterclockwise, the beveled edge of the latch should contact the wedge, holding the right door snug against the left. When you find the proper position, glue the wedge to the inside surface of the stile.

18

Mount the door catch on the bottom side of the top shelf, just behind the left inside stile. The catch should hold the left door closed.

19

Remove the doors and the hardware from the case. Do any necessary touch-up sanding, then apply a finish to the completed dry sink. Finish *all* sides of the project — inside and out, top and bottom. Then reassemble the doors to the case.

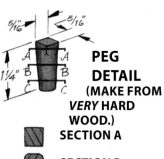

5/16" 5/16"
1¼" A A
B B
C C

PEG DETAIL (MAKE FROM VERY HARD WOOD.)

 SECTION A

 SECTION B

SECTION C

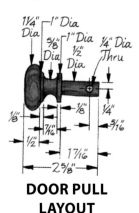

1¼" Dia   1" Dia
5/8" Dia   1" Dia   ½" Dia   ¼" Dia Thru
1/8"   1/8"   ¼"
7/16"   5/16"
½"   1 7/16"
2 5/8"

DOOR PULL LAYOUT

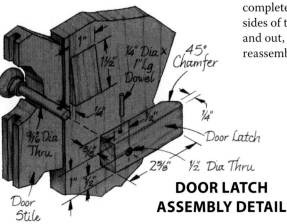

1"
1½"   ¼" Dia x 1" Lg Dowel   45° Chamfer
¼"   ½"   ¼"
Door Latch
9/16" Dia Thru   5/8"
2 5/8"   ½" Dia Thru
1"   ½"
Door Stile

DOOR LATCH ASSEMBLY DETAIL

COUNTRY CRAFTSMAN'S KNOW-HOW:
MAKING BACKBOARDS

Country craftsmen often assembled wide panels at the backs of cupboards and cabinets from several boards. For strength and aesthetics, they rabbeted the edges of these boards, then lapped the rabbets. They did *not* glue the boards together, but left each backboard free to expand and contract independently of the others. This prevented the boards from cracking or splitting.

The boards did, however, show their seams. When the backboards contracted, the lapped rabbets opened up. This was especially distracting if the boards were stained or painted a dark color. Wherever the rabbets pulled apart, they would reveal raw, light-colored wood. To make these gaps less noticeable, cabinetmakers stained the rabbeted edges a dark brown or black.

1 Rabbet the adjoining edges of backboards so you can lap them when you assemble the case. This prevents light from showing through the back, and adds strength to the assembly.

2 Apply a dark stain to the rabbets *before* you attach the backboards to the cabinet.

3 Scrape the faces of the backboards to remove any stain that bleeds over onto the surfaces from the edges.

4 After staining the edges and scraping the faces, nail the backboards in place. Do *not* glue them to the case. The nails allow the backboards to move freely, flexing slightly as the wood expands and contracts.

Salt Box

Salt was a precious commodity in colonial America. The colonists needed it not only for cooking, but to preserve food. In the days before refrigeration, salting meat and canning vegetables in brine (a salt solution) was the only way to keep the food from going bad.

Cooks kept their salt in a "salt box." There were no salt shakers — kitchen salt came in clumps or large crystals. For convenience, this small box usually hung near the stove. A lid kept soot and grease from settling in the salt.

Although salt was precious, craftsmen rarely wasted much effort or materials in making salt boxes. Owing to constant use and the chemical action of the salt, these boxes wore out quickly. So they were usually made simply, using inexpensive wood and as little hardware as possible. The hinges on this salt box are fashioned from linked cotter pins and were known as "snipe" hinges. This was a popular method of making inexpensive hinges for small, utilitarian projects during the eighteenth and early nineteenth centuries.

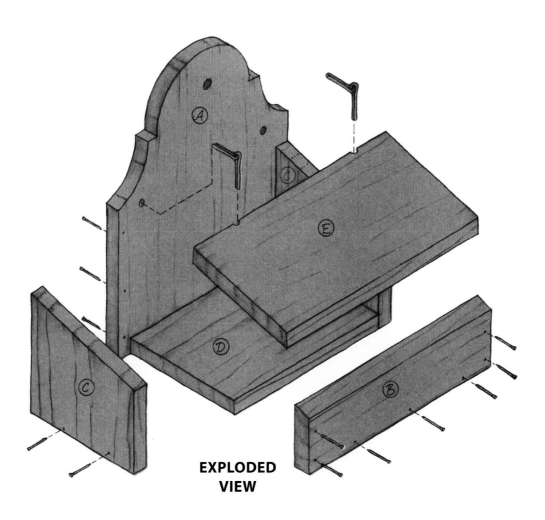

**EXPLODED
VIEW**

BILL OF MATERIALS

WOODEN PARTS/*FINISHED DIMENSIONS*

A.	Back	⅜" × 5¼" × 6½"
B.	Front	⅜" × 1⅞" × 5¼"
C.	Sides (2)	⅜" × 2½" × 3"
D.	Bottom	⅜" × 2½" × 4½"
E.	Lid	⅜" × 3¾" × 5¾"

HARDWARE

1¼" Headless brads (12–16)
1" Cotter pins (4)

PLAN OF PROCEDURE

1

Plane, rip, and cut the parts to the sizes shown in the Bill of Materials. Bevel both edges of the lid and the top edge of the front at 25°. Miter the top ends of the sides at 65°, as shown in the *Side View*.

2

Lay out and cut the shape of the back, as shown in the *Back Pattern*. Sand the sawed edges.

3

Dry assemble the parts and mark where the lid touches the back. Then drill the necessary holes:

- ¼"-diameter hole through the back, as shown in the *Front View*

- ⅛"-diameter holes through the lid and the back, as shown in the *Side View* and *Hinge Detail*

Note: The holes in the lid are angled slightly. These holes and those in the back hold the cotter pin hinges. The location and spacing of these holes are not critical, but they should be equidistant from each side.

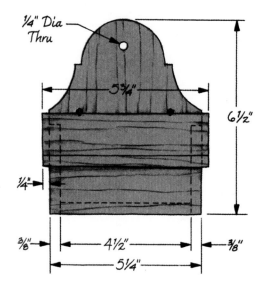

FRONT VIEW

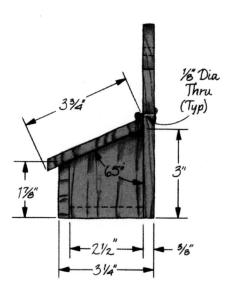

SIDE VIEW

4

Finish sand the parts of the salt box and dry assemble them to check the fit. Reassemble the parts with glue and square-cut headless brads. Set the heads of the brads and cover them with putty.

5

Do any necessary touch-up sanding and apply a finish to the completed project.

6

Link two pairs of cotter pins as shown in the *Hinge Detail*. Insert one pin from each pair through the ⅛"-diameter holes in the lid, and bend over the ends. Insert the other pins through the ⅛"-diameter holes in the back. Once again, bend over the ends.

7

If you wish, hang the salt box from a nail. If you want to secure the project to the wall, drive a screw or Molly anchor through the ¼"-diameter hole in the back.

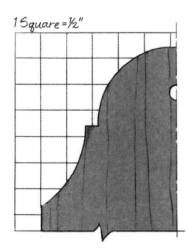

BACK PATTERN

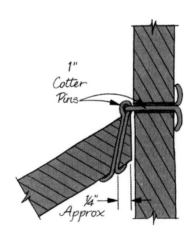

HINGE DETAIL

SPICE CUPBOARD

Spices and herbs were precious commodities in centuries past. Country folk didn't have the variety of foods that we do today, and without a store of spices, their meals would have been bland and monotonous. They didn't have over-the-counter medicines, either. Instead, they collected and stored many different herbs to treat a wide assortment of ailments. For this reason, the cupboard where these commodities were stored was an important fixture in the early American home. It was a spice rack, a first-aid center, and a medicine cabinet all rolled into one.

Country folks often made these small, hanging cupboards with just the simplest tools. The parts were butt jointed and nailed together. The paneled doors were flat and plain; there were few decorations. The hinges were usually homemade, and the latch was a simple brass hook. Some craftsmen even used strips of leather for hinges and latches.

This reproduction preserves this simplicity. It has just a little decoration — an arched back and a double-paneled door. The construction is authentic; even the shelves are spaced to hold old-time spice boxes. The one contemporary addition is that the shelves sit loosely in dadoes. Only the middle and bottom shelves are fixed; the others can be moved — or removed completely. This allows you to rearrange the space inside the cupboard.

Variations: You can alter the height of the cupboard, if you wish, simply by changing the length of the vertical parts. (Don't make it too much longer than shown, or it will be too heavy to hang on the wall.) You may also turn the panels around in the door frame so the raised area faces out. This will give the piece a more formal appearance.

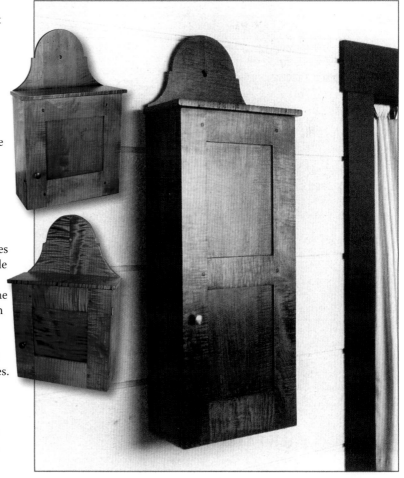

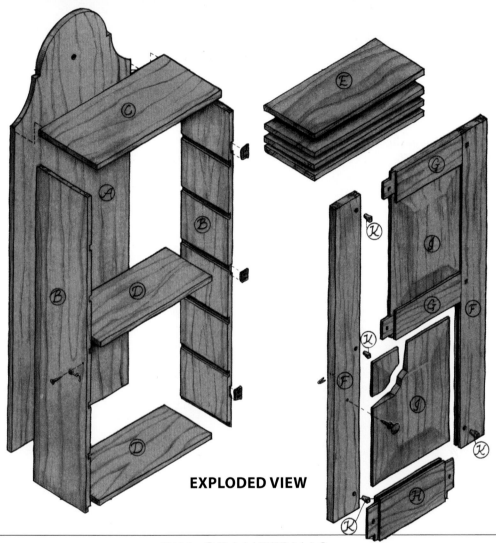

EXPLODED VIEW

BILL OF MATERIALS

WOODEN PARTS/*FINISHED DIMENSIONS*

A.	Backboard	⅝" × 14" × 40"
B.	Sides (2)	⅝" × 5¾" × 31½"
C.	Top	⅝" × 7" × 15"
D.	Bottom/middle shelves (2)	½" × 5¾" × 13½"
E.	Adjustable shelves (2–4)	½" × 5¾" × 13⅜"
F.	Door stiles (2)	¾" × 3" × 31½"
G.	Upper door rails (2)	¾" × 3" × 10"
H.	Lower door rail	¾" × 4" × 10"
J.	Door panels (2)	⅝" × 8⅝" × 11⅜"
K.	Pegs (6)	⁵⁄₁₆" × ⁵⁄₁₆" × 1"*

HARDWARE

Brass hook and eye
1" Door pull
4d Square-cut nails (24–30)
1½" × 2" Butt hinges and mounting screws (3)

*Make the pegs at least this long, then cut them to length after you install them.

PLAN OF PROCEDURE

1

Plane, rip, and cut the parts to the sizes shown in the Bill of Materials, except for the pegs. Cut these about ¼" longer than specified.

2

Cut ½"-wide, ¼"-deep dadoes and rabbets in the sides, as shown in the *Side Panel Layout.*

3

Cut the shape of the backboard as shown in the *Front View,* and drill a hole in the center of the arch so you can hang the cupboard on a peg or a nail.

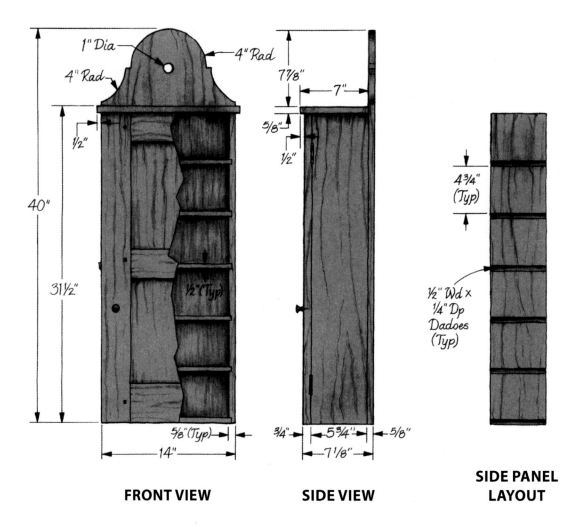

FRONT VIEW   **SIDE VIEW**   **SIDE PANEL LAYOUT**

4

Finish sand the parts of the case, then assemble the backboard, top, sides, middle shelf, and bottom shelf with glue and square-cut nails. Set the heads of the nails.

5

Cut ¼"-wide, ⅜"-deep grooves in the *inside* edges of all the door parts. Cut grooves in *both* edges of the middle rail.

6

Drill holes to rough out ¼"-wide, 1"-deep mortises in the door stiles, as shown in the *Door Frame Joinery Detail*. Square the sides and corners of the mortises with a chisel.

7

Cut ¼"-wide, 1"-long tongues on the ends of the door rails to fit the mortises in the stiles. Cut haunches on the upper and lower rails as shown in the *Door Frame Joinery Detail*.

8

Raise the door panels, as shown in the *Door Panel Detail*.

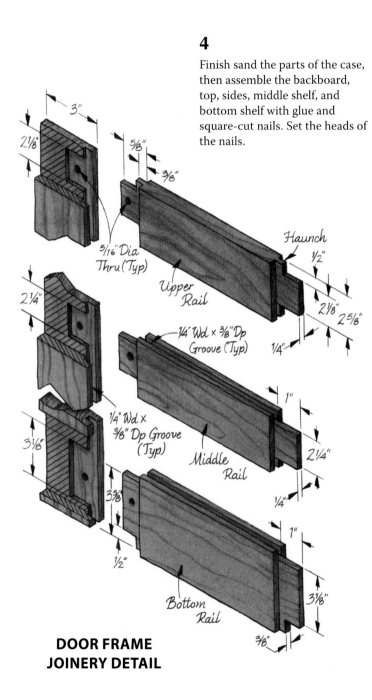

**DOOR FRAME
JOINERY DETAIL**

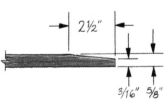

**DOOR PANEL
DETAIL**

PLAN OF PROCEDURE

9

Finish sand the parts of the door and assemble the rails and stiles with glue. Put the panels in place as you glue up the door frame, but do not apply glue to them. The panels must float in the grooves.

10

Round the bottom portion of the pegs, as shown in the *Peg Detail*.

11

Drill a ⁵/₁₆"-diameter hole through each mortise and tenon in the door frame. Drive a peg into the hole to secure the tenon in the mortise, then cut off the peg flush with the inside surface of the door frame.

12

Mortise the door and the side of the cupboard for hinges, then mount the door to the cupboard.

13

Fit the adjustable shelves in the dadoes, shaving and rounding the shelf ends so the shelves will slide smoothly in and out of the case.

14

Remove the door from the case and all hardware from the cupboard. Do any necessary touch-up sanding and apply a finish to complete the cupboard.

15

Reassemble the cupboard and, if desired, mount it on a wall or hang it on a peg rail.

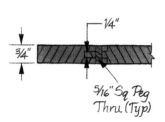

SECTION A

 SECTION B

 SECTION C

SECTION D

(MAKE PEGS FROM *VERY* HARD WOOD.)

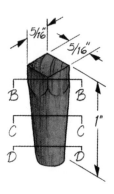

PEGS DETAIL

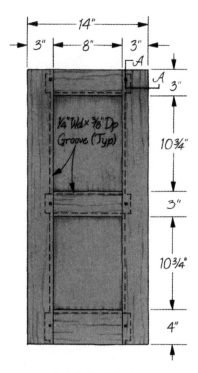

DOOR DETAIL

COUNTRY CRAFTSMAN'S KNOW-HOW:
DRIVING SQUARE PEGS IN ROUND HOLES

The country craftsman often pinned his door frames and other furniture assemblies together by driving square pegs into round holes. This method works much better than using round pegs or dowels. The corners of the square pegs wedge themselves in the holes and can't work loose.

1 Make the pegs from a wood much harder than the one you used to make the frame. Rock maple and hickory are the materials most country craftsmen used.

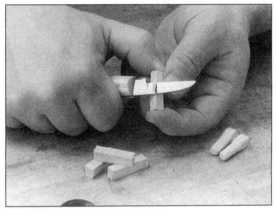

2 Cut each peg to a length you can comfortably grip. Whittle about three-quarters of its length, making it more and more round toward one end. When you're finished, one end should be round and the other square. The square portion should be just ¼"–½" long.

3 Assemble the joint. Drill a hole, as big around as the peg is square, through the parts that are to be pegged together.

4 Coat the peg with glue, and drive it into the hole, rounded end first, with a mallet. Tap it in so the top is *almost* (but not quite) flush with the surface of the wood. (About $^1/_{16}$" should protrude.) Make sure the square portion is wedged in the hole. Be careful, however, not to hit the peg so hard that it splinters.

(Continued) ✦ **235**

COUNTRY CRAFTSMAN'S KNOW-HOW:
DRIVING SQUARE PEGS IN ROUND HOLES—CONTINUED

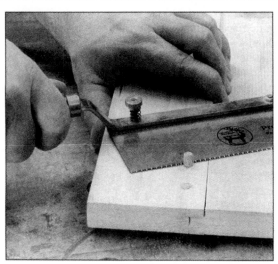

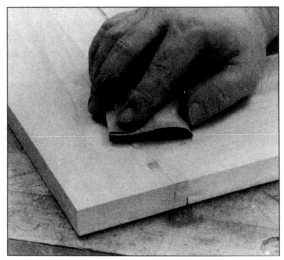

5 If the rounded portion protrudes from the back of the assembly, cut it flush with the surface of the wood. Leave the square end alone — don't sand it or cut it flush.

6 Lightly sand the front surface, rounding over the peg slightly. Do *not* sand it flush. If you inspect the pegs on old country pieces, you'll see that most of the pegs protrude. As the wood frame expands and contracts for a century or more, it begins to push the pegs out of the holes.

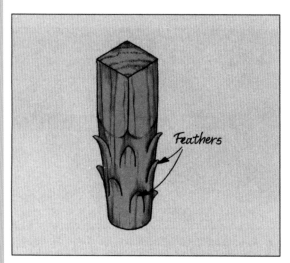

Feathers

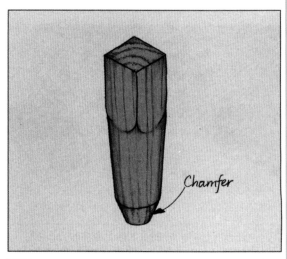

Chamfer

7 To help hold the pegs in their holes, some craftsmen "feathered" them, as shown, with a pocketknife. These feathers always faced toward the "head" of the peg.

8 If the peg is to be driven through several parts, chamfer the round end. This will prevent it from catching on the edge of a board and possibly splitting the joint.

FOR STORING
& KEEPING

HANGING CORNER CABINET

While cupboards were popular in the country, cabinets were less common. The reason has to do with the traditional difference between cupboards and cabinets, and how they were used: Solid-door cupboards were for storage whereas glass-door cabinets were for display. Cupboards are utilitarian; cabinets are special and tend to be more finely crafted. This distinction is why fine furnituremakers of the seventeenth century began to use the title *cabinetmaker*.

Early country life was a great deal like a cupboard — plain and practical. Country folks had lots to store, but little to display. The decorative knickknacks and collectibles that we take for granted would seem rare treasures to our great-great grand-parents. Consequently, cabinets were few and far between. If a country family had a cabinet, it was likely to be a small one, such as the cabinet shown. It has just three shelves, one of them open — probably more than enough for the treasures of simple country folks.

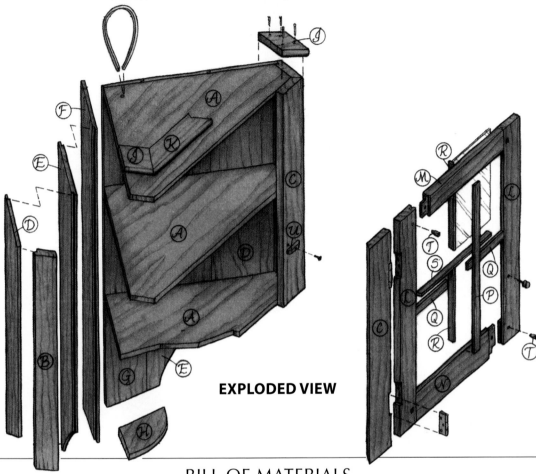

EXPLODED VIEW

BILL OF MATERIALS

WOODEN PARTS/*FINISHED DIMENSIONS*

A.	Top/middle shelves (3)	$\frac{1}{2}$" × 12" × 20 $\frac{3}{4}$"
B.	Side stiles (2)	$\frac{3}{4}$" × 3" × 19 $\frac{3}{4}$"
C.	Front stiles (2)	$\frac{3}{4}$" × 2 $\frac{1}{4}$" × 19 $\frac{3}{4}$"
D.	Front backboards (2)	$\frac{3}{8}$" × 5 $\frac{3}{4}$" × 21 $\frac{1}{4}$"
E.	Middle backboards (2)	$\frac{3}{8}$" × 5 $\frac{3}{4}$" × 30"
F.	Right rear backboard	$\frac{3}{8}$" × 4 $\frac{3}{4}$" × 30"
G.	Left rear backboard	$\frac{3}{8}$" × 4 $\frac{3}{8}$" × 30"
H.	Bottom shelf	$\frac{1}{2}$" × 5" × 7 $\frac{1}{16}$"
J.	Side top moldings (2)	$\frac{3}{4}$" × 2 $\frac{1}{4}$" × 3 $\frac{1}{4}$"
K.	Front top molding	$\frac{3}{4}$" × 2 $\frac{1}{4}$" × 20 $\frac{1}{8}$"
L.	Door stiles (2)	$\frac{3}{4}$" × 2" × 19 $\frac{11}{16}$"
M.	Top door rail	$\frac{3}{4}$" × 2" × 11 $\frac{5}{8}$"
N.	Bottom door rail	$\frac{3}{4}$" × 2 $\frac{3}{4}$" × 11 $\frac{5}{8}$"
P.	Mullion	$\frac{1}{4}$" × $\frac{3}{4}$" × 14 $\frac{15}{16}$"
Q.	Sashes (2)	$\frac{1}{4}$" × $\frac{3}{4}$" × 4 $\frac{7}{16}$"
R.	Vertical glazing bars (2)	$\frac{1}{4}$" × $\frac{1}{2}$" × 7 $\frac{23}{32}$"
S.	Horizontal glazing bar	$\frac{1}{4}$" × $\frac{1}{2}$" × 10 $\frac{3}{8}$"
T.	Pegs (4)	$\frac{5}{16}$" × $\frac{5}{16}$" × 1"*
U.	Door latch	$\frac{1}{4}$" × $\frac{1}{2}$" × 1 $\frac{1}{4}$"

**Make the pegs at least this long, then cut them to
length after you install them.*

HARDWARE

$\frac{1}{2}$" Door pull
1 $\frac{1}{2}$" × 2" Butt hinges and mounting screws (2)
4d Square-cut nails (18)
4d Finishing nails ($\frac{1}{4}$ Ib.)
5" × 7 $\frac{5}{8}$" Glass panes (4)
Glazing points (24)
#8 × 1" Flathead wood screw
Leather thong (12")

PLAN OF PROCEDURE

1

Plane, rip, and cut the parts to the sizes shown in the Bill of Materials, except for the moldings, mullion, sashes, glazing bars, and pegs. Plane and rip the moldings, mullion, sashes, and glazing bars to the proper thickness and width, but don't cut them to length yet. Make the pegs about ¼" longer than specified.

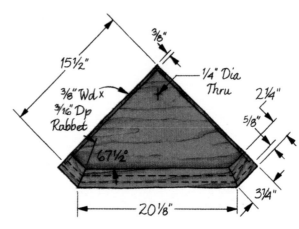

TOP VIEW

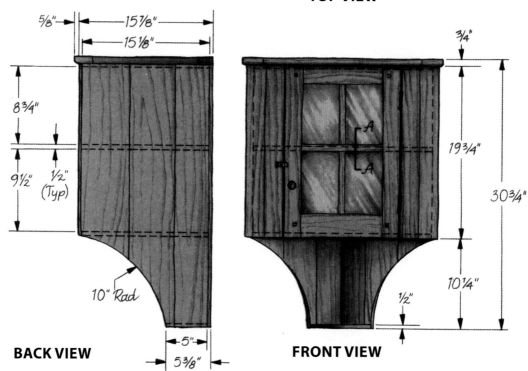

BACK VIEW

FRONT VIEW

2

Bevel the adjoining edges of the front and side stiles at 67½°, as shown in the *Bottom View*.

3

Cut the shapes of the top and middle shelves, as shown in the *Middle Shelf Layout*.

4

Cut the shape of the bottom shelf.

5

If you wish, cut or rout dovetail notches to hold spoons in the front edges of the middle shelves, as shown in the *Spoon Holder Layout*. These notches are optional.

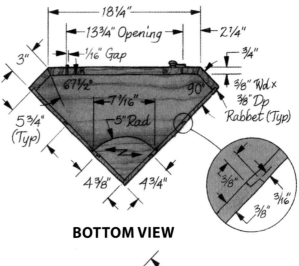

BOTTOM VIEW

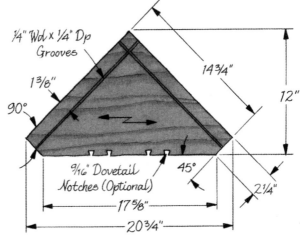

MIDDLE SHELF LAYOUT

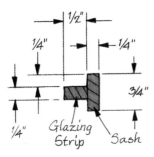

SECTION A

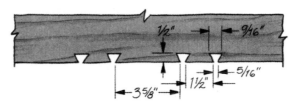

SPOON HOLDER LAYOUT

PLAN OF PROCEDURE

6

Cut the grooves and rabbets needed to assemble the case:

- ⅜"-wide, ⅜"-deep rabbets in the back edges of the side stiles
- ⅜"-wide, ⅜"-deep rabbets in the adjoining edges of the backboards
- ¼"-wide, ¼"-deep grooves in the middle shelves, 1⅜" from the back edges

7

Drill a ¼"-diameter hole for the thong in the top, as shown in the *Top View.*

8

Finish sand the parts of the case, then assemble them with glue, finishing nails, and square-cut nails. Drive the finishing nails in the back of the case, where they won't be seen, and the square-cut nails in the sides and front. Set the nails. Don't attach the bottom shelf yet.

9

Cut a 10"-radius curve in the lower portion of the backboards, as shown in the *Back View.* Sand the cut edges.

10

Attach the lower shelf with glue and finishing nails. Set the nails.

11

Round the edge of the top molding, as shown in the *Molding Detail.*

12

Cut the molding to length, mitering the adjoining ends at 67½°.

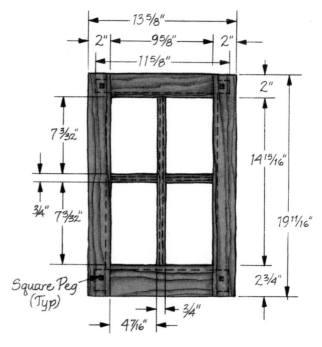

DOOR LAYOUT

13

Finish sand the molding, then attach it to the case with glue and finishing nails. Set the nails.

14

Cut the joinery needed to assemble the door, as shown in the *Door Assembly Detail:*

- 1"-long, ¼"-thick tenons the full width of the rails

- ⅜"-wide, ½"-deep rabbets in the inside edges of the rails

- ¼"-wide, ⅜"-deep grooves centered in the inside edges of the stiles

- ¼"-wide, 1"-deep, 1¼"-long mortises in the upper ends of the stiles

- ¼"-wide, 1"-deep, 2"-long mortises in the lower ends of the stiles

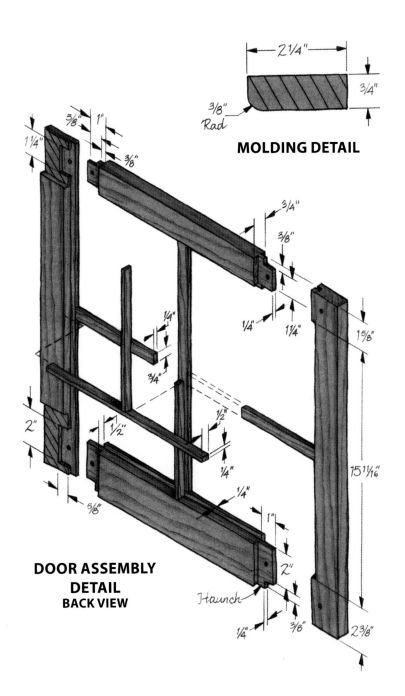

MOLDING DETAIL

DOOR ASSEMBLY DETAIL
BACK VIEW

PLAN OF PROCEDURE

15

Cut a haunch in the tenons, as shown in the *Door Assembly Detail.*

16

Cut away the inside edge of the stiles to make double-blind rabbets for the glass, as shown in the *Door Assembly Detail.*

17

Finish sand the door frame parts, then assemble the door frame with glue.

18

Round the bottom portion of the pegs, as shown in the *Peg Detail.*

19

Drill a ⁵⁄₁₆"-diameter hole through each mortise-and-tenon joint, then drive the pegs through the holes from the outside. Cut the pegs off flush with the inside surface of the door frame.

20

Cut the mullion, sashes, and glazing bars to the proper length, finish sand them, and glue them in the door frame. (They are attached with simple butt joints.)

21

Cut hinge mortises in the door frame and left front stile, then mount the door in the case.

 **SECTION B**

 **SECTION C**

 **SECTION D**

(**MAKE PEGS FROM *VERY* HARD WOOD.**)

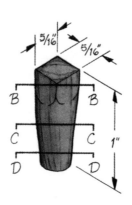

PEG DETAIL

THONG DETAIL

22

Chamfer the outside corners of the latch, as shown in the *Latch Detail.*

23

Drill a pilot hole and a countersink in the latch, then attach the latch to the right front stile with a flathead wood screw, as shown in the *Front View.*

24

Remove the door and the latch from the case, and remove all hardware.

25

Do any necessary touch-up sanding, then apply a finish to the case, door, and latch.

26

Mount panes of glass in the door with glazing points and glazing compound. After the compound dries, paint it or stain it to match the cabinet.

27

Remount the door and the latch on the case.

28

Insert a leather thong through the hole in the top, and knot it as shown in the *Thong Detail.*

29

Reassemble the cabinet. Drive a nail into the corner where you want to mount the cabinet, and hang it by the thong. Fasten the cabinet securely to the wall with screws or Molly anchors. (**Note:** The thong is an *aid* to help mount the cabinet on the wall. It shouldn't be used as the sole support for the cabinet.)

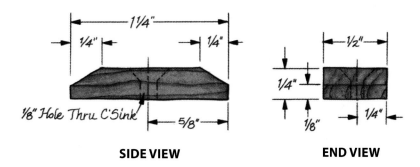

SIDE VIEW　　　**END VIEW**

LATCH DETAIL

COUNTRY CRAFTSMAN'S KNOW-HOW:
USING SQUARE-CUT NAILS

Much country furniture was assembled with nails. Craftsmen didn't often have the time, tools, or expertise to make fancy joinery, and metal screws were expensive. So they used common nails. These nails, however, were very different from modern common nails. They were hand forged, with square shanks and heads. You can still purchase hand-forged nails from: *www.tremontnail.com*

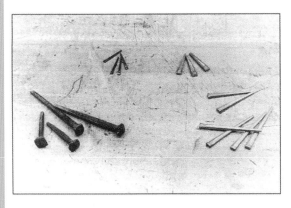

Tremont offers several sizes and styles of hand-forged nails, including a fine finishing nail. They cost a little more than regular hardware-store variety nails, but they have a more aesthetic look to them. And they will make your reproductions more authentic.

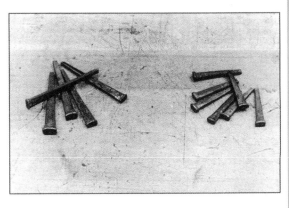

If you don't want to purchase special hand-forged nails, the closest type that's commonly available in most hardware stores is the *square-cut nail* (or, simply, cut nails). These are stamped from a sheet of thick steel, so they have square, tapered shanks and square heads. They are made to be used in cement and concrete, but will also work well in wood.

1 Whether you use a hand-forged nail or square-cut nail, you can't simply drive it into a board (particularly a hardwood board) because it acts like a small wedge and splits the wood. Instead, you must first drill a pilot hole. This hole should be slightly smaller than the width of the nail, measured about halfway along the shank.

2 Hammer the nail into the pilot hole until it protrudes just $1/16$"–$1/8$" from the surface. If the nail is rectangular, rather than truly square, make sure the widest part of the shank is parallel to the wood grain.

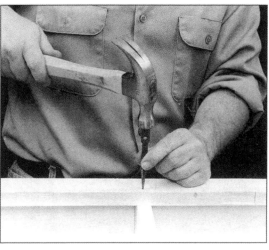

3 Drive the nail the rest of the way into the wood with a nail set, so the head rests $1/16$"–$1/8$" below the surface.

4 Cover the exposed head of the nail with wood putty, such as Durham's Water Putty. You can also make your own putty by mixing sawdust with clear epoxy glue. When the putty hardens, sand it flush with the surface. *Tip*: If you use a commercial putty, mix it with a stain or aniline dye to match the final finish on your project.

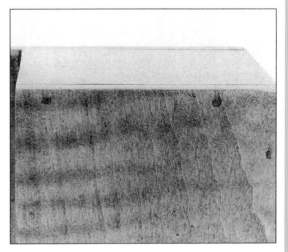

5 After you paint or finish the project, the nail holes will only be visible on close inspection. They will look as if you assembled the piece with old-time hand-forged nails.

PEWTER BENCH

In medieval Europe, it was the custom for a nobleman to display his "plate" or dinnerware on open shelves. These shelves were perhaps the most important piece of furniture in his inventory — the number of "steps" in the shelving unit showed his rank, and the quality of his plate indicated his success.

These shelves were designed to be light and transportable — European nobles and their courts often traveled to administer far-flung territories. As time went on, Europe became more politically integrated and nobles did less traveling. The plate shelves stayed put. Craftsmen began to elaborate on this form for their well-to-do clients, making it larger and heavier. By the seventeenth century, it had evolved into an ornate floor-to-ceiling cabinet with glass doors.

Country folks, however, continued to use the simpler, open shelves to store their dinner-ware. These were called by many names — *open dresser, delft rack,* and *pewter bench,* to list a few — but they all referred to the same basic design.

They were particularly popular in early colonial America, where lack of tools and time prevented the colonists from building more stylish pieces. This pewter bench is patterned after a New England plate rack built in the first half of the eighteenth century.

EXPLODED VIEW

BILL OF MATERIALS

WOODEN PARTS/_FINISHED DIMENSIONS_

A. Sides (2)   ¾" × 13" × 63¼"
B. Top   ¾" × 6¾" × 51½"
C. Valance   ¾" × 1½" × 50"
D. Top shelf   ¾" × 6" × 49¼"
E. Bottom shelves (3)   ¾" × 13" × 49¼"
F. Plate rests (4)   ¾" × ¾" × 50"

HARDWARE
6d Square-cut nails (36–40)

PLAN OF PROCEDURE

1

Plane, rip, and cut the parts to the sizes shown in the Bill of Materials.

2

Cut ¾"-wide, ⅜"-deep dadoes in the sides, as shown in the *Side Layout*.

3

Lay out and cut the shape of the sides, as shown in the *Side Layout*. Also cut the ¾" × ¾" notches for the plate rests.

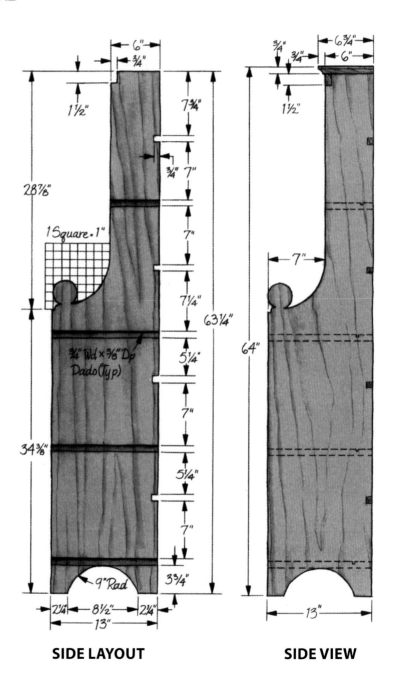

SIDE LAYOUT

SIDE VIEW

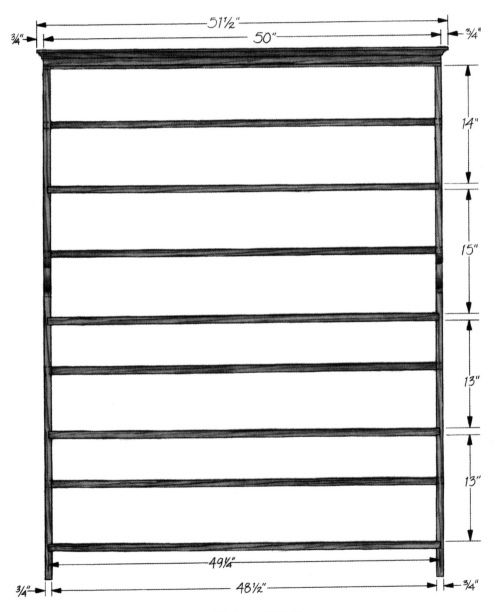

FRONT VIEW

PLAN OF PROCEDURE

4

Shape the front edge and both ends of the top shelf, as shown in the *Top Shelf Profile.*

5

Cut a ³⁄₁₆" bead in the front face of the valance, near the bottom edge, as shown in the *Valance Profile.*

6

Cut ³⁄₈"-wide, ³⁄₈"-deep grooves in the top and all bottom shelves, 1⅛" from the back edges as shown in the *Plate Groove Detail.* These grooves hold the edges of the plates.

7

Finish sand the parts of the pewter bench and dry assemble them to check the fit of the joints. Reassemble the parts with glue and square-cut nails.

8

Set the heads of the nails. If you wish, cover them with putty.

9

Do any necessary touch-up sanding and apply a finish to the completed project.

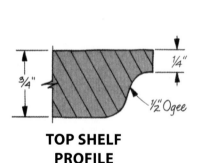

TOP SHELF PROFILE

¾"
¼"
½" Ogee

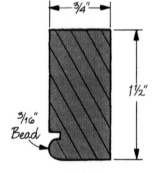

VALANCE PROFILE

¾"
1½"
³⁄₁₆" Bead

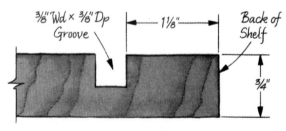

PLATE GROOVE DETAIL

³⁄₈" Wd × ³⁄₈" Dp Groove
1⅛"
Back of Shelf
¾"

OHIO CORNER CABINET

During the eighteenth century, collecting fine ceramics — particularly Oriental porcelain or "china" — became the vogue among the upper class in colonial America. Cabinetmakers began to build *cabinets* — large case pieces with shelves and glass doors — to display these collections. The fad spread to the middle class, and displaying one's "good china" became a tradition. By the early nineteenth century, the china cabinet was a common sight in American homes, both city and country.

This cabinet is patterned after one built in Cincinnati, Ohio, between 1810 and 1820. It had the same basic form as a corner cupboard, a design that evolved in England several centuries earlier. And, in typical country fashion, it displayed a mix of styles. For example, the tapered Hepplewhite legs were characteristic of Federal period craftsmanship, but the fretwork skirt showed the lingering influence of Queen Anne and Chippendale design. Yet all the elements blended well.

The original cabinet was atypical in one respect — it was smaller than most. Country corner cabinets and cupboards tended to be monstrous affairs. This small size is better suited for modern homes.

BASE DOOR
EXPLODED VIEW

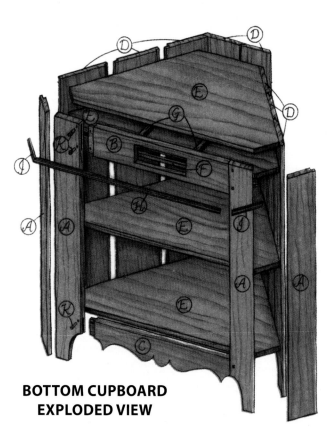

BOTTOM CUPBOARD
EXPLODED VIEW

DRAWER
EXPLODED VIEW

BILL OF MATERIALS

WOODEN PARTS/*FINISHED DIMENSIONS*

Base

A.	Front/corner stiles (4)	¾" × 4⅛" × 40"
B.	Top rail	¾" × 5" × 26½"
C.	Bottom rail	¾" × 4" × 26½"
D.	Side/back panels (8)	½" × 6½" × 40"
E.	Shelves (4)	¾" × 15" × 36⅜"
F.	Cleat	¾" × ¾" × 33⅝"
G.	Drawer guides (2)	½" × ⅞" × 14"
H.	Front middle molding	¼" × ⅝" × 32⅞"
J.	Corner middle moldings (2)	¼" × ⅝" × 4¼"
K.	Pegs (6)	$^5/_{16}$" × $^5/_{16}$" × 1¼"*

Base Door and Drawer

K.	Pegs (8)	$^5/_{16}$" × $^5/_{16}$" × 1¼"*
L.	Drawer front	⅞" × 2$^{15}/_{16}$" × 9$^{11}/_{16}$"
M.	Drawer sides (2)	½" × 2$^{15}/_{16}$" × 13½"

N.	Drawer back	½" × 2$^5/_{16}$" × 9$^{11}/_{16}$"
P.	Drawer bottom	½" × 9$^1/_{16}$" × 15⅛"
Q.	Top/bottom cock beading (2)	⅛" × ½" × 9$^{11}/_{16}$"
R.	Side cock beading (2)	⅛" × 1/2" × 2$^{15}/_{16}$"
S.	Outside base door stiles (2)	¾" × 2$^{15}/_{16}$" × 28⅞"
T.	Middle base door stile	¾" × 3" × 23⅞"
U.	Top door rail	¾" × 3" × 20½"
V.	Bottom door rail	¾" × 4" × 20½"
W.	Base door panels	½" × 8⅜" × 22½"

Cabinet Top

A.	Front/corner stiles (4)	¾" × 4⅛" × 40"
C.	Top rail	¾" × 5" × 26½"
D.	Side/back panels (8)	½" × 6½" × 40"
E.	Shelves (4)	¾" × 15" × 36⅜"
K.	Pegs (6)	$^5/_{16}$" × $^5/_{16}$" × 1¼"
X.	Bottom rail	¾" × 1½" × 26½"

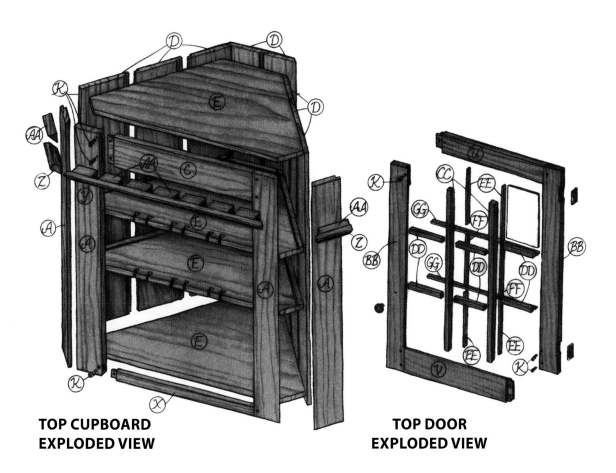

**TOP CUPBOARD
EXPLODED VIEW**

**TOP DOOR
EXPLODED VIEW**

Y.	Front top molding	¾" × 3½" × 35"
Z.	Corner top moldings (2)	¾" × 3½" × 5"
AA.	Glue blocks (6)	1⁷/₁₆" × 1⁷/₁₆" × 3½"
Top Door		
K.	Pegs (8)	⁵/₁₆" × ⁵/₁₆" × 1¼"
U.	Top door rail	¾" × 3" × 20½"
V.	Bottom door rail	¾" × 4" × 20½"
BB.	Top door stiles (2)	¾" × 2¹⁵/₁₆" × 33⅜"
CC.	Sash stiles (2)	⅜" × ⅝" × 26⅜"
DD.	Sash rails (6)	⅜" × ⅝" × 5¾"
EE.	Long vertical glazing bars (4)	⅛" × ⅜" × 9"
FF.	Short vertical glazing bars (2)	⅛" × ⅜" × 8⅞"
GG.	Horizontal glazing bars (2)	⅛" × ⅜" × 19¼"

HARDWARE
1" Door/drawer pulls (3)
1¾" × 2" Butt hinges and mounting screws (2 pairs)
Door latches (2)
6⁵/₁₆" × 9⅛" Glass panes (4 — for corners)
6⁵/₁₆" × 8¹⁵/₁₆" Glass panes (2 — for right/left middle)
6⅛" × 9⅛" Glass panes (2 — for top/bottom middle)
6⅛" × 8¹⁵/₁₆" Glass pane (1 — for middle)
Glazing compound
6d Square-cut nails (1 lb.)
⅞" Wire or headless brads (12–16)

*Make the pegs at least this long, then cut them to length
after you install them.*

PLAN OF PROCEDURE

To help this project progress smoothly, build it in two parts. First, build the cases — base and top. Then build the doors and drawer to fit the cases.

Making the Top and Base Cases

1

Glue up stock for the shelves. Then plane, rip, and cut the parts for the base and top to the sizes shown in the Bill of Materials, except the moldings. Cut the top molding stock to the proper thickness and width, but don't cut it to length yet. *Plane* the middle molding stock to the proper width (⅝"), but don't cut it to thickness or length. Bevel the adjoining edges of the front and corner stiles at 22½°, as shown in the *Top View*.

2

Cut the drawer opening in the top base rail, as shown in the *Front View*. Sand the sawed edges.

3

Cut the joinery necessary to assemble the cases:

- ½"-wide, ⅜"-deep rabbets in the square edges of the corner stiles, as shown in the *Top Back Panel Detail* and *Base Back Panel Detail*, to hold the back panels

- ⅜"-wide, ¼"-deep rabbets in the adjoining square edges of the side and back panels, so the panels will overlap

- ¼"-wide, 1"-deep, 4¼"-long mortises in the inside edges of all four front stiles, ⅜" from the top ends

- ¼"-wide, 1"-deep, ¾"-long mortises in the inside edges of the top front stiles, ⅜" from the bottom ends

- ¼"-wide, 1"-deep, 1¼"-long mortises in the inside edges of the base front stiles, 4⅜" from the bottom ends

- ¼"-thick, 1"-long tenons in the ends of all the rails; notch the tenons to fit the mortises.

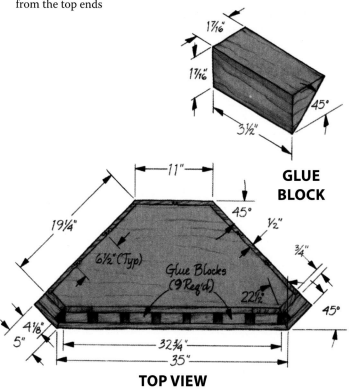

GLUE BLOCK

TOP VIEW

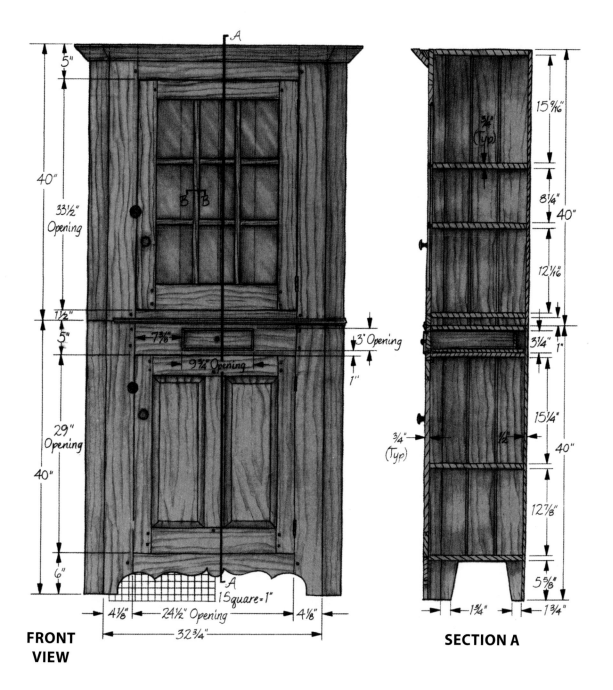

FRONT VIEW

5"

40"

33½" Opening

1½"

5"

7⅜"

9¾" Opening

29" Opening

40"

6"

4⅛"

24½" Opening

4⅛"

32¾"

15 square = 1"

A

A

B B

3" Opening

1"

SECTION A

15 9/16"

¾" (Typ)

8¼"

40"

12 1/16"

3¼"

1"

¾" (Typ)

15¼"

40"

½"

12⅞"

5⅝"

1¾"

1¾"

PLAN OF PROCEDURE

Note: You must cut ⅜"-wide notches in *most* of the tenons to fit them to their mortises, as shown in the *Case Joinery Detail*. When the stiles and rails are assembled, the outside edges of *most* of the rails should be flush with the ends of the stiles. The exception is the *bottom base rail*. Cut a ⅜"-wide notch in the top cheeks of the tenons, and 1⅜"-wide notches in the bottom. When assembled, the outside (or bottom) edge of this rail should be 3" above the bottom ends of the stiles.

4

Lay out the shapes of the shelves, as shown on the *Top Shelf Layout* and *Base Shelf Layout*. Cut the shapes and sand the sawed edges.

5

If you wish, rout or cut dovetail notches on the front edges of the top middle shelves, as shown in the *Top Shelf Layout*. You can use the notches to hold spoons.

6

Rout ¼"-wide, ¼"-deep plate grooves near the back edges of the top middle shelves.

7

Rout or cut ³/₁₆" beads near the adjoining edges of the top side and back panels, as shown in the *Top Back Panel Detail*.

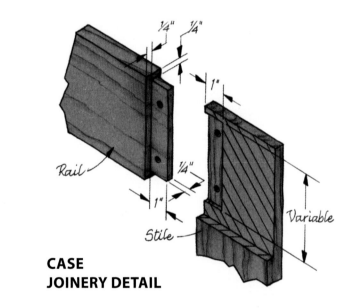

CASE JOINERY DETAIL

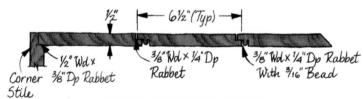

TOP BACK PANEL DETAIL

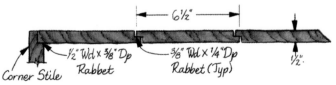

BASE BACK PANEL DETAIL

8

Finish sand the parts of the cases. Assemble the front stiles and rails with glue.

9

Round the bottom portion of 12 pegs, as shown in the *Peg Detail*.

10

Drill $5/16$"-diameter holes through the mortise-and-tenon joints in the face frames, as shown in the *Front View*. Note that the wider joints get two holes each, while the narrower joints get one. Drive the pegs through the holes from the outside. Cut the pegs off flush with the inside surfaces of the face frames.

11

Enlarge the foot pattern shown in the *Front View* and trace it on the base face frame. Cut the pattern, then sand the sawed edges.

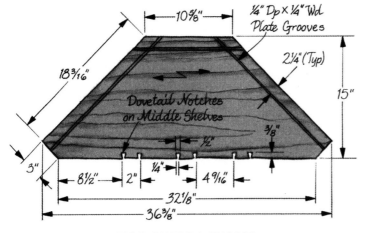

TOP SHELF LAYOUT

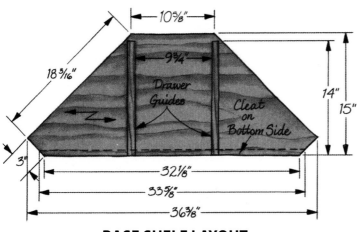

BASE SHELF LAYOUT

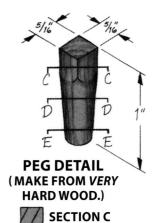

PEG DETAIL
(MAKE FROM *VERY* HARD WOOD.)

 SECTION C

SECTION D

SECTION E

PLAN OF PROCEDURE

12

Miter the ends of the cleat at 45°, then glue it to the inside surface of the base face frame.

13

Nail the drawer guides to the upper middle base shelf (the shelf that supports the drawer), as shown in the *Base Shelf Layout*.

14

Measure the positions of the shelves in the inside surfaces of the face frames. Remember, you must position the top middle shelves so they will be even with the horizontal sashes when the top door is installed. Attach the frames to the shelves with glue and nails. Temporarily, nail strips of wood to the back edges of the shelves to hold them parallel during the next few steps.

15

Apply a dark stain or black paint to the rabbeted edges of the panels. If the panels should shrink, the stain will make the gaps between them less noticeable. Otherwise, you would see strips of light-colored, raw wood in the gaps.

16

Attach the corner stiles and side panels to the shelves with nails and glue. When installing the two rearmost side panels, fit them to the cases. Mark the back edges and rip these panels to the proper width. Bevel the back edges at 45°, as shown in the *Top View*, then nail and glue them in place.

17

Remove the wooden strips that temporarily held the shelves parallel. Fit the back panels to the cases, mark the edges, and rip them to width. Once again, bevel the edges at 45°, then nail and glue them to the back edges of the shelves.

18

Sand all joints clean and flush, then rest the top assembly on the base.

19

Rout or cut the shape of the middle molding in the edges of the stock, as shown in the *Middle Molding Profile*. Rip the middle molding from the stock. Finish sand the molding.

20

Fit the middle molding to the base assembly, mitering the adjoining ends at 22½°. Using brads and glue, attach the molding to the base so it straddles the joint between the base and top. Do *not* attach the molding to the top. You should be able to remove the top from the base easily, when necessary.

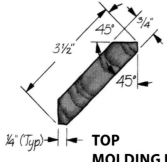

TOP MOLDING PROFILE

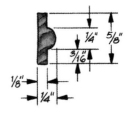

MIDDLE MOLDING PROFILE

21

Bevel the edges of the top molding stock at 45°, as shown in the *Top Molding Profile.* Finish sand the molding.

22

Fit the top molding to the top assembly, mitering the adjoining ends at 22½°. Using nails and glue, attach the molding to the top. The top edge of the molding must be flush with the top of the case. Reinforce the molding with glue blocks, as shown in the *Top View.*

23

Set the heads of all the nails and brads. Cover them with putty.

Making the Drawer and Doors

24

Measure the openings for the drawer and doors — the dimensions may have changed slightly. If so, adjust the dimensions of the door and drawer parts. Plane, rip, and cut them to size, except the drawer bottom, cock beading, sash rails, sash stiles, and glazing bars. Cut the drawer bottom about ½" longer than specified in the Bill of Materials. Cut the remaining parts to the proper thicknesses and widths, but don't cut them to length yet.

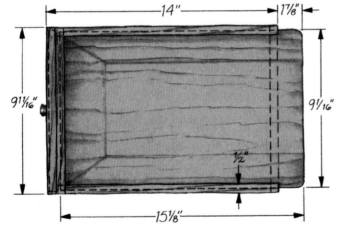

BOTTOM VIEW

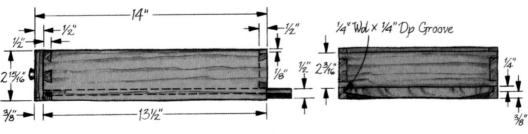

SIDE VIEW **END VIEW**

DRAWER

PLAN OF PROCEDURE

25

Cut the joinery needed to assemble the drawer:

- Half-blind dovetails to join the front to the sides, and through dovetails to join the sides to the back. (See Making Hand-Cut Dovetails on page 48.

- ⅜"-wide, ⅛"-deep rabbets all around the drawer front, as shown in the *Cock Beading Detail*, to hold the cock beading

- ¼"-wide, ¼"-deep grooves in the inside faces of the drawer front and sides, as shown in the *Drawer/End View*, to hold the drawer bottom

26

Finish sand the drawer front, sides, and back, then assemble them with glue. Sand the joints clean and flush.

27

Round one edge of the cock beading stock, then fit the beading to the drawer front. Miter the adjoining ends at 45°. Glue the beading in the top and bottom drawer front rabbets. Secure it with brads in the side rabbets.

28

Bevel the front end and both edges of the drawer bottom, so they taper to ¼", as shown in the *Drawer/End View*. Finish sand the bottom and slide it in place in the grooves. Secure it to the drawer by driving several brads through the bottom and into the drawer back.

29

Install a pull in the drawer front, then test fit the drawer in the base. If it binds, sand or plane away small amounts of stock until it slides smoothly. Cut the drawer bottom to length so when it butts against the back panels, the drawer front will be flush with the face frame. (The cock beading should protrude ⅛".)

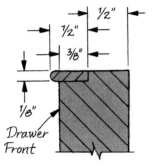

COCK BEADING DETAIL

30

Cut the joinery needed to assemble the doors:

- ¼"-wide, ⅜"-deep grooves in the inside edges of the base door rails and stiles; cut grooves in *both* edges of the base door middle stile

- ¼"-wide, ⅜"-deep *blind* grooves in the inside edges of the top door stiles — each groove should be 1"–2" long, open to the end of the board; make two grooves in each stile, cutting in from each end

- ¼"-wide, 1"-deep, 2¼"-long mortises in the inside edges of all outside stiles, ⅜" from the top ends

- ¼"-wide, 1"-deep, 3¼"-long mortises in the inside edges of all outside stiles, ⅜" from the bottom ends

- ¼"-wide, 1"-deep, 2¼"-long mortises in the inside edges of the base door rails, equally distant from either end

- ¼"-thick, 1"-long tenons in the ends of the rails and base door middle stile, where necessary; notch the tenons to fit the mortises, as shown in the *Top Door Frame Joinery Detail* and *Base Door Frame Joinery Detail*

31

Raise the base door panels, as shown in the *Base Door Panel Profile*.

32

Finish sand the door stiles, rails, and panels. Assemble them with glue. Slide the panels in place in the base door, but do *not* glue them to the door frames. The panels must float in the grooves.

33

Round the bottom portion of the remaining pegs, as shown in the *Peg Detail.*

34

Drill ⁵/₁₆"-diameter holes through the mortise-and-tenon joints in the door frames, as shown in the *Top Door Layout* and *Base Door Layout*. Drive the pegs through the holes from the outside. Cut the pegs off flush with the inside surfaces of the frames.

35

Rout a ⅜"-wide, ⅜"-deep rabbet around the inside edges of the top door frame, on the back surface. Square the corners of the rabbet with a chisel.

36

Cut and install the sash rails, sash stiles, and glazing bars, following the procedure in Installing Glass in Cabinet Doors on page 299. Sand all the joints clean and flush.

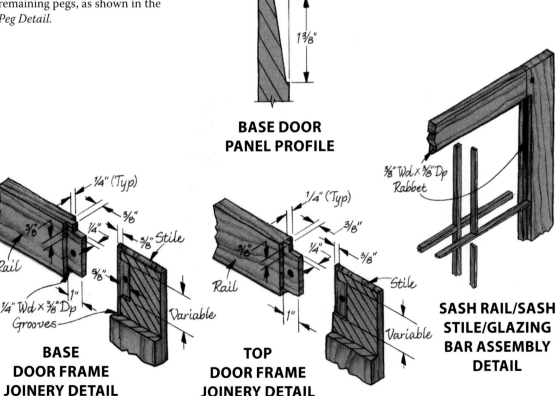

BASE DOOR PANEL PROFILE

BASE DOOR FRAME JOINERY DETAIL

TOP DOOR FRAME JOINERY DETAIL

SASH RAIL/SASH STILE/GLAZING BAR ASSEMBLY DETAIL

PLAN OF PROCEDURE

37

Mortise the left front stiles and left door stiles for hinges, then hang the doors in the cabinet. Install pulls and catches for both doors.

38

Remove the doors and drawer from the cabinet, and remove all the hardware from the doors and drawer. Take the top case off the base. Do any necessary touch-up sanding, then apply a finish to the cabinet. Coat all wooden surfaces — inside and out, front and back.

39

Put the top back on the base. Replace the hardware, then hang the doors and slide the drawer back in the cabinet.

40

Install glass panes in the top door, holding the glass in place with glazing compound. Mix paint or stain with the compound to match the finish.

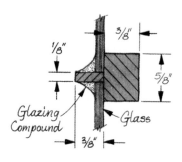

SECTION B

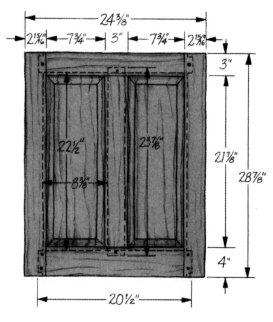

BASE DOOR LAYOUT

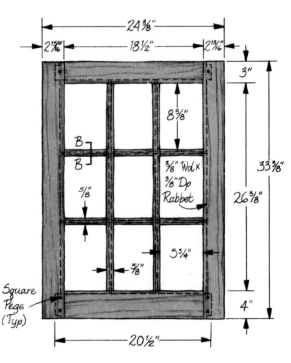

TOP DOOR LAYOUT

CHIMNEY CUPBOARD

Cabinetmakers sometimes custom made cupboards for their clients to fit the available space. One oft-heard request was for a tall, narrow storage piece to fill the otherwise unusable area between two large objects. To satisfy this request, cabinetmakers sometimes made a "chimney cupboard" — so-called because its shape reminded folks of a chimney.

This cupboard is a copy of a Shaker piece built in the New Lebanon, New York, community. The original, which now resides at the Metropolitan Museum of Art in New York City, was made in the early nineteenth century to hold tinware.

The cupboard design shows the simplicity and utility characteristic of Shaker furniture, but the construction is puzzling. Why is the top door so much larger and why does it have more panels than the bottom one? Why not three doors? This, too, may have been due to customizing. In addition to simplicity and utility, Shaker craftsmen also believed in the virtue of economy. By building just two doors, even though three would seem the logical choice, the builder eliminated the need for a third pair of hinges.

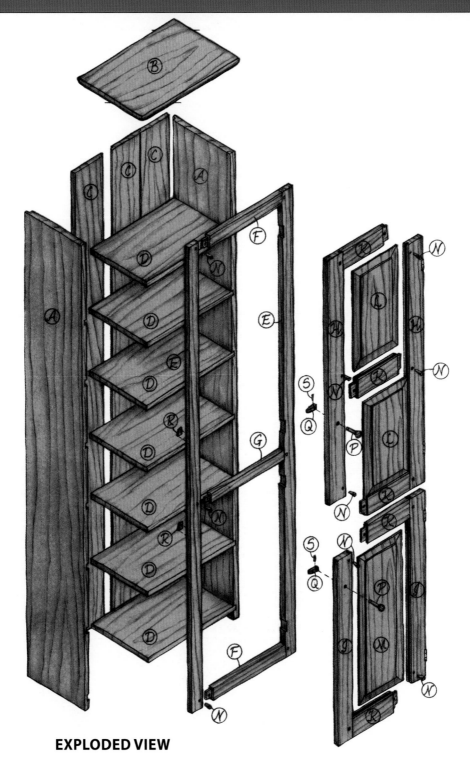

EXPLODED VIEW

PLAN OF PROCEDURE

1

If necessary, glue up stock to make the wide parts — sides, top, and shelves. Plane, rip, and cut the parts to the sizes shown in the Bill of Materials.

2

Cut the joinery needed to assemble the case:

- ¾"-wide, ⅜"-deep dadoes in the sides to hold the shelves, as shown in the *Side Layout*

- ½"-wide, ⅜"-deep rabbets in the back edges of the sides

- ½"-wide, ⅜"-deep, 17¹/₄"-long double-blind rabbet in the back edge of the top, as shown in the *Top Layout*

- ⅜"-wide, ¼"-deep rabbets in *both* edges of the middle backboard and one edge of the right and left backboards, as shown in the *Backboard Joinery Detail/ Top View*

- ¼"-wide, 1"-deep, 1¼"-long mortises in the inside edge of each face frame stile, as shown in the *Face Frame Joinery Detail*

- ¼"-wide, 1"-long tenons in the ends of the face frame rails

3

Notch the tenons on the top and bottom face frame rails to fit the mortises. Do *not* notch the tenons on the middle rail.

4

Round the front edge and both ends of the top, as shown in the *Top Edge Detail*. Sand the shaped edges.

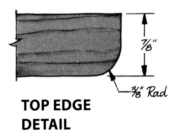

⅞"

⅜" Rad

TOP EDGE DETAIL

BILL OF MATERIALS

WOODEN PARTS/*FINISHED DIMENSIONS*

A.	Sides (2)	¾" × 11¼" × 74⅛"
B.	Top	⅞" × 12¾" × 19½"
C.	Backboards (3)	½" × 6" × 73"
D.	Shelves (7)	¾" × 10¾" × 17¼"
E.	Face frame stiles (2)	¾" × 2" × 74⅛"
F.	Top/bottom face frame rails (2)	¾" × 2" × 16"
G.	Middle face frame rail	¾" × 1¼" × 16"
H.	Top door stiles (2)	¾" × 3" × 37¾"
J.	Bottom door stiles (2)	¾" × 3" × 29⅞"
K.	Door rails (5)	¾" × 3" × 9⅞"
L.	Top door panels (2)	½" × 8½" × 15¹/₁₆"
M.	Bottom door panel	½" × 8½" × 24⁹/₁₆"
N.	Pegs (16)	¼" × ¼" × 1¼"*

P.	Door pulls (2)	1¼" dia. × 2⅝"
Q.	Door latches (2)	⅝" × 1" × 2⅝"
R.	Wedges (2)	¼" × 1" × 1½"
S.	Pins (2)	¼" dia. × 1"

*Make the pegs at least this long, then cut them to length after you install them.

HARDWARE

1½" × 2" Butt hinges and mounting screws (2 pairs)
6d Square-cut nails (36–40)
4d Square-cut nails (12–18)

PLAN OF PROCEDURE

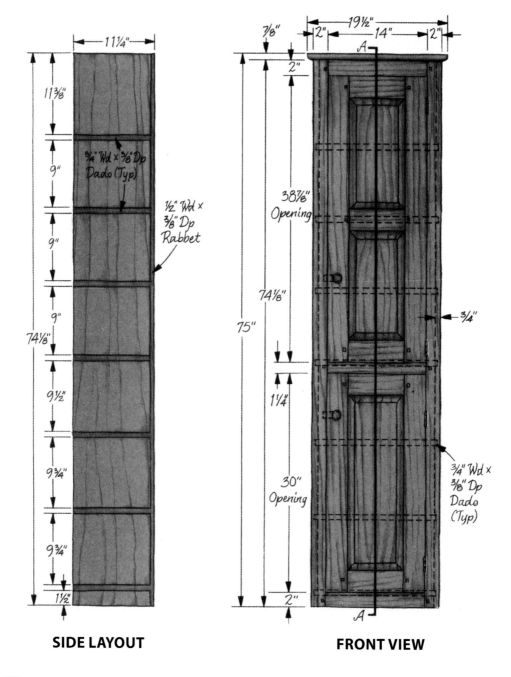

SIDE LAYOUT

FRONT VIEW

5

Stain the rabbeted edges of the backboards a dark brown or black.

6

Finish sand the parts of the face frame. Glue them together, inserting the tenons in the mortises.

7

Round the bottom portion of the pegs, as shown in the *Peg Detail*.

8

Drill a ¼"-diameter hole through each mortise and tenon in the face frame. Drive a peg into each hole to secure the tenon in the mortise, then cut off the peg flush with the inside surface of the frame.

9

Finish sand the remaining parts of the case and assemble them in the following order:

- Glue the shelves to the sides and reinforce the joints with 6d square-cut nails.

- Glue the assembled face frame to the case. Reinforce it with 6d nails.

- Attach the top to the face frame and sides with glue and 6d nails.

- Attach the backboards to the sides, top, and shelves with 4d nails. Do *not* glue the backboards in place.

As you work, sand all joints clean and flush. Set the heads of the nails. If you wish, cover the heads of the nails in the sides and front with putty.

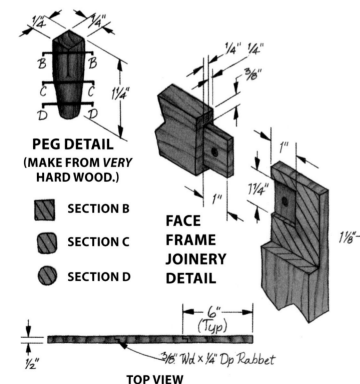

PEG DETAIL
(MAKE FROM *VERY* HARD WOOD.)

SECTION B

SECTION C

SECTION D

FACE FRAME JOINERY DETAIL

6" (Typ)

½"

⅜" Wd × ¼" Dp Rabbet

TOP VIEW
BACKBOARD JOINERY DETAIL

19½"

17¼"

1⅛"

1⅛"

½" Wd × ⅜" Dp Double-Blind Rabbet

12¾"

TOP LAYOUT

PLAN OF PROCEDURE

10

Cut the joinery needed to assemble the doors:

- ¼"-wide, ⅜"-deep grooves in the inside edges of all door rails and stiles, as shown in the *Door Frame Joinery Detail*

- ¼"-wide, 1"-deep, 2¼"-long mortises in the inside edges of the door stiles

- ¼"-wide, 1"-long tenons on the ends of the door rails

11

Notch the tenons in the rails as shown in the *Door Frame Joinery Detail*, creating a haunch in each tenon and fitting it to its mortise.

12

Raise the door panels, beveling the edges and ends to fit the grooves in the rails and stiles, as shown in *Section A*.

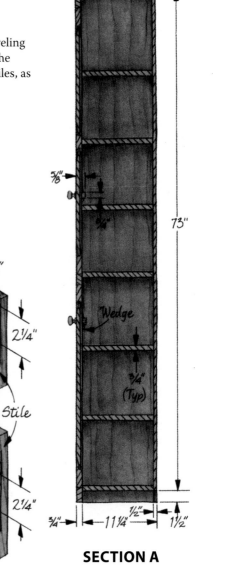

DOOR FRAME JOINERY DETAIL

Top or Bottom Rail

¼" (Typ)

⅜"

⅜"

½"

⅝" (Typ)

1"

¼" Dia (Typ)

Middle Rail

2¼"

¼"

1"

Stile

2¼"

PANEL PROFILE

1"

½"

3/16"

Wedge

¾" (Typ)

⅝"

73"

12¾"

12"

½" Wd × ⅜" Dp Rabbet

¾"

11¼"

½"

1½"

SECTION A

13

Drill a ⁹/₁₆"-diameter hole in each left door stile for the door latch assembly, as shown in the *Top Door Layout* and *Bottom Door Layout*.

14

Finish sand the door parts and assemble the rails and stiles with glue. Put the panels in place as you glue up the door frames, but do *not* apply glue to them. The panels must float in the grooves.

15

Reinforce the mortise-and-tenon joints in the door frames with pegs, as you did on the face frame.

16

Mortise the door stiles and face frame stiles for hinges, then mount the doors to the case.

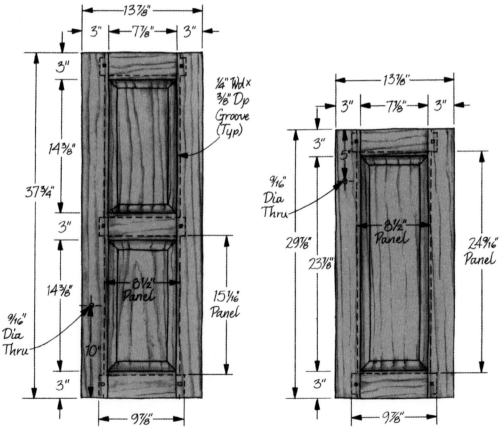

TOP DOOR LAYOUT

BOTTOM DOOR LAYOUT

PLAN OF PROCEDURE

17

Turn the door pulls as shown in the *Door Pull Layout*. Finish sand the pulls on the lathe.

18

Drill a ½"-diameter hole through each door latch, ½" from one end, as shown in the *Door Latch Assembly Detail*.

19

Bevel the end of each latch opposite the hole you just drilled. Also, cut a taper in the wedge.

20

Insert a door pull through the hole in each left door stile. Glue the latch on the pull shaft. Don't press the latch too tightly on the shaft — the pull must turn freely. Drill a ¼"-diameter hole through the latch and pull, and glue a pin in the hole.

21

Experiment with the position of the wedges on the inside face of the left face frame stile. Temporarily tape each wedge in place with double-faced tape. When you turn the pull counterclockwise, the beveled edge of the latch should contact the wedge, holding the door closed. When you find the proper position, glue the wedge to the inside surface of the stile.

22

Remove the doors and the hardware from the case. Do any necessary touch-up sanding, then apply a finish to the completed chimney cupboard. Finish *all* sides of the project — inside and out, top and bottom. Then mount the doors to the case.

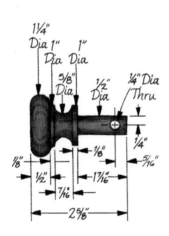

DOOR PULL LAYOUT

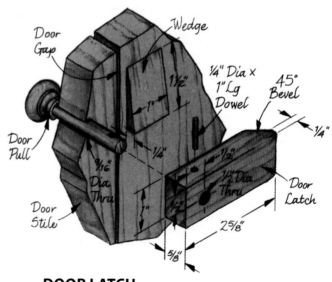

DOOR LATCH ASSEMBLY DETAIL

HANGING CORNER SHELF

Corner furniture —
triangular shelves, cup-
boards, tables, and chairs
designed to fit in a corner — was
popular in country homes.
Eighteenth- and nineteenth-
century rural cabins and houses
tended to be small, while families
were large. Consequently, folks
couldn't afford to waste an inch
of space. So when the walls and
floors filled up with furniture,
they began to use the corners.

This small shelving unit was
designed to hang in a corner,
possibly filling the space above
a table or chair. Shelves of this
size were usually more
decorative than practical
— this unit has just
three small shelves, of
three different sizes.
When every inch counts,
however, three shelves
of any size can be a
welcome addition.

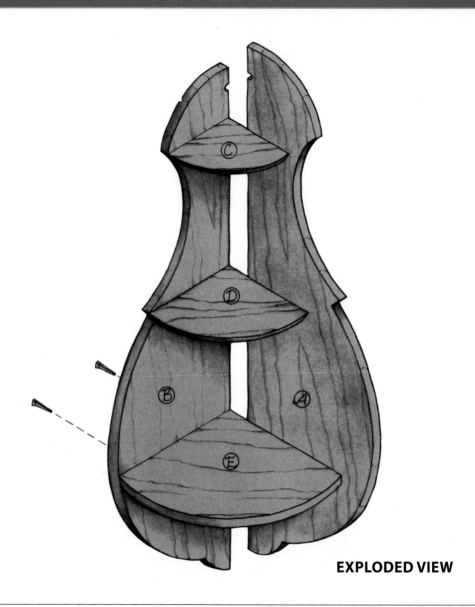

EXPLODED VIEW

BILL OF MATERIALS

WOODEN PARTS/*FINISHED DIMENSIONS*

A.	Right side	⅜" × 8¹¹⁄₁₆" × 24¾"
B.	Left side	⅜" × 8⁵⁄₁₆" × 24¾"
C.	Top shelf	⅜" × 3⅛" × 3⅛"
D.	Middle shelf	⅜" × 4¾" × 4¾"
E.	Bottom shelf	⅜" × 8⁵⁄₁₆" × 8⁵⁄₁₆"

HARDWARE
4d Square-cut nails (16–18)

PLAN OF PROCEDURE

1

Plane, rip, and cut the parts to the sizes shown in the Bill of Materials.

2

Lay out and cut the shape of the sides, as shown in the *Side View Pattern.*

3

Cut the curved edges of the shelves, beveling the top and middle shelves at 45° and the bottom shelf at 84°, as shown in the *Shelf Edge Profiles.*

4

Finish sand the parts of the corner shelf, and assemble them with glue and square-cut nails. Set the heads of the nails.

5

Drill a ¼"-diameter hole through the project, near the top where the two sides meet.

6

Do any necessary touch-up sanding and apply a finish to the completed project.

7

Drive a nail in the corner where you want the shelf. (The head of this nail must be less than ¼" in diameter, so it will fit through the hole near the top of the piece.) Hang the finished shelves from the nail.

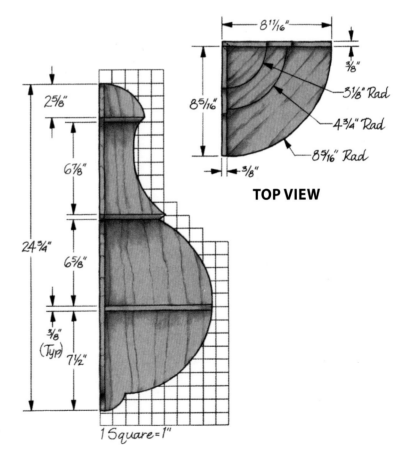

TOP VIEW

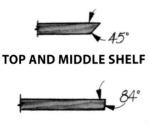

TOP AND MIDDLE SHELF

BOTTOM SHELF

SHELF EDGE PROFILES

SIDE VIEW PATTERN

PLATE SHELF

Families once kept all their dinnerware on racks like these. To save space, they made the shelves very narrow. The plates stood on edge, leaning against a rail at the back of the shelves. A shallow groove or a small molding running the length of each shelf prevented the plates from slipping off. Sometimes the craftsman added pegs or hooks underneath the shelves to hang cups and other eating or cooking utensils.

Today, most families couldn't fit their dinner service on a small rack. Plates and cups are easier to come by — and more numerous — than they once were. However, the old racks are still useful. They make good places to display collections of small items — keepsakes, boxes, dolls, old tools, and (of course) plates.

The rack shown is a small set of hanging shelves, with several pegs below the bottom shelf. The sides are shaped slightly at the bottom, and the edges of the top are molded, adding just a little decoration to an otherwise utilitarian design.

EXPLODED VIEW

BILL OF MATERIALS

WOODEN PARTS/*FINISHED DIMENSIONS*

A.	Top	½" × 5¾" × 35½"
B.	Sides (2)	½" × 5" × 32¾"
C.	Shelves (2)	½" × 5" × 33½"
D.	Valances (2)	½" × 2½" × 34"
E.	Stretchers (2)	½" × 2½" × 33"
F.	Plate rails (2)	½" × ¾" × 34"

G.	Pegs (5)	⅞" dia. × 3½"*

*Make the pegs at least this long, then cut them to length after you install them.

HARDWARE
4d Square-cut nails (16–20)

PLAN OF PROCEDURE

1

Plane, rip, and cut the parts to the sizes shown in the Bill of Materials. You can purchase pegs from most woodworking suppliers. If you plan to turn them, cut the pegs about 1" longer than specified.

2

Cut the joinery necessary to assemble the project:

- ½"-wide, ¼"-deep dadoes in the sides, as shown in the *Side Layout,* to hold the shelves

- ½"-wide, 2½"-long notches in the upper ends of the sides, to hold the valances

- ½"-wide, ¾"-long notches in the back edges of the sides to hold the plate rails

- ½"-wide, ¾"-long notches in the back edges of the sides to hold the plate rails

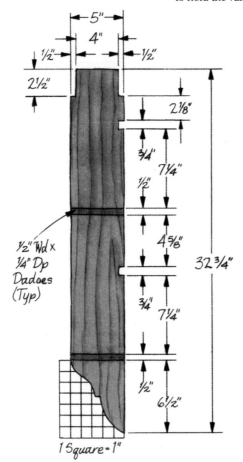

½" Wd x ¼" Dp Dadoes (Typ)

1 Square = 1"

SIDE LAYOUT

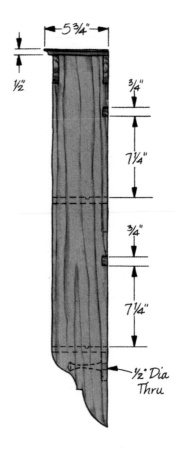

½" Dia Thru

SIDE VIEW

3

Lay out and cut the shape of
the sides, as shown in the
Side Layout.

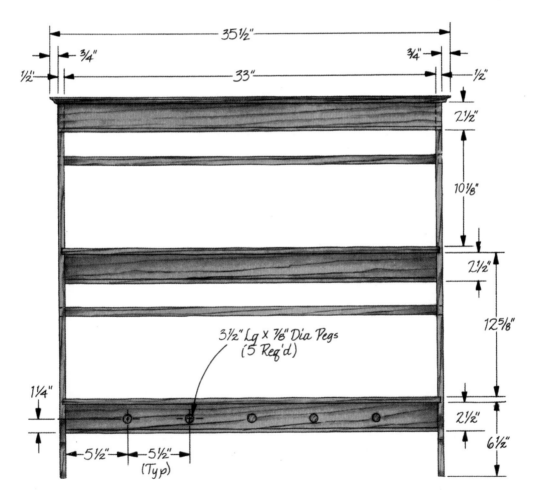

FRONT VIEW

PLAN OF PROCEDURE

4

Rout or cut the molded shapes:

- ■ ³/₁₆"-diameter beads in the lower front of the front valance and both stretchers, as shown in the *Stretcher/Valance Profile*

- ■ ⅛"-radius cove in the front and ends of the top, as shown in the *Top Edge Profile*

- ■ ¼"-wide round-bottom groove in the top surface of the shelves, as shown in the *Plate Groove Detail*

5

If you're turning your own pegs, turn them to the profile shown in the *Peg Detail*.

6

Drill ½"-diameter holes through the bottom stretcher to hold the pegs, as shown in the *Front View* and *Side View*.

7

Finish sand the parts of the plate rack and dry assemble them to check the fit of the joints. Reassemble the parts with glue and square-cut nails. Set the heads of the nails.

8

Do any necessary touch-up sanding and apply a finish to the completed project.

9

Hang the finished plate rack on the wall by driving screws or Molly anchors through the back top valance.

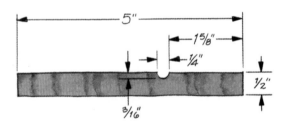

PLATE GROOVE DETAIL

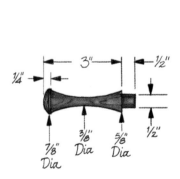

PEG DETAIL

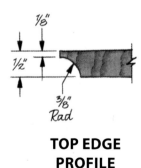

TOP EDGE PROFILE

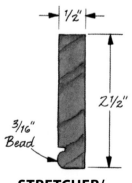

STRETCHER/ VALANCE PROFILE

WHALE SHELF

To add decoration to racks and shelves, country craftsmen often shaped the sides. Some of these contours were simple geometric patterns, laid out with a compass and a rule. Others mimicked the prevailing furniture styles or incorporated traditional folk patterns. Still others were flights of individual fancy.

During the mid-eighteenth century — the Queen Anne period — craftsmen began to incorporate flowing S-curves (also called cyma curves or *ogees*) into their furniture designs. Small sets of shelves with delicate ogee supports became very popular and continued to be made into the early nineteenth century. These shelves are an example of this motif. Folks called them "whale-end shelves" or simply "whale shelves," because the sides looked like silhouettes of surfaced whales. The shelves were cut and attached to the whale shapes so each shelf was a different width and each compartment a different height.

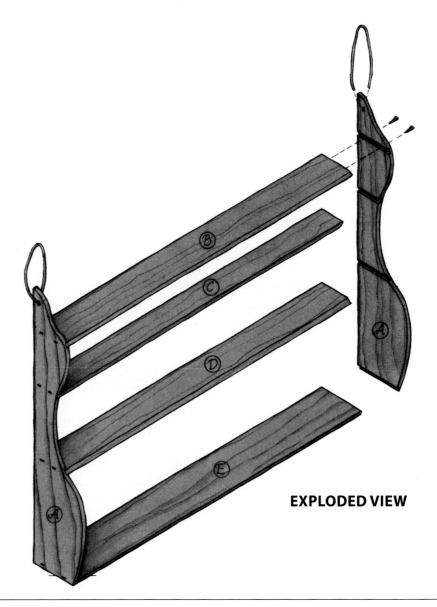

EXPLODED VIEW

BILL OF MATERIALS

WOODEN PARTS/*FINISHED DIMENSIONS*

A.	Sides (2)	½" × 7" × 33¼"
B.	Top shelf	½" × 4½" × 41½"
C.	Top middle shelf	½" × 2¾" × 41½"
D.	Bottom middle shelf	½" × 4½" × 41½"
E.	Bottom shelf	½" × 5½" × 41½"

HARDWARE
4d Square-cut nails (16)
Leather thong (12")

PLAN OF PROCEDURE

1

Plane, rip, and cut the parts to the sizes shown in the Bill of Materials. Bevel the front edge of the top, bottom middle, and bottom shelves at 65°, as shown in the *Shelving Profiles*.

2

Cut ½"-wide, ¼"-deep dadoes in the sides, as shown in the *Front View* and *Side Pattern*.

3

Lay out the *Side Pattern* and cut the shape of the sides. Sand the sawed edges.

4

Drill a ³/₁₆"-diameter hole through each side, near the top end, as shown in the *Side Pattern*.

5

Finish sand the parts of the whale shelf and dry assemble them to check the fit of the joints. Reassemble the parts with glue and square-cut nails.

6

Set the nails and cover the heads with putty.

7

Do any necessary touch-up sanding and apply a finish to the completed project.

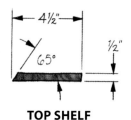

TOP SHELF

TOP MIDDLE SHELF

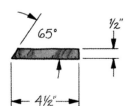

BOTTOM MIDDLE SHELF

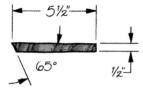

BOTTOM SHELF

SHELVING PROFILES

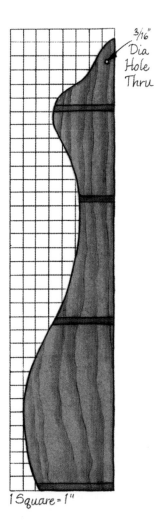

³/₁₆" Dia Hole Thru

1 Square = 1"

SIDE PATTERN

Plan of Procedure

8

Cut two 6" lengths of leather thong. Insert a thong through the hole in each side, as shown in the *Thong Detail*. Tie a knot to secure the thong.

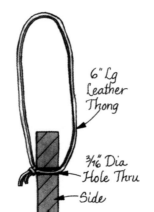

6" Lg Leather Thong

³⁄₁₆" Dia Hole Thru

Side

THONG DETAIL

9

Drive nails or install Molly anchors in the wall where you want to hang the shelf. Paint the heads to match the wall, then suspend the shelf from the nails or anchors, looping the leather thongs over them.

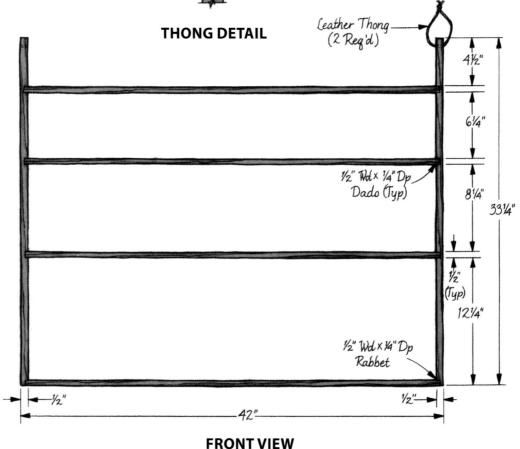

Leather Thong (2 Req'd)

4½"

6¼"

½" Wd × ¼" Dp Dado (Typ)

8¼"

33¼"

½" (Typ)

12¼"

½" Wd × ¼" Dp Rabbet

½"

½"

42"

FRONT VIEW

STEP-BACK CABINET

In the sixteenth century, Europe began to import fine porcelain from the Orient. So folks could display these treasures in a protective enclosure, joiners developed a cupboard with glass doors. The French called this a *cabinette* (which the English shortened to "cabinet"), after the word cabin, a one-room house with windows.

The techniques needed to make cabinets were more difficult than those required to make other pieces of furniture. Joiners who possessed these skills advertised themselves as "cabinetmakers." The term quickly became synonymous with makers of fine furniture.

Although American craftsmen were advertising themselves as cabinetmakers in the early 1700s, cabinets were rare in the colonies until much later. Glass was a luxury. But as America began to industrialize, it became less expensive and cabinets more common. By the nineteenth century, many country homes had glass-front cabinets in which to display their china.

There were many different styles of cabinets, but one of the most popular was this "step-back" cabinet. It's actually a cabinet top on a cupboard base. The top isn't as deep as the base, so the cabinet seems to "step back" from the wider cupboard.

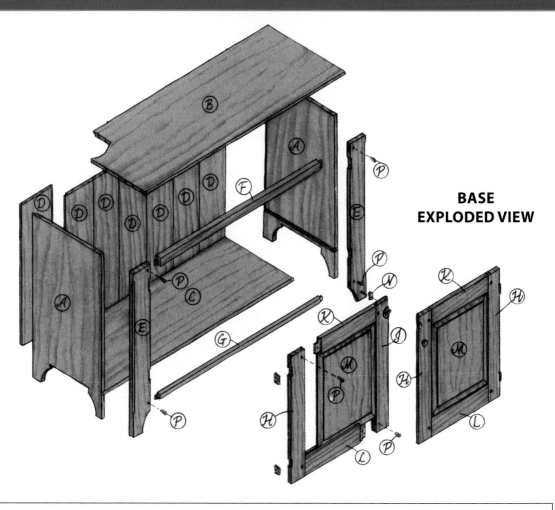

**BASE
EXPLODED VIEW**

BILL OF MATERIALS

WOODEN PARTS/*FINISHED DIMENSIONS*
Base

A.	Base sides (2)	¾" × 17¼" × 34¼"
B.	Counter	¾" × 19" × 50"
C.	Base shelf	¾" × 16¾" × 47¼"
D.	Base backboards (7)	½" × 7 1/16" × 29"
E.	Base face frame stiles (2)	¾" × 4" × 34¼"
F.	Top face frame rail	¾" × 2" × 42"
G.	Bottom face frame rail	¾" × 1" × 42"
H.	Base door stiles (3)	¾" × 3" × 26⅛"
J.	Left inside base door stile	¾" × 3⅜" × 26⅛"
K.	Top door rails (2)	¾" × 3" × 15 15/16"
L.	Bottom door rails (2)	¾" × 4" × 15 15/16"
M.	Base door panels (2)	½" × 14½" × 19 13/16"

N.	Door catch	⅝" × 1" × 1½"
P.	Pegs (12)	¼" × ¼" × 1¼"*

Cabinet

G.	Bottom face frame rail	¾" × 1" × 42"
K.	Top door rails (2)	¾" × 3" × 15 15/16"
L.	Bottom door rails (2)	¾" × 4" × 15 15/16"
N.	Door catch	⅝" × 1" × 1½"
P.	Pegs (14)	¼" × ¼" × 1¼"*
Q.	Cabinet sides (2)	¾" × 11¼" × 48½"
R.	Top	½" × 15⅜" × 54¾"
S.	Cabinet shelves (3)	¾" × 10¾" × 47¼"
T.	Cabinet backboards (7)	½" × 7 1/16" × 48¾"

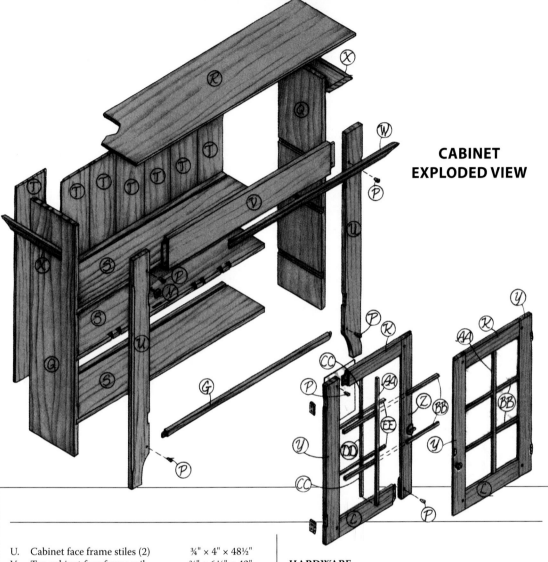

**CABINET
EXPLODED VIEW**

U.	Cabinet face frame stiles (2)	¾" × 4" × 48½"
V.	Top cabinet face frame rail	¾" × 6½" × 42"
W.	Front molding	¾" × 4⁷/₁₆" × 54¼"
X.	Side moldings (2)	¾" × 4⁷/₁₆" × 15⅛"
Y.	Cabinet door stiles (3)	¾" × 3" × 34⅞"
Z.	Left inside cabinet door stile	¾" × 3⅜" × 34⅞"
AA.	Sash stiles (2)	¾" × ⅝" × 27⅞"
BB.	Sash rails (8)	¾" × ⅝" × 6²¹/₃₂"
CC.	Top/bottom vertical glazing bars (4)	¼" × ⅜" × 9⁵/₁₆"
DD.	Middle vertical glazing bars (2)	¼" × ⅜" × 9¼"
EE.	Horizontal glazing bars (4)	¼" × ⅜" × 14⁷/₁₆"

HARDWARE

1½" × 2" Butt hinges and mounting screws (4 pairs)
Door latches (2)
Door pulls (2)
6d Square-cut nails (36–42)
4d Square-cut nails (36–42)
#8 × 1¼" Flathead wood screws (12)
⅛" × 7¹/₁₆" × 9³/₁₆" Glass panes (12)

Make the pegs at least this long, then cut them to length after you install them.

PLAN OF PROCEDURE

To help this project progress smoothly, build it in two parts. First build the base, then the cabinet to sit on top of the base.

Making the Base

1

If necessary, glue up stock to make the wide parts of the base — sides, shelf, counter, and door panels. Plane, rip, and cut the base parts to the sizes shown in the Bill of Materials, except the door parts. Cut these after you've built the base case.

2

Cut the joinery needed to assemble the base:

- ¾"-wide, ⅜-deep dadoes in the sides to hold the shelf, as shown in the *Base Side Layout*

- ½"-wide, ⅜-deep rabbets in the back edges of the sides to hold the backboards

- ½"-wide, ⅜"-deep, 47¼"-long double-blind rabbet in the back edge of the counter, as shown in the *Counter Layout,* to hold the backboards

- ⅜"-wide, ¼"-deep rabbets in *both* edges of the middle backboards, and one edge of the right and left backboards, as shown in the *Back Joinery Detail*

- ¼"-wide, 1"-deep, 1¼"-long mortises in the inside edges of the base face frame stiles, near the top ends, as shown in the *Face Frame/ Cabinet Door Joinery Detail* and *Base Face Frame Layout*

- ¼"-wide, 1"-deep, 1"-long mortises in the inside edges of the face frame stiles, near the bottom ends

- ¼"-thick, 1"-long tenons on the ends of the face frame rails

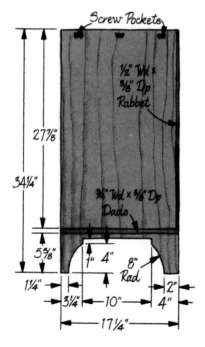

BASE SIDE LAYOUT

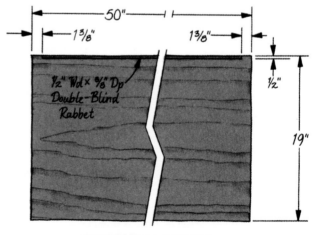

COUNTER LAYOUT

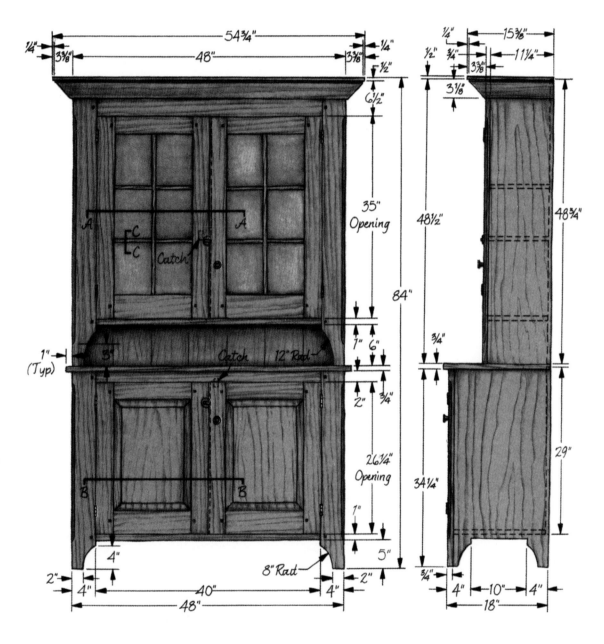

FRONT VIEW

SIDE VIEW

Plan of Procedure

3

Notch the tenons of the top base rail to fit the 1¼"-long mortises.

4

Drill screw pockets with ³⁄₁₆"-diameter pilot holes in the sides, as shown in the *Counter Joinery Detail*. Make 3 pockets in each side, near the top end. The placement of these holes is not critical, but they should be evenly spaced along each side.

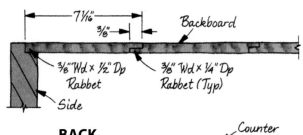

7¹⁄₁₆" ⅜" Backboard

⅜" Wd × ½" Dp Rabbet   ⅜" Wd × ¼" Dp Rabbet (Typ)

Side

BACK JOINERY DETAIL

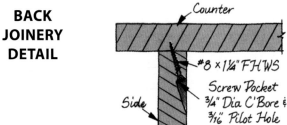

Counter

#8 × 1¼" FHWS Screw Pocket ¾" Dia C'Bore & ³⁄₁₆" Pilot Hole

Side

COUNTER JOINERY DETAIL

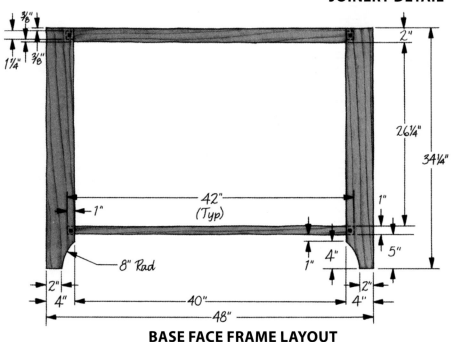

¾" ⅜"

1¼" ⅞"

2"

26¼"

34¼"

42" (Typ)

1"

1"

8" Rad

1" 4"

5"

2" 4" 40" 2" 4"

48"

BASE FACE FRAME LAYOUT

5

Lay out and cut the shapes of the sides and face frame stiles, as shown in the *Base Side Layout* and *Front View*. Chamfer the outside corners of the stiles, stopping 2" from the top ends and 5" from the bottom ends. Sand the saw and mill marks smooth.

6

Stain the rabbeted edges of the backboards a dark brown or black.

7

Finish sand the parts of the face frame. Glue them together, inserting the tenons in the mortises.

8

Round the bottom portion of the pegs, as shown in the *Peg Detail*.

9

Drill a ¼"-diameter hole through each mortise and tenon in the face frame. Drive a peg into each hole to secure the tenon in the mortise, then cut off the peg flush with the inside surface of the frame.

10

Finish sand the parts of the base case and assemble them as follows:

- Glue the shelf to the sides and reinforce the joints with 6d square-cut nails.

- Glue the assembled face frame to the case. Reinforce it with 6d nails.

- Attach the counter to the sides with screws.

- Nail the backboards to the sides, top, and shelf with 4d nails. Do *not* glue the backboards in place.

As you work, sand all joints clean and flush. Set the heads of the nails. Cover the heads of the nails in the sides and front with putty.

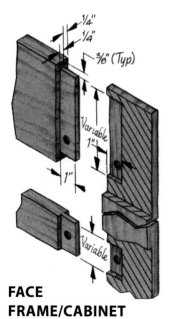

FACE FRAME/CABINET DOOR JOINERY DETAIL

SECTION D

SECTION E

SECTION F

(MAKE FROM *VERY* HARD WOOD.)

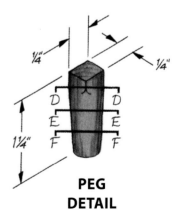

PEG DETAIL

PLAN OF PROCEDURE

11

Measure the door opening and make any necessary changes in the dimensions of the door parts. Cut the door parts to size, then cut the joinery needed to assemble the doors:

- ⅜"-wide, ⅜"-deep rabbets in the adjoining edges of the inside door stiles
- ¼"-wide, ⅜"-deep grooves in the inside edges of all door rails and stiles
- ¼"-wide, 1"-deep, 2¼"-long mortises in the inside edge of each door stile, ⅜" from each end
- ¼"-thick, 1"-long tenons on the ends of the door rails

12

Notch the tenons in the rails as shown in the *Base Door Frame Joinery Detail,* creating a haunch in each tenon and fitting it to its mortise.

13

Raise the door panels, beveling the edges to fit the grooves in the rails and stiles, as shown in *Section B.*

14

Finish sand the door parts and assemble the rails and stiles with glue. Put the panels in place as you glue up the door frames, but do not apply glue to them. The panels must float in the grooves.

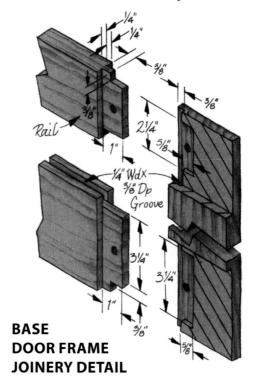

BASE DOOR FRAME JOINERY DETAIL

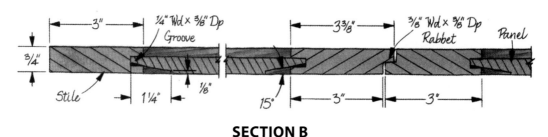

SECTION B

15

Reinforce the mortise-and-tenon joints in the door frames with pegs, as you did on the face frame.

16

Mortise the door stiles and face frame stiles for hinges, then mount the doors to the case.

17

Chamfer the top corners of the base door catch, as shown in the *Base Door Catch Detail.*

18

Using a wood screw, attach the door catch to the inside surface of the left inside base door stile (as you face the assembly), near the top end. The catch must turn freely on the screw. When turned so the chamfered end is up, it should overlap the top base face frame rail.

19

Mount a door latch on the outside surface of the left inside base door stile and a door pull on the right inside base door stile.

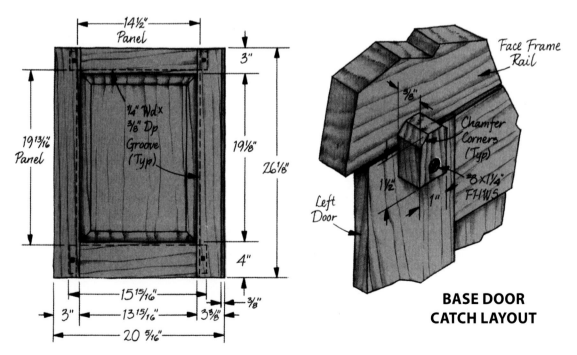

BASE LEFT DOOR LAYOUT

BASE DOOR CATCH LAYOUT

PLAN OF PROCEDURE

Making the Cabinet

20

Plane, rip, and cut the cabinet parts to the sizes shown in the Bill of Materials, except the door parts. Cut these after you've built the cabinet case.

21

Cut the joinery needed to assemble the cabinet:

- ¾"-wide, ⅜"-deep dadoes in the sides to hold the shelves, as shown in the *Cabinet Side Layout*

- ½"-wide, ⅜"-deep rabbets in the back edges of the sides to hold the backboards

- ½"-wide, ¼"-deep, 47¼"-long double-blind rabbet in the back edge of the top, as shown in the *Top Layout*, to hold the backboards

- ⅜"-wide, ¼"-deep rabbets in *both* edges of the middle backboards, and *one* edge of the right and left backboards, as shown in the *Back Joinery Detail*

- ½"-wide, ⅜"-deep dovetail notches in the front edges of the top and middle shelves, as shown in the *Cabinet Shelf Layout*, to hold spoons

- ¼"-wide, ⅜"-deep, 1¾"-long mortise in the middle shelf for the cabinet catch

- ⅜"-wide, ⅜"-deep grooves in the shelves, 1¼" from the back edges, to hold plates

- ¼"-wide, 1"-deep, 5¾"-long mortises in the inside edges of the face frame stiles, near the top ends, as shown in the *Face Frame/Cabinet Door Joinery Detail* and *Cabinet Face Frame Layout*

- ¼"-wide, 1"-deep, 1"-long mortises in the inside edges of the face frame stiles, near the bottom ends

- ¼"-thick, 1"-long tenons on the ends of the face frame rails

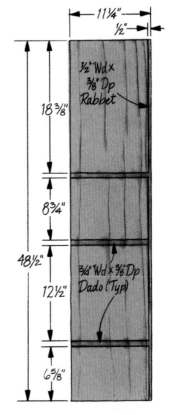

CABINET SIDE LAYOUT

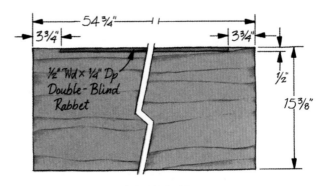

TOP LAYOUT

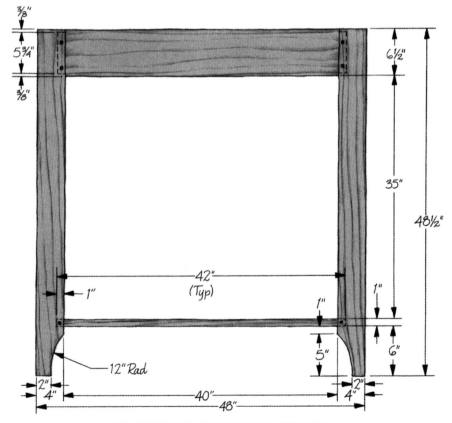

CABINET SHELF LAYOUT

CABINET FACE FRAME LAYOUT

PLAN OF PROCEDURE

22

Notch the tenons of the top cabinet rail to fit the mortises.

23

Lay out and cut the shapes of the face frame stiles, as shown in the *Front View*. Chamfer the outside corners of the stiles, stopping 6½" from the top ends and 3" from the bottom ends. Sand the saw and mill marks smooth.

24

Finish sand the parts of the face frame. Glue them together, inserting the tenons in the mortises. Reinforce the mortise-and-tenon joints with pegs.

25

Finish sand the parts of the cabinet case and assemble them as follows:

- Glue the shelves to the sides and reinforce the joints with 6d square-cut nails. (The plate grooves in all the shelves and the mortise in the middle shelf must face up.)

- Glue the assembled face frame to the case. Reinforce it with nails.

- Attach the top to the sides with nails. Don't drive the nails all the way in, so you can adjust the position of the top later.

26

Cut the 45° bevels in the moldings, as shown in the *Molding Detail*.

27

Fit the top moldings to the case, compound-mitering the adjoining ends at 45°.

28

Finish sand the moldings. Attach the front molding to the case with glue and nails. Attach the side moldings with nails only — do *not* glue them in place. If necessary, shift the position of the top to center it over the moldings.

29

Stain the rabbeted edges of the backboards a dark brown or black.

30

Nail the backboards to the sides, top, and shelves with 4d nails. Do *not* glue the backboards in place.

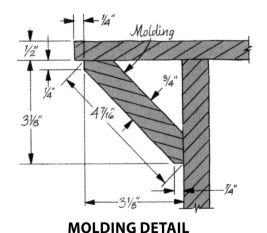

MOLDING DETAIL

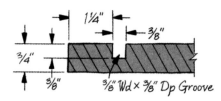

PLATE GROOVE DETAIL

31

Sand all joints clean and flush. Set the heads of the nails. Cover the heads of the nails in the sides and front with putty.

32

Measure the door opening and make any necessary changes in the dimensions of the door parts. Cut the door rails and stiles to size, then cut the joinery needed to assemble the door frames:

- ½"-wide, ⅜"-deep rabbets in the adjoining edges of the inside door stiles

- ¼"-wide, 1"-deep, 2¼"-long mortises in the inside edge of each door stile, ⅜" from each end

- ¼"-thick, 1"-long tenons on the ends of the door rails

33

Notch the tenons in the rails as shown in the *Face Frame/ Cabinet Door Joinery Detail*, fitting each tenon to its mortise.

34

Finish sand the door parts and assemble the rails and stiles with glue. Reinforce the mortise-and-tenon joints with pegs.

35

Rout a ¼"-wide, ⅜"-deep rabbet all around the inside edges of the cabinet door frames. Square the corners where the rabbets meet with a chisel.

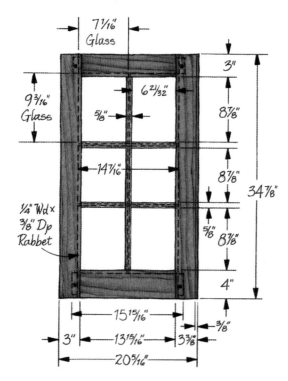

TOP LEFT DOOR LAYOUT

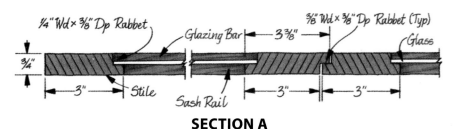

SECTION A

PLAN OF PROCEDURE

36

Cut and install the sash rails, sash stiles, and glazing bars, following the procedure in Installing Glass in Cabinet Doors. Sand all the joints clean and flush.

37

Mortise the door stiles and face frame stiles for hinges, then mount the doors to the case.

38

Taper one end of the cabinet door catch, as shown in the *Cabinet Door Catch Detail.*

39

Using a wood screw, attach the door catch to the inside surface of the left inside cabinet door stile, just above the middle shelf. The catch must turn freely on the screw. When turned so the tapered end is down, it should rest in the shelf mortise.

40

Mount a door latch on the outside surface of the left inside cabinet door stile and a door pull on the right inside cabinet door stile.

Finishing Up

41

Remove the doors from the base and cabinet and remove all the hardware from the doors. Do any necessary touch-up sanding, then apply a finish to the base, cabinet, and doors. Coat all wooden surfaces — inside and out, front and back.

42

Put the cabinet on the base. Replace the hardware, then hang the doors.

43

Install glass panes in the cabinet doors, holding the glass in place with glazing compound. Mix paint or stain with the compound to match the finish.

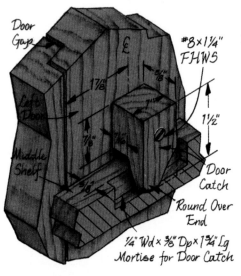

CABINET DOOR CATCH DETAIL

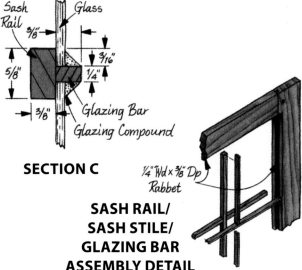

SECTION C

SASH RAIL/ SASH STILE/ GLAZING BAR ASSEMBLY DETAIL

COUNTRY CRAFTSMAN'S KNOW-HOW:
INSTALLING GLASS IN CABINET DOORS

Country craftsmen never mounted large panes of glass in their cabinets, for a very good reason: There weren't any available. The technology needed to cast large, flat panes wasn't developed until the late nineteenth century, well after the country furniture era. Instead, when they wanted to make a large glass cabinet door, they arranged several smaller panes in a delicate wooden frame usually in multiples of 3 or 4. This framework was called sash work or *glazing*.

There is no one way to make glazing. The glass panes can be configured many different ways, and the wooden parts can be lapped, mitered, mortised, or simply butted together. Country craftsmen, as you might expect, usually kept the glazing simple. They configured the glass in a simple grid, often in multiples of three or four. Four-, nine-, and twelve-pane doors were the most common. This, in turn, simplified the joinery. The glazing shown is assembled with ordinary butt joints.

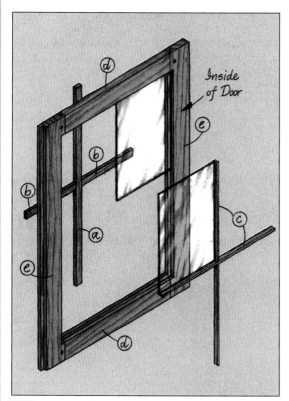

1 This glazing consists of three parts: The vertical outside moldings are called *sash stiles (a)*, the horizontal outside moldings are *sash rails (b)*, and the narrow, inside strips that actually support the glass are *glazing bars (c)*. These are set into an ordinary door frame consisting of *rails (d)* and *stiles (e)*.

2 Before you can install the glazing, you must have something to set it in. Make a door frame, then rout a deep rabbet all around the inside. Square the corners of the rabbet with a chisel.

COUNTRY CRAFTSMAN'S KNOW-HOW:
INSTALLING GLASS IN CABINET DOORS—*CONTINUED*

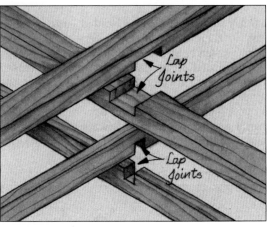

3 Carefully measure the inside dimensions of the frame, then cut the sash stiles, sash rails, and glazing bars to fit it. The sash stiles should span the opening from top to bottom. The sash rails, because they are interrupted by the stiles, will be somewhat shorter. Likewise, the horizontal glazing bars span the opening from side to side, and the vertical bars will be shorter. These parts must fit snug, but not so tight that they bow.

4 Some craftsmen prefer to lap the sash rails and stiles — or vertical and horizontal glazing bars — for extra strength. If you choose to do this, you must measure the position of these lap joints very precisely.

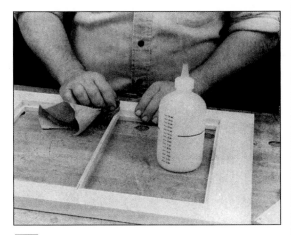

5 Rest the frame on its front surface. Dry assemble the parts in it. Carefully arrange them so the openings in the grid are the sizes required. (In most projects, the grid openings should all be the same size.) Mark the locations of the parts on the door frame and each other, then remove the parts.

6 Glue the horizontal glazing bars in the frame first. Apply the glue generously, and wipe away any that squeezes out with a wet rag. The inside edges of the bars must be flush with the inside surfaces of the door frame.

7 Next, install the sash stiles, gluing them to the door rails and the glazing bars. Check that all the parts are square to one another and properly positioned — the outside surfaces of the sash stiles must be flush with the outside surfaces of the door frame. Let the glue dry completely.

8 Glue the vertical glazing bars to the door frame, sash stiles, and horizontal bars. Make sure the bars are centered on the sash stiles.

9 Finally, glue the sash rails to the horizontal glazing bars, sash stiles, and door frame. Once again, make sure the sash rails and bars are centered — this will create many small ledges and lips in which to rest the glass panes.

10 Complete the cabinet and apply a finish. Then install the glass panes in the door, holding them in place with glazing compound. Mix this compound with paint, stain, or dye to match the finish on the cabinet.

Note: For an accurate country reproduction, use "antique" glass. This glass is cast with imperfections to mimic old-time glass. It's available through most glass shops.

PIPE BOX

Although we remember these small, hanging boxes as "pipe boxes," they weren't originally intended to hold pipes. Most country gentlemen had only one or two pipes — hardly enough to fill a box — and those usually had short stems. Only in taverns and inns, where the proprietor kept a selection of long-stem clay pipes for guests, did pipe boxes really hold pipes.

Originally, these boxes had another purpose altogether — and another name. Folks built them to hold "candles" — not the wax candles we think of, but slender sticks of candlewood (resinous pine) or lengths of dried, pithy rush soaked in tallow. Wax candles were a luxury in colonial America; common people usually burned these strips of pine and rush for light at night. Because they burned quickly — each candle lasted no more than fifteen or twenty minutes — folks had to keep a large supply at hand. They filled their "candle boxes" before dusk each day.

The box shown is an original design, but it's typical of early American candle boxes — or pipe boxes, if you prefer. A deep bin, open at the top, held the candlewood or rush. A small drawer at the base held flint, an iron striker, and "punk" to help light the candles.

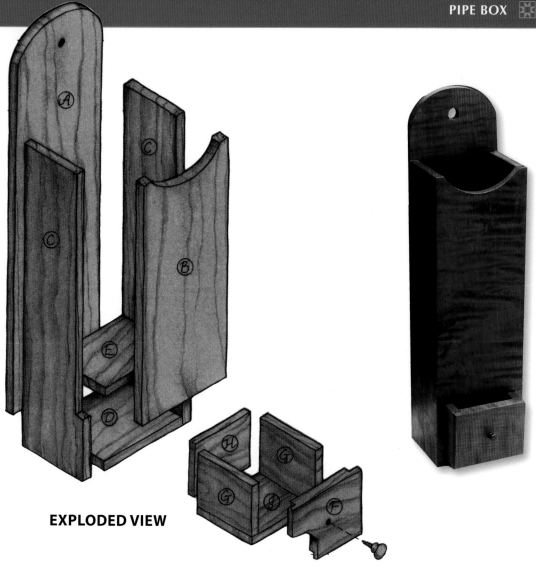

EXPLODED VIEW

BILL OF MATERIALS

WOODEN PARTS/*FINISHED DIMENSIONS*

A.	Back	$\frac{3}{8}" \times 4\frac{1}{4}" \times 16"$
B.	Front	$\frac{3}{8}" \times 4\frac{1}{4}" \times 9\frac{3}{4}"$
C.	Sides (2)	$\frac{3}{8}" \times 2\frac{7}{8}" \times 12\frac{5}{8}"$
D.	Bottom	$\frac{3}{8}" \times 2\frac{7}{8}" \times 3\frac{1}{2}"$
E.	Bin bottom	$\frac{3}{8}" \times 2\frac{1}{2}" \times 3\frac{1}{2}"$
F.	Drawer front	$\frac{3}{8}" \times 2\frac{13}{16}" \times 3\frac{7}{16}"$
G.	Drawer sides (2)	$\frac{3}{8}" \times 2\frac{9}{16}" \times 2\frac{3}{4}"$
H.	Drawer back	$\frac{1}{4}" \times 2\frac{9}{16}" \times 2\frac{11}{16}"$
J.	Drawer bottom	$\frac{1}{4}" \times 2\frac{3}{4}" \times 3\frac{7}{16}"$

HARDWARE

$\frac{1}{2}"$ Brass knob
$\frac{7}{8}"$ Wire or "headless" brads (30–40)

PLAN OF PROCEDURE

1

Plane, rip, and cut the parts to the sizes shown in the Bill of Materials.

2

Cut ⅜"-wide, 9¾"-wide notches in the sides, as shown in the *Side View*.

3

Lay out and cut the shapes of the back and front, as shown in the *Front View*.

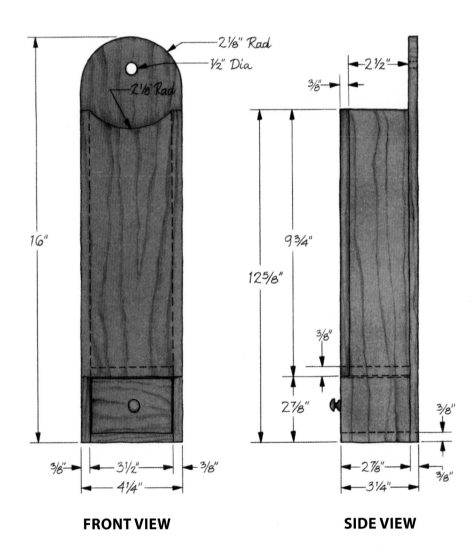

FRONT VIEW   **SIDE VIEW**

4

Finish sand the parts of the pipe box that you have made so far. Assemble them with glue and wire brads. Set the heads of the brads.

5

Cut ⅜"-wide, ¼"-deep rabbets in the ends of the drawer front, as shown in the *Drawer Detail/ Top View.*

6

Lightly sand the drawer parts, then assemble them with glue and brads. Set the brads.

7

Finish sand the drawer front and install a drawer pull. Place the drawer in the pipe box to check the fit, and make any necessary adjustments.

8

Remove the drawer from the box and the pull from the drawer. Do any necessary touch-up sanding and apply a finish to the completed project.

9

Replace the pull on the drawer and rub the bottom of the drawer with soap or wax to help it slide more easily. Replace the drawer in the finished pipe box.

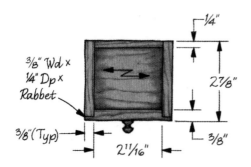

⅜" Wd × ¼" Dp × Rabbet

¼"

2⅞"

⅜" (Typ)

2¹¹⁄₁₆"

⅜"

TOP VIEW

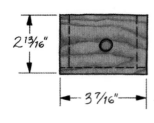

2¹³⁄₁₆"

3⁷⁄₁₆"

FRONT VIEW

¼" Wd × ¼" Dp Rabbet

2³⁄₄"

2⅞"

2⁹⁄₁₆"

¼"

SIDE VIEW

DRAWER DETAIL

FINISH

FINISHING PHILOSOPHY

Of the three important elements in American country furniture — design, construction, and finish — the finish, most of all, decides the effect that a project has on its viewer. Design and construction determine the purpose of a project, but finish bestows its "look" — the mood, feeling, and ambience of a piece.

To illustrate, imagine that you've made two small cupboards following the same plan. One is built from an elegant hardwood, such as cherry or walnut, and the other from a plainer wood such as poplar. You outfit the fancy hardwood cupboard with brass hardware and the other with iron. Finally, you apply a natural finish to the hardwood piece, and paint the plain piece.

Even though these two cupboards are designed and constructed identically, they will have different effects on an observer. The naturally finished piece will look much more sophisticated. The painted piece will have a down-home, utilitarian appearance. The fancier piece would best

be placed in a formal dining room or living room, while the plainer one would look more at home in a kitchen or family room.

Before you finish a country piece, consider the effect or look you want — *how you want it to appear to a viewer* — then choose from the many different finishes available to you. Choose carefully! You can ruin days, weeks, even months of work by applying the wrong finish to properly designed and constructed furniture.

NATURAL VERSUS ARTIFICIAL AGING

Perhaps the most important question you must answer when choosing a finish is whether or not you want it to look aged immediately upon finishing it. There are two schools of thought on this question.

The first maintains that historical and historically inspired furniture should be finished in a *traditional* manner and allowed to age naturally. Apply old-time country finishing materials using country methods, appropriate to the same period in which the furniture would have been built. Then let the piece develop a natural patina over many years —just as an antique would have aged.

The second (and currently most popular) school holds the opposite view: An antique reproduction ought to look like an antique. Use both traditional and modern finishing materials and methods to create an artificial patina, complete with dings and scratches. A finish that successfully imitates the natural aging process is sometimes called a *museum-quality finish*.

The finishing philosophy that's right for you will depend on your tastes and the look you want your project to have. You might even switch philosophies now and again, depending on what

These two sofa tables are similar in size and design. However, they were finished differently. One was stained and lacquered, the other grain-painted. This gives them a completely different look. The stained piece appears reserved and formal, the painted piece festive and folksy.

you build and how you use it. The Workshops is best known for the museum-quality finishes that they apply to their furniture, but they sometimes apply a traditional finish on request.

EXPERIMENTATION AND EXPERIENCE

No matter what effect you're after, whether you use a clear, natural varnish or paint the wood, whether you let the piece age naturally or age it artificially, every finish requires a singularly important first step: You must experiment with the planned finishing procedure and the materials *before* you apply the finish to the completed project. This may save a great deal of refinishing later on.

As you build, save the larger scraps from your project. Finish sand these at the same time you sand the other parts, then set them aside. When you've completed the project, get out the scraps again. Use them to experiment with finishing materials. If you're undecided as to what look you want, finish several different scraps using different methods. If you've never tried a finish technique before, practice on a scrap to gain experience.

These practice runs are especially important if you decide to apply a museum-quality finish. Artificially aging a project generally requires several different materials and methods — more so than other finishes. Some materials may be incompatible, causing a chemical reaction that could ruin your project. Or you may have unanticipated problems with your equipment. Unless you're an experienced finisher, always try the finish on a scrap first.

Both of these salt boxes have milk paint finishes. One, however was painted with an old-time recipe and will age naturally. The other was finished with more modern materials and aged artificially.

This scrap was used to experiment with grain-painting techniques. In each experiment, the craftsman used the same tool and the same colors; he just applied them differently. As you can see, a little change in finishing technique can make a big difference. If you're in doubt as to how the finish will turn out, practice first on a scrap.

TRADITIONAL FINISHES

You might expect that the choice of finishes in eighteenth- and nineteenth-century America was more limited than it is now, but this was not the case. Although country craftsmen didn't have ready-mixed finishes as we do, they had plenty of ingredients for mixing their own. Furthermore, they often experimented with different mixes before settling on something they liked.

As a result, there were no truly "traditional" finishing materials. Each craftsman had one or more mixtures that he preferred, and these were as unique as his own signature. There were, however, several finishing methods that became popular during the Country era (1690 to 1860) in America. It's these techniques that we remember as traditional country finishes.

A BRIEF HISTORY OF FINISHING

Finishing was a relatively new practice among American *country* craftsmen. Furniture finishing, of course, had begun with furniture making. The Egyptians, Greeks, and Romans used a variety of materials to protect the surface of their furniture and enhance its appearance. These included varnishes (a mixture of resins and oils or spirits) and paints (pigments suspended in oils). However, all but the most basic finishing techniques were forgotten in Europe during the Dark Ages. For over 1,000 years the sparse, crude furniture of the medieval era was either painted or left unfinished.

As Europe climbed out of the Dark Ages and furniture styles once again began to evolve, so did finishing techniques. During the Gothic period, joiners began to polish the surface of their furniture by rubbing it with a liquid or semi-liquid material such as linseed oil, walnut oil, or a mixture of turpentine and beeswax. The harder they rubbed, the more oil or wax built up on the surface of the wood. After a lot of elbow grease had been expended, the surface became smooth as glass. This painstaking rubbing technique was the first to be called *finishing*. By the sixteenth century, finishing had largely replaced painting on stylish European furniture, although most country pieces were still painted.

With the Renaissance, European craftsmen experimented with dozens of new finishing materials and techniques. They rediscovered varnishes, which quickly replaced oils and waxes as the preferred finish on quality furniture. Varnish, they found, preserved the wood better and held its gloss longer than previous materials.

Trade with the Orient introduced Europe to many exotic varnishes, most importantly lacquer. Lacquer was made from the resin of the Chinese sumac tree, *Rhus vemiciflua*. Although it needed special conditions to harden (it was often applied in a damp basement or cave), it dried quickly and allowed the craftsmen to build up many layers in a short time. Oriental craftsmen used this property to build up three-dimensional pictures on the lacquered surfaces of their furniture.

European cabinetmakers began to imitate this technique, but true Chinese lacquer was rare. They invented several substitute finishes such as *gesso,* a mixture of plaster of paris and sizing. Gesso could be applied much thicker than lacquer; the surface built up much more rapidly. However, if skillfully done, the result was very similar to true lacquer. The art of applying three-dimensional, pictorial finishes with gesso and other lacquer substitutes became known as *japanning,* since most lacquered furniture was imported from Japan.

During the late Renaissance, France began to import another varnish finish, *shellac*. Shellac was the resinous excrement of the lac bug, an insect native to India and Ceylon. When dissolved in alcohol, the mixture dried so quickly that multiple layers could be built up in minutes. French cabinetmakers took advantage of this property and developed the *French polish*. Use of shellac quickly spread to other countries.

This was the state of the finishing art as Europe began to colonize America. Cabinetmakers were in the midst of an explosion of new finishing materials and techniques, although much of this was confined to city craftsmen. Most country furnituremakers continued to use hand-rubbed oil or that ancient stand-by, paint. But a few had begun to experiment with innovative varnish mixtures. They brought all of these ideas, both old and new, with them to the New World. By the time of the American Revolution, country craftsmen were using most of the same techniques as their counterparts in the city.

DUPLICATING TRADITIONAL FINISHING MATERIALS

Perhaps the most difficult task in duplicating a traditional country finish is obtaining the same materials a country craftsman might have used. However, you can find most of these if you look around—consult the Sources section for names and addresses.

You also have to know what you're looking for. For example, most eighteenth- and nineteenth-century varnishes were made from *copal* resin. Copal was extracted from the copa tree, a variety of cedar that grew in Central America and Africa. You can't use modern varnishes for a traditional finish. Most of these are distilled from flax seed or the tung tree.

Paints, too, have changed. To make old-time paints opaque, craftsmen added *lime paste* (hydrated or "slaked" lime and water) to their paint recipe. Today, paint manufacturers use titanium dioxide and silicates for the same purpose. However, several finishing companies still sell powdered mixes that use lime.

A few traditional finishes, such as hand-rubbed oils and shellac, haven't changed in 200 years. You can purchase these right off the shelf in most paint or hardware stores. And you can come close to re-creating others by making them from scratch.

APPLYING TRADITIONAL FINISHES

Hand-Rubbed Oil — The most common material used for hand-rubbed oil finishes was boiled linseed oil. (The oil was boiled to prevent it from going rancid.) However, cabinetmakers also employed walnut oil, cottonseed oil, and other plant oils. Add 2 tablespoons of japan drier per pint of oil.

1 Carefully remove all mill marks and other evidence of power tools, then finish sand the surface to 220#.

2 Apply a generous coat of oil and rub into the wood with your hands. (The warmth of your hands helps the oil to penetrate deeply.) Allow it to soak in for a few hours, then wipe off the excess.

3 Apply yet more oil and polish the wood with 320# wet/dry paper. (Old-time craftsmen used sharkskin.) The sandpaper will create a fine sawdust, which mixes with the oil to make a paste. This, in turn, fills imperfections in the wood and creates a glass-smooth surface. Wipe off the excess.

4 Allow the oil to dry overnight, then apply another coat. Rub it in vigorously with a clean cloth.

5 Allow the second coat to dry overnight, and repeat as needed until you build up the gloss you want.

Hand-Rubbed Beeswax — You can purchase beeswax from dental supply outlets, crafts stores, and some hardware stores. Cut or break the beeswax into small chunks, pack it into a jar, and add just enough turpentine to cover the wax. You may also want to add a small amount of carnauba wax to make the finish harder. Allow the mixture to sit overnight. In the morning you'll find the beeswax has turned into a soft paste. If the paste is too stiff, add more turpentine; if it's runny, a=dd more wax. (If you add carnauba, gently warm the mixture in a pan of water over an electric burner to melt the two waxes together. **Warning:** Do *not* use an open flame.)

1 Carefully remove all mill marks and other evidence of power tools, then finish sand the surface to 220#.

2 Apply the beeswax paste to a small area with a soft cloth, rubbing vigorously.

3 Allow the wax to set for a few minutes, then polish it with clean cheesecloth. Continue rubbing until you remove all the streaks and the wax is buffed to a high gloss.

4 Repeat, applying wax to just one small area at a time until you've finished the entire project.

Brushed-On Varnish — Varnishes are more finicky than most finishes and require the proper conditions. The finishing room must be relatively free of dust, and the temperature should be between 65° and 85°F. Use a good animal bristle brush and prepare it by soaking the brush in turpentine for a day or so. Just before you use it, remove the brush from the turpentine and wipe it clean on a rag or paper. This will remove any loose bristles.

1 Carefully remove all mill marks and other evidence of power tools, then finish sand the surface to 220#.

2 "Fill" the brush by dipping half the length of the bristles into the varnish. Do *not* wipe the brush on the sides of the container.

3 Let the varnish "flow" onto the surface of the wood, wiping the brush *across* the grain until the bristles are fairly dry.

When mixing waxes for a hand-rubbed wax finish, melt them together in a water bath over an *electric* burner. Do *not* use an open flame.

After you apply the varnish across the grain, smooth it with just the tip of the brush, wiping with the grain. Hold the brush nearly vertical as you do this.

4 Repeat, starting the next set of brush strokes 1"–2" inside the area you covered with the first set. Wipe toward the unvarnished area. Continue until you've covered the entire surface.

5 While the varnish is still wet, smooth it with the very tip of the brush, wiping *with* the grain.

6 Allow the first coat to dry completely (usually 6–12 hours). The varnish will look awful. There will be dimples, specks, and other marks, but this is normal. Sand out the imperfections with wet/dry 320# sandpaper. To prevent the sandpaper from loading, dip it in linseed oil from time to time as you work.

Note: Be careful not to sand through the varnish at the edges and corners. Use a sanding block to apply even pressure over the entire surface.

7 Repeat Steps 2 through 6 to build up several coats of varnish.

8 Rub out the last coat with linseed oil and pumice stone. Fold a soft, clean cloth into a pad and soak it in oil. Press the pad into the pumice, then rub the varnish vigorously. Replenish the oil and pumice on the pad as needed. Periodically, wipe away the grime from the surface to check your progress. Continue until the varnished surface has a smooth, even sheen.

9 Apply a paste wax, such as a beeswax/carnauba mixture, to the varnished surface and buff it.

French Polish — You can apply shellac with a brush in a similar manner as varnish. However, many country craftsmen preferred to apply it with a pad, using a technique known as French polish. To make this polish, purchase orange shellac flakes — these are available from some paint stores and many mail-order woodworking suppliers. Mix 5 ounces of flakes with 1 cup of denatured alcohol for a "5-pound cut." Then fold a clean, soft cloth around a wad of cotton balls to make an egg-sized pad.

1 Carefully remove all mill marks and other evidence of power tools, then finish sand the surface to 220#.

2 Sprinkle a few drops of alcohol on the pad and work it in with your hand. Next, add a few drops of shellac, followed by a few drops of linseed oil. The pad should feel moist to the touch.

3 Begin rubbing the surface of the wood in a circular or figure-8 pattern. This pattern should be about 12" across.

4 Refill the pad with alcohol and shellac as needed. If the pad begins to stick to the surface, add a few more drops of linseed oil to lubricate it.

5 In a short time, the finish will begin to accumulate on the surface as you rub. Cover the entire surface, building up the finish to the desired depth.

6 Shake a few drops of alcohol onto the pad and wipe the finish in the direction of the grain. This will remove any circular marks.

7 Allow the finish to dry overnight, then rub it out with linseed oil and pumice stone.

8 Apply paste wax to the surface and buff it to a high gloss.

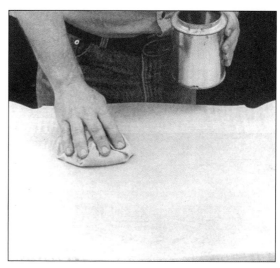

To build up a French polish, rub a thick (5-pound cut) shellac onto the surface in a circular or figure-8 motion. Keep the shellac from drying on the pad by sprinkling it with alcohol now and then. Lubricate the pad with linseed oil to prevent it from sticking to the surface.

Staining — Old-time craftsmen often stained their furniture for effect. They stained light woods, such as oak and maple, dark brown or black. Even darker woods, such as walnut, were sometimes stained a bright red color known as "Dragon's Blood." These stains were either thinned varnishes tinted with colored resins, or "spirit stains" — vegetable dyes dissolved in alcohol, turpentine, or oil.

1 Carefully remove all mill marks and other evidence of power tools, then finish sand the surface to 220#.

2 Wipe the varnish, oil, or spirit stain on the surface with a cloth or brush, then wipe off the excess with a clean cloth dipped in thinner. Take care to coat the wood evenly. If any areas appear darker than the others, apply a little extra thinner to the clean cloth and rub until the wood lightens.

3 If you want a darker stain, wait a few minutes before you wipe the excess stain off, or apply successive coats.

When sanding a stained, varnished, or shellacked surface, be careful not to sand through the finish to the raw wood, especially at the edges and corners. Use a sanding block to apply even pressure over the entire surface.

4 If you want to apply varnish or shellac over the stain, seal the stain with a "wash coat" of shellac. Mix 2 ounces of shellac flakes in 1 cup of alcohol (to make a 2-pound cut) and brush this over the stain. Lightly sand with 220# paper, then apply a "top coat" of varnish or shellac as you would normally. The wash coat prevents the stain from bleeding into or clouding the clear top coat.

Note: When sanding stained, varnished, or shellacked surfaces, be careful not to sand through the finish to the raw wood. You may choose to ignore this advice when applying museum-quality finishes, however. You may *want* to sand through the finish in certain areas to simulate wear.

Milk Paint — One of the most popular country finishes was milk paint, which came into general use in the last half of the eighteenth century. There were many different recipes for milk paint, but most combined skim milk, lime paste, linseed oil, and pigment. (Sometimes cottage cheese was substituted for milk.) The casein in the dairy product bound the pigment to the wooden surface, producing a hard, waterproof finish. The milk paint finish on some historical country furniture — particularly Shaker furniture — has lasted for almost 200 years with no noticeable signs of fading or wear!

Today, several manufacturers offer powdered milk paint that you simply mix with water. These can be purchased at most paint and craft stores. The choice of colors is limited, but you can combine colors to get different hues. You can also mix white milk paint with fresco colors or water-soluble aniline dies to produce your own colors.

When you mix milk paint, be careful to mix only as much as you need. It will keep in your refrigerator for a few days, but not much longer than that. Before using the paint, strain it through a cheesecloth or nylon stocking to remove any lumps of undissolved powder.

1 Carefully remove all mill marks and other evidence of power tools, then finish sand the surface to 150#.

2 Dampen the surface of the wood with a wet rag. This will help the paint adhere to the surface of the project.

3 Apply a coat of milk paint with a brush. Put the paint on thickly if you want the finish to have some texture; use less if you want it to be smooth.

4 Allow the first coat to dry (usually 4–8 hours), then apply a second. You don't need to sand the surface between coats.

5 Allow the second coat to dry overnight, then sand with wet/dry 320# sandpaper to smooth out the brush strokes. As you work, wet the paper with water to prevent it from loading.

6 Mix a teaspoon of japan drier to a pint of linseed oil, and apply this mixture to the painted surface. Allow the oil to soak in for a few minutes, then wipe away the excess with a soft, clean cloth.

7 Allow the oil to dry overnight. If you want a glossy finish, apply a coat of paste wax and buff.

Note: You can make a semi-opaque paint stain or "wash" by mixing milk paint with more water than the recipe calls for. Apply this wash as you would a spirit stain, using water as the thinner. If you want to apply clear varnish or shellac over the wash, seal it with thin (2-pound cut) shellac.

Grain Painting — In the late eighteenth century, as classic furniture styles began to incorporate exotic woods with highly figured grains, many country cabinetmakers began to "grain" their furniture with paint. Ostensibly, this grain painting was intended to imitate expensive woods and hide inferior materials. However, the technique soon evolved into a folk art form. Many "grainers" applied bold patterns and colors — fanciful caricatures of wood grain. This became known as *faux bois,* French for "false wood."

To grain a piece of furniture, you need a special tool (or combination of tools) to either apply the paint or partially wipe it off. The sorts of tools used by grainers are as fanciful as their work. In addition to a variety of "graining combs," you can also use brushes, feathers, putty, corncobs, sponges, a wad of newspaper, almost anything.

1 Carefully remove all mill marks and other evidence of power tools, then finish sand the surface to 150#.

2 Apply a "base coat" of paint. This can be any color, light or dark.

3 Seal the base coat with a wash coat of shellac (2-pound cut).

4 Fill the bottom of a bowl with a small amount of mineral spirits or varnish. On the edge of the bowl, put a small amount of an artist's oil color. This color must contrast with the base coat. Mix the color and the spirits — you must experiment to get just the right mixture.

5 At this point, you have two choices: (1) Apply the color/spirits mixture with your graining tools, creating a pattern, or (2) paint the mixture onto the surface, covering it completely. Before it dries, wipe part of it off with the graining tools, exposing the base coat and creating a pattern.

6 Let the grain painting dry completely. Then seal it with a wash coat of shellac.

7 Follow with more coats of shellac or a coat of varnish. This will protect the grain paint from wear.

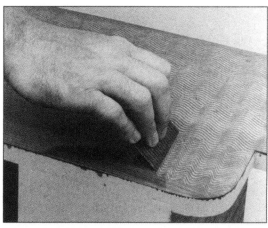

You can use many, many different tools to grain paint, and with each tool you can achieve different effects. This shows just one of the many possible effects of traditional graining combs.

You can paint realistic wood grain with a molded rubber "grainer" — these are available at most crafts stores. Rock the tool back and forth as you drag it through the wet paint.

Use a feather to imitate the grain pattern of a crotch burl. Swirl the feather through the wet paint, drawing parallel arcs.

Not all grain paintings imitated wood grain. Some were fanciful patterns that were invented by the finisher. This half-moon pattern was used on several historical pieces. It's applied with a brush.

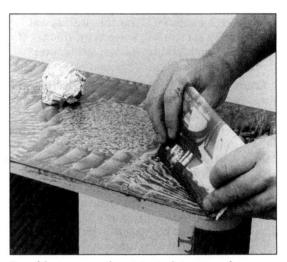

One of the most versatile graining tools is a piece of newspaper. Crumple it into a ball and dab it into the wet paint to mimic burls. Or fold it so you have a straight edge and make a series of parallel dabs to imitate curly grain. You can also dab in quarter-circles or half-circles to create fan shapes.

MUSEUM-QUALITY FINISHES

In a museum-quality finish, the effect — the antique look — is more important than the materials you use. The final finish must protect the surface of the wood, but you can use any material, traditional or modern, that correctly simulates the effects of age. At the Workshops, the finishers commonly use latex paints, aniline die stains, and spray lacquer. (Contemporary lacquer bears little resemblance to old-time Chinese lacquer. The resin is made from nitrocellulose, and many of the vehicles are distilled from petroleum products.) Yet the final effect is almost indistinguishable from traditional materials that have been naturally aged.

To achieve the right effect, you must first understand the natural aging processes. The wood, the finish, and the hardware all show their age in different ways. The surface of the wood changes color and collects chips and dings. Traditional finishes dry out, shrink, and become discolored and scratched. Hardware rusts or tarnishes.

Think about each detail of your project. If it *had* been built during the Country era, what would have happened to it over the centuries? If you want, make up a history — whom it belonged to, how it was used, where it was kept. Create 150— 200 years of fictional use and abuse. This fantasy will help you to build a believable *surface history*.

ARTIFICIAL AGING

There are many different processes that affect the appearance of every antique. For each process, there are one or more ways to simulate its effects on a reproduction:

Patina — Wood reacts with both light and air. When the surface is exposed to sunlight, it often changes color. It may also oxidize in the open air, which also alters the hue. Each wood changes in a different way. Most species become darker; walnut

becomes lighter. This color shift happens, for the most part, only on the surface of the wood. This layer of exposed dark (or light) wood is called the *patina*.

To discover how the patina of a particular wood develops, study antiques that were built from this species. Purchase or mix a stain that simulates the color of this patina. In some cases, you may be able to create an artificial patina by treating the wood with chemicals. Cherry, for example, will darken when you apply ammonia. Pine, poplar, and maple develop a patina when you paint them with diluted (10 percent) nitric acid, then gently warm the surface with a heat gun. To simulate the patina of walnut, lighten it with wood bleach.

Accumulation of Dirt and Grime — Although a piece of furniture may be periodically cleaned and waxed, dirt eventually becomes ground into thesurface. The dirt may also mix with oils on the surface to become grime. This grime accumulates

To simulate dirt and grime, apply a dark glaze and wipe most of it away before it dries. Leave the areas that would have accumulated more dirt a little darker than the rest of the project.

in cracks and crevices, and around door pulls and latches. Where the wood is unfinished, dirt collects in the pores of the wood, staining it a brownish gray. You can duplicate all of these effects by wiping the finished surface with glaze — a thick, dark stain.

There are several commercial glazes available, but you can easily make your own. Mix 2 ounces of Burnt Umber and 2 ounces of Burnt Sienna artist's oil paints with 8 ounces of turpentine, 3 ounces of boiled linseed oil, and ¼ ounce of japan drier. Apply the glaze with a rag or brush, let it soak into the wood for a few minutes, then wipe it off. Wipe away as much glaze as possible in the center of broad areas, but leave some at the edges. (More dirt and grime accumulate at the edges

than in the center.) When properly glazed, a surface should be lighter at the center, then darker and darker toward the edges.

Rounding — As a piece of furniture is used, the hard edges wear and round over. This doesn't happen evenly. For example, if you study an antique cupboard door, you'll find that the edges are worn more in the vicinity of the latch or pull. The corners of tabletops, top edges of drawer fronts, front edges of shelves and chair seats, inside edges of doors, and bottom ends of legs are all areas that wear faster on most furniture. Round over or "break" most of the hard edges and corners on an antique reproduction with sandpaper. Then use a rasp and file to round over and remove stock from the areas that would have seen the most wear.

Many of the edges on a piece of country furniture will become rounded with normal use. Identify these areas, decide how much they would have worn, then round them over with a rasp, file, or sandpaper.

Make a distressing tool by wiring 30–40 keys to a wooden handle. (Most hardware stores will be glad to give you their mis-cut key blanks.) *Lightly* beat the surface with the keys to create dents and scratches.

Distressing — Although wooden furniture is durable, the surface is not particularly resilient. It shows every dent and scratch. Over the years these accumulate, especially in the areas that see the most wear — around feet or legs, on tabletops, chest lids, shelves, and the seats of chairs. You can duplicate these marks by lightly beating the surface of a reproduction with a small ball peen hammer, a light chain, or a collection of keys. Be careful not to leave too many marks or make them too deeply; it's easy to over-distress a surface. Remember, the wear and tear should be believable.

Chips, Gnaw-Marks, and Other Damage — Occasionally, the wood is damaged rather than just dented or scratched. The corner of a drawer or the tip of a pendant may break off. Cabriole legs sometimes crack at the ankles. Rats and mice gnaw the backs of drawers, particularly if those drawers were used to hold foodstuffs or clothes. You can simulate all of this damage with a hammer, chisel, rasp, or other suitable tool. Once again, don't overdo it. Country furniture should look worn, but not as if it's been through a war.

Worn Finish — Just as the corners and the edges of wood wears, so will finish. Most antiques show areas where the finish has worn away completely, showing the bare wood underneath. These areas are the same as mentioned previously under "Rounding" — the surfaces around door pulls and latches, corners of tabletops, front edges of shelves and chair seats, and so on. To simulate this wear, sand away the finish on these areas with 320# wet/dry sandpaper. Wet the sandpaper with water or linseed oil to prevent it from loading.

Discolored and Cracked Finish — As a finish ages, it often darkens. Sometimes, it becomes stained, mildewed, or collects "fly specks." Old varnish and paint often become brittle, shrink, split, and appear "crackled."

To darken or stain a finish, wipe it with a dark glaze, let the glaze set a few minutes, then wipe it off again. If you want it darker yet, repeat. To add fly specks, dip a toothbrush in the glaze. Hold the brush about 12" from the surface of the wood and run your thumb through the bristles, spattering the surface of the project. Don't overdo this — a few fly specks go a long way.

There are several ways to simulate a crackled finish. The easiest, perhaps, is to apply a base coat of ordinary lacquer, then spray this with special "crackle lacquer." The crackle lacquer is a chemical agent that cracks the lacquer coat directly underneath it, showing the wood, stain, or paint beneath that. You can control the crackling effect (making larger or smaller cracks) by varying the amount of crackle lacquer you apply or by mixing it with varying amounts of thinner.

Note: Crackle lacquer must be applied over clear lacquer, tinted lacquer, or lacquer paint. For the best effect, seal the wood, stain, or paint you want to show through the cracks with clear lacquer or a wash coat of shellac. Apply the lacquer you want to crack over the sealant, then apply the crackle lacquer.

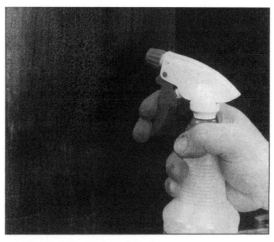

Crackle lacquer is especially formulated to react with the lacquer coat immediately underneath it and cause it to crack. It's normally applied with a spray gun, but you can also use a spray bottle.

You can also achieve a crackle finish with latex paint. Apply a base coat of latex and cover this with a thin, even coat of hide glue. Let the glue dry completely, then paint over the glue. As the second coat of latex dries, it will begin cracking. You can control the crackling by thinning the paint or covering the crackled latex with enamel. "Set" the cracks by covering the paint with clear shellac or varnish.

Finally, you can purchase several different types of "crackle paint" at most crafts stores. They may also have chemical agents to crack acrylic paint. These work well for small projects, but they're not economical for large ones.

Accumulated Layers of Finish — Many antiques are finished several times during their lifetimes. A typical early nineteenth-century Windsor chair,

Antique furniture often accumulates several layers of paint. Each of these may be worn or chipped, showing the bare wood or colors underneath. To duplicate this effect, apply several coats of contrasting paint. After applying each coat, sand it or chip it away in the areas that would have seen the most wear.

for example, might have been finished with a thin, green milk paint when it was first made. Later in the century, it could have been covered with the black lacquer that was so popular in Victorian decor. In the 1920s or 1930s, it might have been painted once more with colored enamel. Each of these layers would have worn away partially, revealing bare wood or the colors underneath them.

To simulate this history, you must apply successive layers of paint. Sand and chip away a layer in the areas that are prone to wear, then wipe it with glaze to discolor it. Repeat for each layer. This is a painstaking process, but there are no good shortcuts for simulating this particular type of aging.

Liming — Country furniture made in the mid-Atlantic and southern colonies was often finished with an inexpensive whitewash, a mixture of lime paste and salt. As this whitewash wore off, the wood showed through, looking as if it had been stained white. To duplicate this look, mix oil-based white paint with mineral spirits to make a semi-transparent stain. Use this stain as you would a glaze — wipe it on the wood, allow it to set a few minutes, then wipe it off again.

Rusting and Tarnishing — Hardware also shows its age. Iron rusts, brass tarnishes. Pins, pivots, and other working parts come loose. Cast metal may break — it's very common to find old willow-and-bail pulls with one or more of the points missing.

To age iron hardware, including screws and nails, dip the metal in a 30 percent solution of nitric acid for 10–15 minutes. (**Warning:** Do this *outside*, wear rubber gloves and eye protection, and be careful not to breathe the fumes.) This will remove the rust-resistant zinc chromate coating. Rinse the hardware in distilled water. Dip it in gun bluing for 2–3 minutes, or until the surface turns black. Allow it to dry overnight — don't blot it dry. The metal will look used and worn, and there will be a thin layer of rust in the crevices.

To age brass hardware, first soak it in lacquer thinner. This will remove the lacquer coating that most hardware manufacturers apply to keep the brass bright. Blot the hardware dry. Make a salt water solution, adding 2 tablespoons of salt to 1 cup of water. Also, fill an old coffee can full of ammonia. Dip the hardware in salt water, then suspend it *above* the ammonia on a string or in a wire basket. (Do *not* dip it *in* the ammonia.) Put the lid on the can, and gently warm it with a heat gun. As the ammonia fumes accumulate inside the can, the brass will begin to darken. (**Warning:** Do this *outside,* and avoid breathing the fumes.)

As soon as the darkening stops (in one or two minutes), repeat — dip the hardware in salt water and suspend it over the ammonia again. After several repetitions, the brass will be almost black. Dip it in salt water one final time and let it dry.

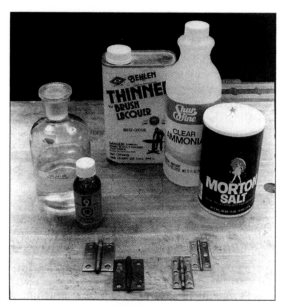

To artificially age iron hardware, strip the protective coating off with nitric acid, and apply gun bluing. For brass, strip it with lacquer thinner, and tarnish it with salt water and ammonia. All of these chemicals are available from hardware stores, grocery stores, or chemical supply houses.

Buff the flat areas bright with #0000 steel wool, allowing the tarnish to stay in the crevices.

If you decide to break off a portion of a brass pull or escutcheon, remember that the wood underneath the brass will likely be lighter than the rest of the surface. Also, the outline of the brass will be defined by a thin line of accumulated grime. To duplicate this, fasten the brasses in place, and lightly score the finish around them with a scratch awl. Wipe a glaze over the project, including the brasses. Before the glaze dries completely, remove the brasses and wipe them clean. Break off a *few* small pieces from one or two brasses. When you replace the brasses, the broken pieces will be outlined in simulated grime. Furthermore, the wood will be a shade lighter where the brass had covered it.

STICKING TO HISTORY

Although there are a lot of processes that age a piece of country furniture, none of them is complex. They can all be duplicated simply, using a few special techniques and a lot of horse sense. There are only two tricks: First, come up with a finishing plan that includes all the details. Second, arrange the various steps of this plan in the *proper chronological order.*

This chronology is extremely important! For the aging to appear authentic, you must carry out the simulation just as it might have happened in history. For instance, when you distress the wood, do so *after* you have applied a finish. If you're applying several layers of finish to build up a paint history, do a little distressing after each layer. This is the way it would have happened in real life.

The following procedures are outlines of finishing plans that are commonly used at the Workshops. The steps are arranged so the work flows easily, but they add the effects of age in the same order that history would have done so.

Museum-Quality Natural Finish — This finish is appropriate for formal furniture made from hardwoods such as walnut, cherry, and maple. It's transparent, so you can enjoy the wood grain. If your project is made from figured woods, you can take advantage of optional procedures to enhance the grain pattern.

1 Carefully remove all mill marks and other evidence of power tools, then finish sand the surface to 220#.

2 If the wood is figured, stain it a dark brown. Let the stain dry, then sand the surface again with 220# paper. Figured wood normally presents a swirl of end grains and long grains on its surface. Where the stain penetrates the end grain, the wood will remain dark. The long grains, which absorb less stain, will be lighter after sanding. This duplicates the way in which the end grains would have absorbed oil, wax, and grime over the years, growing darker than the long grains. It also accents the figuring.

3 Apply the "patina" stain — the color that the wood would otherwise achieve over time with exposure to sunlight and air. Note: If you're using a chemical stain, such as ammonia or nitric acid to create a patina, switch Steps 2 and 3.

4 If you want a crackle finish, first apply a coat of ordinary lacquer to seal the stain. This lacquer may be clear or tinted with aniline dyes. Then apply crackle lacquer to crack the ordinary lacquer.

5 Allow the lacquer (or the patina stain, if you skipped Step 4) to dry completely. Then do the rounding, distressing, and re-create any other wear and tear that might have happened to the wood or finish over time. As mentioned previously, be careful not to overdo this step.

6 Apply glazing to the surface, allow it to set for a few minutes, then wipe it off. Let it dry for at least 6 hours.

7 Apply the "top" coat — clear lacquer, shellac, or varnish.

8 Fasten the hardware in place, then rub out the finish with #0000 steel wool and oil soap. You may substitute dark paste wax for the soap, if you wish. Buff the surface until you get the sheen you want.

Museum-Quality Painted Finish — This finish is best suited for informal projects made from utilitarian woods such as poplar or for folk designs that are meant to be painted. You can also use it to disguise the grain of projects made from several different wood species.

1 Carefully remove all mill marks and other evidence of power tools, then finish sand the surface to 150#.

2 Apply a base coat of latex paint, milk paint, or lacquer paint.

3 Seal the base coat with clear shellac, varnish, or lacquer.

4 For a crackle finish, apply a coat of lacquer paint that contrasts with the base coat, then apply crackle lacquer over that. This second coat will crack, letting the base coat show through the cracks.

5 If you want to "grain paint" the project, skip Step 4. Apply the graining, let it dry thoroughly and seal it with a clear finish. (If you want to crack the grain painting, seal the graining with clear lacquer, then apply crackle lacquer.)

6 Allow the previous finish or sealer to dry completely. Then do the rounding, distressing, and re-create any other wear and tear that might have happened to the wood or paint over time. Be careful not to overdo.

7 If you want to build up multiple layers of paint, repeat Steps 2, 3,4, and 6 as desired.

8 Apply glazing to the surface, allow it to set for a few minutes, then wipe it off. Let it dry for at least 6 hours.

9 Apply a final coat of clear lacquer, shellac, or varnish.

10 Fasten the hardware in place, then rub out the finish with #0000 steel wool and oil soap. Substitute dark paste wax for the soap, if desired. Buff the surface.

SOURCES

If you need sources of country furniture supplies—tools, hardware, finishes, or other materials—here's a list of companies and the products they provide:

COMPANY	PRODUCT
Deco Art, Inc. PO Box 386 Stanford, KY 40484 (606) 365-319 www.decoart.com	Finishes
Connecticut Cane & Reed Co. P.O. Box 762 Manchester, CT 06045 (860) 646-6586 www.caneandreed.com	Seating materials
Country Accents 1723 Scaife Road Williamsport, PA 17701 (570) 478-4127 www.piercedtin.com	Tin
Eisenbrand Hardwoods, Inc. 4100 Spencer Street Torrance, CA 90503 (310) 542-3576 www.eisenbran.com	Wood
Garrett Wade 5389 E. Provident Drive Cincinnati, OH (800) 221-2942 www.garrettwade.com	Tools, hardware, finishes, general woodworking supplies
Horton Brasses 49 Nooks Hill Road Cromwell, CT 06416 (800) 754-9127 www.horton-brasses.com	Brass hardware
Mohawk Finishes PO Bo 22000 Hickory, NC 28603 (800) 545-0047 www.mohawk-finishing.com	Finishes

COMPANY	PRODUCT
Olde Mill Cabinet Shoppe 1660 Camp Betty Washington Road York, PA 17402 (717) 755-8884 www.oldemill.com	Finishes
Shaker Workshops P.O. Box 8001 Ashburnham, MA 01430 (978) 829-9900 www.shakerworkshops.com	Seating and finishing materials
Tremont Nail Co. P.O. Box 31 Mansfield, MA 02048 (508) 339-4500 www.tremonnail.com	Nails
Woodcraft Supply Co. 1177 Rosemon P.O. Box 1686 Parkersburg, WV 26102 (800) 225-1153 www.woodcraft.com	Tools, hardware, general woodworking supplies
The Woodworker's Store 4365 Willow Drive Medina, MN 55340 (800) 279-4441 www.woodworkerstore.com	Tools, hardware, general woodworking supplies
Woodworker's Supply 5604 Alameda Place Albuquerque, NM 87113 (505) 821-0500 www.woodworker.com	Tools, hardware, general woodworking supplies
The Workshops of David T. Smith 3600 Shawhan Road Morrow, OH 45152 (513) 932-2472 www.davidtsmith.com	Hand-forged iron hardware

INDEX

CREDITS

A friend of ours who has written several enormous books once observed: "Authors often write acknowledgments that go on for pages, and you wonder whether it's necessary. Well, it is. All those thank-you-kindly's are well-deserved. No one person can write a book; no *two* people can write it. The task is too mind-boggling. A good book is *always* a team effort."

This book is no different. It has been a mind-boggling task, and we would never have finished it without the help of many good people. We have a lot of thank-you-kindly's to deliver, so bear with us. In particular, we have relied on the craftsmen, craftswomen, and other folks at The Workshops. We have been awed by their artistry, enlightened by their woodworking savvy, and genuinely astonished by their patience. But most of all, we have been warmed by their good company. Thank you, Clare Allen, Kent Allen, Joe Bradley, John Buchanan, Ed Campbell, Jerry Cook, Kelly Cook, Loretta Cooper, Patty Cramer, Cathy Gatch, Eric Hancock, Kelly Holliday, Larry Hough, Todd Hough, Cathy McFarland, Walt Miller, Elzo Morgan, Dawn Morningstar, Jerry Parker, Harold Pauley, Jerry Ratliff, Bobby Rooks, John Rose, Dixie Rose, Marilee Rose, Rex Rose, Troy Sexton, Greg Shooner, David T. Smith, Grace Smith, Jason Smith, Julie Smith, Lora Smith, Mary Spellmire-Shooner, Beth Stephenson, Susan Swearigen, Tom Thompson, Chris Woods, Luke Woods, and Warren Young. Whew!

But wait, there's more! We have also depended on many other people, organizations, and institutions who've tracked down historical trivia, lent photographs, checked woodworking procedures, and have helped us with the thousands of details that make up this book. Many thanks to Rich and Sue Burmann, Thomas Clark, Jane Sikes Hageman, Gordon Honeyman, Tom Kuhns, Bob Menker, Mary Myers, Larry Owrey, Ruth Penewit, Tom and Ann Workman,

Ohio Historical Society, Warren County Museum, and Winterthur Museum.

And special thanks to that one person whom we probably forgot to include in these acknowledgments but will remember (never to forget again) two days after this book goes to the printer.

ABOUT THE AUTHOR

Nick Engler made traditional American musical instruments professionally before he began to write about woodworking. His articles have appeared in publications such as *Fine Woodworking* and *American Woodworker*. He founded *Hands On!* magazine and has published 48 books on woodworking, including the popular *Workshop Companion* series. Nick has taught wood technology and craftsmanship at the University of Cincinnati and holds several patents on woodworking tools.

Mary Jane Favorite is a prolific folk artist, woodworking designer, and illustrator. She is accomplished in several crafts but is best known for her furniture designs, hundreds of which have been published in woodworking magazines and books. She has also coauthored four books on woodworking. Together, Nick and Mary Jane raise assistance dogs for Canine Companions for Independence.

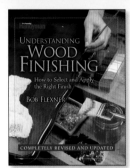

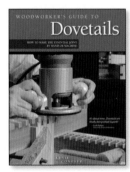
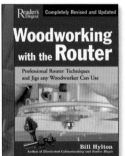
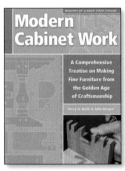